ALSO BY KRIN GABBARD

Black Magic:
White Hollywood and African American Culture

Psychiatry and the Cinema
(with Glen O. Gabbard)

Jammin' at the Margins:
Jazz and the American Cinema

HOTTER THAN THAT

Faber and Faber, Inc.

An affiliate of Farrar, Straus and Giroux

New York

HOTTER THAN THAT

The Trumpet, Jazz,
and American
Culture

KRIN GABBARD

FABER AND FABER, INC.
An affiliate of Farrar, Straus and Giroux
18 West 18th Street, New York 10011

A portion of chapter 4 originally appeared, in slightly different form, in *The Chronicle Review.*

Library of Congress Cataloging-in-Publication Data
Gabbard, Krin.
    Hotter than that : the trumpet, jazz, and American culture / Krin
Gabbard.— 1st ed.
        p.   cm.
    Includes index.
    ISBN-13: 978-0-571-21199-9 (hardcover : alk. paper)
    ISBN-10: 0-571-21199-2 (hardcover : alk. paper)
    1. Trumpet—History.   2. Trumpeters—United States.   3. Jazz
musicians—United States.   I. Title.

ML960 .G33 2008
788.9'209—dc22

                                                            2008031349

Designed by Cassandra J. Pappas

www.fsgbooks.com

10 9 8 7 6 5 4 3 2 1

For my teachers:
Eddie Allen, Laurie Frink, and Don Sickler

Contents

Preface:

A New Horn for a New Era

The twentieth century was barely under way when the grandson of a slave picked up a trumpet and transformed American culture. Before that moment, the trumpet had been a regimental staple in marching bands, a ceremonial accessory for royalty, and an occasional diva at the symphony. Because it could make more noise than just about anything except a bomb blast, the trumpet had been much more declarative than musical for most of its history. Around 1900, however, a man named Buddy Bolden made the trumpet declare in brand-new ways. He may even have invented jazz, or something very much like it. And as an African American, he found a vital new way to assert himself as a man.

Charles "Buddy" Bolden must be counted among the central figures in American history if only because we cannot imagine jazz without the trumpet, just as we cannot imagine modern America without jazz. And while it's impossible to imagine either jazz or the trumpet without Louis Armstrong, Bolden comes first. Because he stands at the tipping point between prejazz and jazz, we would have had to invent Buddy Bolden had he never existed. In fact, so much emphasis has been placed on the singular importance of this un-recorded musician that maybe we did invent him.

Louis Armstrong may have been contributing to that invention when he said he heard Bolden's band in New Orleans at the Union Sons Hall on Perdido Street, a dance joint so hot and crowded that regulars called it "Funky Butt Hall." The name actually came from one of Bolden's songs. Armstrong could not have been more than six at the time, but he lived just down the street from Funky Butt and al-most surely heard Bolden. Young Armstrong was probably listening to the drums, however, which he fancied before he discovered the trum-pet. Nevertheless, it's tempting to connect Bolden, born in New Or-leans in 1877, with Armstrong, born in New Orleans in 1901. A black Sistine God touches the finger of a black Adam. The image is not en-tirely fanciful, since Bolden is as inscrutable and distant as an Old Testament God.

Like so many legendary jazz artists, Bolden's flame burned bright and fast. In 1906, at the age of twenty-nine and his fame at its peak, he became delusional and violent. A year later he was committed to the East Louisiana State Hospital in Jackson, where he spent the rest of his life. In 1931, he died there in obscurity. We have no way of know-ing what Bolden's trumpet sounded like, although his group may have recorded on a primitive wax cylinder sometime before the turn of the century. It may be nothing more than a rumor, but the cylin-der will always be the Holy Grail of jazz history. Without it, the sound of Bolden's horn has lived on only in the music of his disciples, a group that includes, arguably, every single person who has ever played intense, African-inflected music on the trumpet.

In the New Orleans of 1900, the time was right for a sea change in American music. Most significantly, the blues was beginning to emerge as a recognizable musical form. By the end of the nineteenth century it had evolved out of the old field songs and hollers from the plantation, but also from the music of what Southern blacks knew as the Sanctified Church. The uniquely African American genre of the spiritual had begun almost as soon as the first slaves were introduced to Christianity and allowed to worship on Sundays. The spiritual had already been popularized by the clean-cut Jubilee Singers from Fisk University Jubilee, but the intense music of the churches remained an essential part of the black South where Bolden was raised. Ultimately, he was able to improvise the power of the spirituals into the cadences of the blues and make it all work for dancers. Someone may have put all of this together before, but Bolden was the first person to become famous for it. He also played the music loud, so loud it was almost impossible *not* to hear his horn. Soon, he was leading the most popular dance band in New Orleans. Even a few white people hired him for their parties.

In his one surviving photograph, probably dating to 1905, Bolden is surrounded by five members of his band (see figure 1 in insert). He seems to be reasonably tall, well built, and light skinned. For some reason, he is not holding his horn as we might expect, either at his side in the traditional military position or with both hands in front of him, as if he were about to raise it to his lips. Instead, Bolden offers up the instrument for our inspection, flat on his outstretched palm. It's an unusually jaunty gesture that goes well with the insouciant half smile on his face. Or is it a smile? The original photograph has been lost, and the best existing copy is scratched and faded. Like all photographs, it yields only a glimmer of information about Bolden at one brief moment in his life. But in that one precious image, we catch a glimpse of a central figure in the modern history of the trumpet as well as the story of American culture.

Not surprisingly, the Buddy Bolden who holds out his horn with a wry smile was extremely popular with women. He never married, but he lived with two women in succession and had a child by each. He surely had several more women on the side. It would be unfair to Bolden to declare that he played to attract women. Undoubtedly he played because he was good enough to earn a decent living at it and because he loved music. Like many trumpeters before and since, he must have relished his ability to astonish listeners with cascades of notes, from the bleating tones at the bottom to the thrilling shrieks at the top. Nevertheless, he surely enjoyed the trumpet's surplus value as a clarion call to members of the female sex. And he was surely not the first or the last man to discover the power of that call.

Like the Armstrong of two decades later, Bolden could not have created his musical revolution with any instrument other than the trumpet. Bolden undoubtedly understood what the trumpet stood for: it made the grand noise that welcomed kings; it was essential for establishing pomp and circumstance; and it was the inevitable instrument when an event called for a fanfare. For armies, it provided the first sound a soldier hears in the morning and the last sound he hears as he falls on the battlefield. Bolden knew from the Old Testament that a trumpet brought down Jericho, and he knew from the book of Revelation that the End of Days will follow a trumpet call.

So, you see, it wasn't *only* a good way to get women. With his prowess as a trumpeter, Bolden also won the respect of men, both black and white. And even if the black and white men of New Orleans did not always show it, Bolden knew that he was asserting himself in a highly forceful manner. He might have paid with his life for a comparable assertion in almost any other venue. Along with everything else, Bolden was appropriating the instrument's long history as a symbol of manhood, whether it was in battle, in the ceremonies of the royal court, or in the religion of God the Father.

Although women have also played the trumpet, often as well as anyone who has ever held one, the instrument has been essential to masculine expression throughout its history. This book traces that history from Egypt in the fifteenth century BCE to the present, stopping along the way to explore the lives of some of the remarkable individuals who made the trumpet their own, especially in the United States. A few of them changed history by changing the way people thought about the trumpet. Buddy Bolden may have been the first American to make the horn as essential to modern America as to the presentation of manhood. Louis Armstrong, who wrote "Hotter Than That," the song that gives this book its title, took this pursuit several steps farther. A generation later, Miles Davis made the trumpet emanate warmth rather than heat. For many, he made it cool. And even if the electric guitar had not been in the process of becoming the most flamboyantly masculine instrument at midcentury, Davis was much less interested in asserting his manhood with his trumpet. He did that in other ways, not all of them pleasant.

I have tried to write a cultural history of the trumpet, but I am also intrigued by the history of the culture of the trumpet. What did the trumpet mean to American history, but also, what did the trumpet mean to the men and women who played it? Almost any musician will tell you that no other instrument demands so much of the player: one more reason for its association with masculine determination and display. Accomplished saxophonists or pianists can take a few weeks off and then pick up practically where they left off, but not a trumpet player, who must practice daily to maintain good form. And it's not unusual for a trumpeter to suffer from a hernia, a split lip, or a slipped disk. Although the trumpet itself may not always be the immediate cause, there is an appallingly long list of great trumpeters who died before they were thirty. The list of those who never made it to forty is just as distressing. This book devotes separate chapters to Bolden, Armstrong, and Davis, but it also tells the stories of the trumpeters who, like Bolden, burned out early. Beyond that, it looks at inspirational trumpeters who, like Armstrong, raged heroically into old age.

The book also includes a chapter about my own life with the trumpet. As a child, I enjoyed playing cornet in the grade school band, slowly learning to hit the right notes and sight-read the music. But it all changed when I first heard Art Farmer (figure 2) just as I was turning fifteen and discovering jazz. If you talk to jazz devotees, almost all of them will tell you that they began their romance with the music in early adolescence. Unlike pop music, which is for children, jazz is for people coming of age. And it's no surprise that the young people most drawn to the jazz trumpet are male. For a pubescent boy becoming a man, the stirring, often subversive call of the jazz trumpet can be irresistible. Before I began listening assiduously to Art Farmer and many other superb jazz trumpeters, I was a ninth grader trying to sound like the anonymous symphony players with their clear, direct tones and their perfect execution. I was also one of the few in my peer group who had not moved on from the school band to the football and basketball teams. At the urging of parents who wanted their children to be "well-rounded," we had all started out in the fourth grade with cornets, trombones, clarinets, saxophones, and snare drums. The demands of high school athletics gave most of my male friends the license to give up on music. They were taking the usual route to masculinity.

I had my own reasons for resisting high school athletics and for dedicating my time and energy to the cornet. For one thing, my parents were devoted to the arts and regularly expressed contempt for sports. When the local college built a huge new gymnasium, my father referred to it as a "jock palace." Thanks to Art Farmer, my own idea of masculinity took a different form. Art was a large-boned man with sad eyes and a droopy mustache. He had tremendous technique as a trumpeter, but he never flaunted it. Heavily influenced by Miles Davis, Farmer made the trumpet an instrument of romance. He had a beautiful feel for ballads, crafting solos that took familiar melodies into lyrical new directions. At the same time, he was capable of fast runs throughout the range of the trumpet, and he could be highly assertive if he so chose. And then there was his tone. Compared to the directness and clarity of the standard symphonic tone, Farmer's sound was downright fuzzy. Today I would say that his tone was dark and thick, although I've heard him be light and delicate as well. And his sound was always instantly recognizable. Like so many great jazz artists, he had made the trumpet his own.

Although I did not really think about it at the time, Art Farmer's playing showed me how to be masculine and authoritative without being an athlete or a bully. In Farmer's playing, I heard expertise and power but also a gentleness and a playfulness that transcended the macho self-presentation of so many men who are not musicians. Nor was he a "trumpet jock," the kind of player who engages in mine-is-bigger-than-yours games. In other words, Farmer was not just another highly practiced trumpeter who only wants to play high and loud. He was the kind of man I wanted to be. When I finally had a chance to talk with Art a few years before his death in 2000, I told him that he was my childhood idol. He immediately smiled and said, "But now that you're older, you've got more sense." At the time all I could do was laugh, but on some level, he was wrong. My admiration for Art is not something I have outgrown.

In spite of my fascination with the music of Art Farmer and a handful of other esteemed trumpeters, I gave up the cornet when I got to college. I had no intention of taking up the instrument again, thinking I might take piano lessons later in life if I ever had some extra time on my hands. When I began researching this book, however, I quickly realized that you have to "blow to know." As of this writing, I have been taking trumpet lessons for almost four years, and I have a small sense of what it means to devote your life to such a fiendishly demanding instrument. The best trumpeters, living and dead, have inspired me to write their stories as compellingly as possible.

I am especially grateful to the many virtuoso players and teachers who took the time to speak with me as my work took shape. This book is dedicated to the three teachers who taught me most of what I know about the trumpet. They have also taken me from a place where I could barely buzz my lips to where I can now play in public with something other than complete humiliation.

HOTTER THAN THAT

chapter 1

How Buddy Bolden Blew His Brains Out
(But Not Before He Changed the Music Forever)

Actually, Buddy Bolden did not play the trumpet. He played the cornet, an instrument with a unique history of its own but not much different from the longer, sleeker trumpet. Because the cornet was more compact, it was preferred by late-nineteenth-century musicians, who carried it around in parades and in crowded dance halls. Symphony players in France regularly played cornets rather than trumpets, and in the United States, school bands were giving cornets to students as late as the 1970s. The instrument still has its enthusiasts today. Wynton Marsalis played cornet on what may be his finest classical album,[1] and several other eminent jazz and classical artists still prefer the instrument. But the trumpet—like the one Louis Armstrong used to record "West End Blues" and the one with which Miles Davis played "So What"—now has pride of place among jazz, Latin, and symphony players, as well as with schoolchildren just learning to play.

When Bolden was making music in New Orleans, from about

1895 until 1907, a good free-blowing cornet was a necessity for any musician who wanted to play loud, clear, and clean but without too much effort. In the 1880s, a good new cornet cost anywhere from $55 for an American horn to $130 and up for a fancy French import like a Courtois or a Besson. Statistics from 1900 suggest that a white laborer in the United States could make as much as $3 a day. But the average weekly wage for a domestic servant—a job that would surely have gone to an African American—was $3.51, much less than a dollar a day. A new cornet would have cost a black musician at least three months' salary. Even the cheap imports from Eastern Europe that were sold in the Sears and Montgomery Ward catalogs would have set back a black musician by at least two weeks' wages.

Musicians who could not afford a new cornet might overhaul a discarded horn. They might even assemble a serviceable instrument from parts of broken horns and plumbing pipes. We know that Bolden played a Conn cornet, the industry standard in the late nineteenth century. The Conn Wonder from 1888 that I once held and played is a miracle of burnished silver, pearl-capped pistons, and gently curving tubes. It blew easily, and its sound was as clear and bright as any soprano brass instrument. Most important, for a black man like Bolden, a brand-new Conn Wonder sold for as little as $40. By the late 1890s, when Bolden began a serious career as a working musician, Conn Wonders had been around for more than ten years. He could have bought a good used one for less still.

Even if they could afford a good horn, cornet men like Bolden might tinker with their instruments, hoping to get the same sound they were hearing in their heads. Some players filed down their mouthpieces, creating a shallower cup that made the high notes easier. Some found cylindrical pieces of metal or wood that could be forced into the cornet's tubing, enlarging the bore and allowing for a bigger, warmer sound. "Trick" or "freak" players would take a Coke bottle or the business end of a toilet plunger and put it over the bell of the horn, creating strange sounds that delighted audiences.

THE CITY WE LOST

Buddy Bolden could not have made his mark anywhere except in New Orleans. It had a wider variety of music than any other place in the world. In fact, in 1900, New Orleans was still not America. It's better to think of it as the crown of the Caribbean rather than the bottom of the United States.[2] New Orleans was also more French, more Spanish, more pagan, and less Puritan than any other American town. Racially mixed couples, even gays and lesbians, were tolerated to a degree unthinkable elsewhere, especially in Southern cities. All of the peoples that made up New Orleans had their own musical traditions. The Irish brought fiddles and whistles into the mix; Germans brought their heavy brass and oompah-pah rhythms; Italians contributed accordions and operatic airs.

A unique presence in New Orleans were the Creoles, people of the Catholic faith with African and French parentage. Many of the Frenchmen who settled in New Orleans in the eighteenth and early nineteenth centuries took dark-skinned wives and mistresses and did not disown their children. Their descendants looked proudly to France for their musical inspiration. Unlike the darker descendants of slaves, "Creoles of Color" were allowed to study in conservatories, and more than one symphony orchestra in New Orleans was made up entirely of Creoles. As the jazz musicologist Travis Jackson has pointed out, musical traditions in New Orleans can be differentiated by religion and language more effectively than by skin color.[3] Intense, rollicking music was essential to the services in the Protestant churches, where most blacks and some whites worshiped on Sundays. The Creoles and those whose principal language was French were more likely to attend Catholic services, where the music was sedate and Eurocentric.

Nevertheless, no musical tradition in New Orleans remained untouched by the others for long. In the years when Buddy Bolden was making music, brass bands gave public concerts in the parks virtually every weekend. The bands were sponsored by civic associations, fraternal organizations, and loose assemblages of ethnic groups. As if there were not enough diversity already, Mexican military bands gave public performances in New Orleans on three different occasions in the last years of the nineteenth century.[4] Out of civic pride as well as the need for cash, brass bands regularly marched in parades, staged concerts, and appeared at picnics, nightclubs, and private parties. On Sundays, when the furniture stores were not using their horse-drawn wagons for deliveries, musicians would turn them into bandwagons, drive them to neighborhoods where they had a scheduled performance, and give free concerts.

Most famously, musicians played at funerals. In a city where music truly mattered, there was no better way to honor the departed than by sending them off with beautiful music. The funeral homes sometimes paid for the procession to and from the graveyard, but the deceased almost always belonged to a union, a fraternal organization, or some other group that would pay for a marching band. In the late nineteenth century, bands marched at funerals for white people, but by the early twentieth century, the tradition of cemetery parades belonged almost exclusively to African Americans in New Orleans.[5] The black bands played solemn music going in and songs of celebration going out. After the service, the grand marshal would turn his sash around to the brightly colored side, the mourners would remove their armbands, and the snare drummer would take the handkerchiefs off his sticks. A reverential "Just a Closer Walk With Thee" would give way to "Oh Didn't He Ramble." By this time, the mourners would have been joined by the "second line" of spectators, who knew the music better than they knew the person who had just been buried. The musicians themselves, who also may never have met the deceased, did not see the rowdy aftermath of the funeral as in any way disrespectful. Life goes on. To someone looking for a more stolid explanation, the musicians would probably have said something about celebrating the arrival of the spirit in a better world.

In the dance halls, New Orleanians heard waltzes, mazurkas, quadrilles, and schottiches. They listened to popular songs in the traditions of Victorian England as well as to the Tin Pan Alley songs from New York that were just then becoming part of American culture. But the dominant musical culture for whites as well as for blacks was strongly based in the African American vernacular. The songs of Stephen Foster and his acolytes, all of them influenced by black music, were popular in New Orleans. Even more popular was the new ragtime music of the African American composer Scott Joplin and his followers. The blues and spirituals were also flourishing. The Jubilee Singers of Fisk University were transforming homegrown church songs and folk melodies into disciplined performances that delighted even proper bourgeois audiences. Then as now, African American performers were teaching white people how to find new levels of emotion in music.

Buddy Bolden surely knew the spirituals from his days attending the Fourth Baptist Church on First Street in New Orleans with his evangelical Christian family. But he also experienced a more earthy form of church music. Young Bolden would have been well acquainted with the music of the Sanctified Church and the commanding vocal cadences of the black folk preacher. In 1903, when Bolden was near the peak of his career, W.E.B. Du Bois wrote, "The preacher is the most unique personality developed by the Negro on American soil."[6] The black novelist Zora Neale Hurston observed that while the white preacher "lectures," the black preacher creates "drama with music."[7] In a tradition that went back to field songs, hollers, and spirituals, and before that to African communal singing, the black preacher led call-and-response with his congregation, singing as he spoke, often dropping in what we would now call "blue notes," those flatted thirds and fifths that are immediately recognizable as the blues. The preacher demonstrated how one voice could command total attention, soaring above the others, even improvising as he sent out his powerful message. Buddy Bolden was among the first instrumentalists to fully appropriate the sounds and techniques of the black folk preacher.

WAS THAT JAZZ?

New Orleans musicians, some who read music, some who played by ear, could not have known that they were creating a music that would eventually be declared a national treasure and treated as an academic subject throughout the world. At the same time that some players were moving toward jazz, others were experimenting with the popular ragtime tunes. Still others were fusing the old marching band music with dance hall songs. It may have all have sounded the same to people in New Orleans—a uniquely Crescent City musical gumbo.

When a prospector finds a nugget of gold, he bites it and holds it up to the light. He immediately knows that he has something of real value. For the inventors of jazz, there could not have been a eureka moment. The music was too busy being born for anyone to stop and declare that it was now "jazz." In fact, the word did not appear in print until 1913, and even then it first appeared on the sports pages.[8] In the slangy, PG-rated prose of the sportswriter, the word meant enthusiasm or intensity, as in "The pitcher put some of the old jazz on the ball." Ten years earlier, when Buddy Bolden was part of the music scene in New Orleans, *jazz* simply meant sex. Scholars of American slang say that the word probably has an African root and may be related to *jism* or *jizz*, terms for semen. There is nothing unusual about this transfer from sex to music. Rock 'n' roll, boogie-woogie, and funk also took their names from sexual slang. Even if it is now considered art music, jazz had its own humble beginnings as low-down dance music and as a prelude to what dancers did later that night in their bedrooms.

Jazz became gold only after it profoundly affected audiences and inspired new generations of musicians to join in. New Orleans jazz, widely known today as Dixieland, was not a national sensation until much later. But it is the source of just about everything that has happened since, whether it was the big-band swing that kept dancers on their feet, the fiendishly difficult music of the beboppers who saw themselves as true artists, or the good-time jump blues that eventually became rock 'n' roll. All of it evolved from a vaguely defined center that, for lack of a better term, we now call "jazz." The term lives on in spite of its obscene origins and in spite of the many distinguished musicians, including Duke Ellington, Max Roach, Miles Davis, and Anthony Braxton, who have disavowed it. Roach, the drummer whose career began with the birth of bebop in the 1940s and continued throughout the rest of the century, once observed that "Don't give me all that jazz" is synonymous with "Don't give me all that shit." He continued, "Personally I resent the word unequivocally because of our spirituals and our heritage; the work and sweat that went into our music is above shit."[9] For many "jazz" artists, the term inadequately describes the complex and constantly evolving music they play.

Whether or not we wish to call it jazz, the music began in New Orleans because a unique collection of musical traditions was mixed together with peculiarly New Orleanian accents in the early years of the twentieth century. The mixing took place in a crucible of intense competition among musicians who pushed the music forward at a feverish pace. Even listening to another musician perform was seldom benign. If two bands showed up simultaneously at the same park, or if two bandwagons arrived at the same corner, sparks would fly. "I've got my man covered," the cornetist or the clarinetist or the trombonist would say, staring purposefully at his counterpart in the competing band. Audiences loved it. Some fans even tied the wagons together so that the bands were toe to toe. A few years after Bolden's confinement, trombonist Kid Ory brought his band into a competition on a new motorized furniture wagon, scaring the horses and sending the other wagon flying.

The competition was especially intense among African American musicians. Money was drastically tight for blacks in the early 1900s, and though many tried, few were able to make a living entirely with music. Bolden himself listed "plasterer" as his occupation around the time he turned twenty. By 1900, however, he was among a small group of blacks in New Orleans who earned all their money as professional musicians. But it was never easy money. Struggling musicians like Bolden worked hard at bringing in the crowds when they played. Innovation was the key, and Bolden was uniquely equipped to introduce new elements—or to creatively combine old ones—that pleased audiences. He was a born innovator, possessed of the same spirit of discovery and invention that would come of age in the music of Louis Armstrong.

GHOST SOUNDS

We are fortunate that so much of Armstrong's music was recorded. We are not so fortunate in the case of Bolden. We have only the faintest idea of how popular music in New Orleans sounded before 1920. And even if that wax cylinder did turn up somehow, someday, jazz aficionados would probably be disappointed. The music would sound hopelessly archaic. Regardless, people in the business of recording music took their time getting around to the great black artists of New Orleans. This is not to say that other types of black music hadn't been preserved—ragtime was recorded in 1900 and gospel music in 1902. The New York "society" orchestra of the black band-leader James Reese Europe was in a recording studio in 1914 playing a version of ragtime. As part of the long history of minstrelsy and the white appropriation of black music, a group of Caucasian musicians recorded "Nigger Blues" in 1916. A more successful take on black music was recorded in 1917 by a white group from New Orleans, the Original Dixieland Jass Band. Rumor has it that members of the band changed their name to the Original Dixieland *Jazz* Band after a wag crossed out the *J* on one of their posters. "Livery Stable Blues" was their first big hit, probably due more to the band's novel means of reproducing barnyard noises than to catchy rhythms and instrumental virtuosity.

It is, however, impossible to overstate the importance of the first recordings by the ODJB, if only because they sold extremely well and created the first wave of jazz fans throughout the United States. Not least among this group was a young Bix Beiderbecke. As a teenager in Davenport, Iowa, Beiderbecke heard the ODJB's records shortly after their release in 1917. Already a child prodigy at the piano, Beiderbecke picked out the tunes on the keyboard and later on a cornet. Eventually he created a new type of jazz that relied more on understatement and lyricism than on the grand, dramatic gestures of black artists. Comparing the solos of Beiderbecke to those of Louis Armstrong, one critic wrote of "the sonnet rather than the epic."[10]

It took a full three years after the ODJB made the first jazz records for a black artist with real connections to the blues and jazz to make her way into a recording studio. In 1920, Mamie Smith had a hit singing "Crazy Blues" with a group that included the cornetist Johnny Dunn. Before Louis Armstrong arrived in New York in 1924, Dunn was the among the city's most acclaimed black musicians. Born in Memphis, he played with W. C. Handy before joining Mamie Smith in New York. When he performed in major cities throughout the United States and in Europe, Dunn traveled with a valet.

Also in 1920, Paul Whiteman, the appropriately named Caucasian who called himself the "King of Jazz," made his first recordings. In 1922, Kid Ory and his Sunshine Orchestra introduced the record-buying public to New Orleans jazz with "Ory's Creole Trombone." For many true believers, however, jazz did not come of age until 1923, when Louis Armstrong, King Oliver, Jelly Roll Morton, and Freddie Keppard—all from New Orleans—began their recording careers. F. Scott Fitzgerald set the beginnings of the Jazz Age a few years earlier, but most of the world could not hear *real* jazz until 1923.

Much of what we know about unrecorded, pre-1920 New Orleans jazz comes from an archive of oral histories. Diligent researchers were constructing a history of jazz long before most Americans thought of jazz as something that had a history. From the 1950s through the 1970s, William Russell and Richard Allen of the William Ransom Hogan Jazz Archive at Tulane University interviewed more than one hundred New Orleanians who played the first jazz or who were intimate with the music in its infancy. Bolden's name appears repeatedly in these interviews, and not always as the mythical figure that appeared sometime after his death in 1930s.

As Bolden biographer Donald Marquis has demonstrated, most of the myths about Bolden come from Willie "Bunk" Johnson. When jazz purists, disgusted by the commercialized jazz of the Swing Era, went in search of the "real thing," they ran across Johnson. In the early 1930s, Bunk had stopped playing, having lost his teeth and sold his trumpet. In 1939, William Russell and another jazz purist bought Johnson a new set of teeth. The Dixieland trumpeter and bandleader Lu Watters chipped in to buy him a new horn. In a series of interviews, Johnson told Russell that he had played in Bolden's band. He also said that Bolden worked in a barbershop and that he edited a thin gossip magazine called *The Cricket*. None of this turned out to be true. Johnson may have improvised a Bolden biography in order to show how well he knew the man many acknowledged to be the inventor of jazz. More likely, he wanted to gain a bit of notoriety (and manhood) for himself.

Jelly Roll Morton, who insisted that *he* was the inventor of jazz, also told his share of tall tales. He spoke of Bolden when he was interviewed extensively by Alan Lomax at about the same time that Bunk Johnson was being resurrected. "Speaking of swell people," Morton said, "I might mention Buddy Bolden, the most powerful trumpet player I've ever heard of that was known and the absolute favorite of all the hangarounders in the Garden District. Bolden was a light brown-skin boy from Uptown. He drank all the whiskey he could find." [11]

Morton's information has turned out to be more useful. But the myths about Bolden should not be totally discarded. If nothing else, the mythological Bolden who worked as a barber and edited *The Cricket* is the hero of an extraordinary novel, Michael Ondaatje's *Coming Through Slaughter.* For Ondaatje, Bolden's music is inseparable from his sex life. In one of the novel's memorable scenes, Bolden makes passionate love to a woman, digging his fingers into her back as he creates a new version of "Cakewalking Blues." He plays the woman like he plays his cornet. And Ondaatje's Bolden goes mad because he has tried to make the cornet part of his body. His blood pours into the cornet along with his spit, his breath, and his soul. He has destroyed the boundary between trumpet and man. Like so many legendary jazz artists who followed him, Ondaatje's Bolden has also destroyed himself.

BEHIND THE LEGEND

Most of the documentary evidence on Bolden has been assiduously collected by Marquis, who spent years searching archives and old newspapers for every scrap of information about Bolden. In his biography *In Search of Buddy Bolden: First Man of Jazz*, Marquis tells us that Bolden's father died when he was six years old. Bolden did not, however, become a street waif like the young Louis Armstrong, who was abandoned by his father when he was still an infant. And unlike Armstrong, Bolden went to school and learned to read and write at an early age. His mother, Alice, appears to have been a devoted and resourceful woman who made sure that her son was properly schooled. Even though she worked as a housekeeper and laundress to support three children, the widowed Alice made sure that Buddy never had to work until after he had finished school. She built her life around her children and the Baptist church.

Buddy Bolden has much in common with three other central figures in jazz history. Duke Ellington, Charlie Parker, and Thelonious Monk all had mothers who were steadfastly devoted to their sons. Each mother told her son that he was entirely capable of accomplishing anything he set his mind to. In a country where black men were denied almost every opportunity for advancement, and in a musical world where their work was disparaged and even demonized, each musician withstood the racism of his day and persevered to make an essential contribution to music. Bolden should probably be counted among these fearless innovators whose destinies were determined at an early age by the attentions of an extraordinary woman. The trumpet may be a man's instrument, but Bolden could not have taken his first baby steps—or the giant steps that followed—without an inspirational mother.

Bolden may even have taken his first cornet lessons through his mother's efforts. When Buddy was a teenager, his mother had a relationship with a cook in the French Quarter named Manuel Hall who was also a cornetist. He lived near the Boldens and may actually have moved into their apartment at some point. Did Alice Bolden choose Hall because he could tutor her son on his instrument of choice? Although Hall was no virtuoso, he was able to give young Bolden what he needed, and he probably did it for free.

Having learned how to read music and how to play with a little technical polish, Bolden did the rest on his own. His most important resource was a city where music was everywhere, and he was blessed with a good ear. Eventually, Bolden would acquire the ability to hear another band's music, memorize it part by part, and then teach it to the members of his own band. When he was first starting out, Bolden was part of a small string orchestra that played for dances, balls, and parties. As in most Crescent City dance bands during the first two decades of the century, the violin was the dominant instrument, always playing the melody and frequently taking solos. Sometimes a clarinet replaced the violin as the lead instrument and took flowery, ornamented solos. Bolden was one of those most responsible for the demise of the string orchestra, creating a new hierarchy in which a cornet replaced the violin as the lead instrument.

Virtually everyone who heard Bolden remembers that he played *loud*. The claims that he could be heard from one side of town to the other may be only a slight exaggeration. In Bolden's day, New Orleans had no automobiles or heavy industry. As we all know from the tragic events of 2005, New Orleans sits below sea level, a collection of basins surrounded by levees. Essentially, it is a series of echo chambers. The city itself gave power to Bolden's cornet when he wanted to "call the children home." The phrase, with its romantic, slightly biblical resonance, is Bolden's own. He used it to describe the moments when he blew a short, recognizable melody at full blast to summon his audience. No one had ever heard anything like it before, and many New Orleanians dropped whatever they were doing and went in search of that sound. No instrument could have produced that sound except for the cornet and the trumpet.

In one of many legends about Bolden's power as a cornetist, he supposedly blew so hard that the tuning slide shot out of his horn, an impossibility for any horn a professional musician would own, but a great trick if that was what Bolden had in mind. We can, however, believe Paul Barbarin, a New Orleans drummer who was about seven when he saw Bolden's band. Interviewed in 1957, Barbarin remembers his mother telling him, "That's Buddy Bolden. He's gonna blow his brains out some day because he plays too loud."[12] According to Jelly Roll Morton, Bolden *did* blow his brains out, and as Morton implies, it's how he ended up in an insane asylum.

Going mad, however, is not the inevitable result of playing loud. At worst, you lose a few brain cells. Bolden may have been after something more than just earsplitting, mind-blowing volume. He was preaching with his cornet, imitating the gospel preachers who found untapped resources of vocal volume as they called out to their congregations. Bolden's great achievement may have been his ability to combine the rollicking sound of the gospel church with the spirit of the blues and turn it all into great music for dancers. By 1900, when Bolden had become King Bolden, he was working his cornet magic throughout the city. He had learned the art of adapting his style to the different performance venues in New Orleans. He could play sweet, "legitimate" music one night and funky, "ratty" music the next. When New Orleans bassist Pops Foster wrote in his autobiography that Bolden played "blues and all that stink music,"[13] that was only part of the story. Bolden's band might play a demure version of "Home Sweet Home" for groups with social aspirations and on those rare occasions when they played for white audiences. At the Uptown dance halls, where working-class blacks came to party, the band might play songs full of double entendres and out-and-out obscenities: "If You Don't Rock You Get No Cock" and "Stick It Where You Stuck It Last Night."[14] One of his most famous compositions, "Buddy Bolden's Blues," was a backhanded celebration of Funky Butt Hall. Audiences loved to sing "Funky Butt, Funky Butt, take it away" and "Open up that window and let that bad air out," but at least according to the eminent New Orleans clarinetist Sidney Bechet, they were inviting trouble. Bechet told interviewers that the police were likely to come down on crowds who sang the more explicit lines in Bolden's lyric.[15]

At the parties and balls where Bolden's low-down blues was most welcome (Bolden's repertoire actually included a number called "Low Down Blues"), people may have been dancing the slow drag, a step that was coming into its own at the turn of the century. The slow drag probably began in Southern juke joints and barrelhouses when dancers were running out of steam for dancing at the same time that they were looking forward to the pleasures of the flesh later that night. Dancers not only put their arms around each other in a mobile embrace; they brought their stomachs into contact. Sometimes they would grind their bodies together as they danced. Sometimes they would just grind. Since Bolden usually played the blues at a slow tempo—just a bit faster than a funeral march, according to one witness—the romantic possibilities were there for the taking.

Bolden's popularity with women is a large part of his legend. He was still in his teens when he started seeing Hattie Oliver, a young woman a few years older who moved in with him after she gave birth to his son. We don't know how long they stayed together, but census records show that by 1900 Hattie had changed her last name from Bolden back to Oliver. From 1902 until 1906, Bolden was living with Nora Bass, who bore him a daughter. Even if he was too young to have known Bolden, Bechet provides a memorable image of the cornetist walking about town in the company of as many as four women: "one woman, she'd have his trumpet, and another, she'd carry his watch, and another, she'd have his handkerchief, and maybe there'd be another one who wouldn't have nothing to carry, but she'd be there all the same hoping to carry something home."[16] This account is almost surely part of the Bolden myth, if only because most witnesses insist that Bolden never let *anyone* touch his cornet.

Nevertheless, Bolden did have the adulation of women, and he may even have been a pimp for some of the more devoted ones.

Manuel Manetta, who played with Bolden in 1906, told interviewers that Bolden was earning money from streetwalkers. Pimps and New Orleans musicians inhabited many of the same venues, and some musicians imitated the pimp's manly strut and style of dress. Bolden may have been thinking of a pimp when he let his shirt fall open so that audiences could see his red underwear. He was not, however, a regular in the brothels. Blues and ragtime could be heard in New Orleans's whorehouses at the turn of the century, but almost exclusively from a "professor" who sat at the piano in the parlor and who was just as likely to play a Chopin polonaise as a bawdy song. Very few brothels could afford an entire orchestra or even a quartet of musicians. And the rooms in the brothels were small. Even downstairs in the more spacious parlor where women were hustling for customers, a lone pianist, or perhaps one assisted by a guitarist or a clarinetist, could provide the right atmosphere without being too conspicuous. A brass band would have been completely out of place. Bolden did not have to frequent the brothels to be a heavy drinker and a show-off as well as a ladies' man. He may have picked up some musical ideas in the houses, but he was just as likely to take his inspiration from the spirituals and hymns of the Baptist church. Two of his fellow musicians remember seeing him walk out of church with his wife Nora and her sister sometime in 1904 or 1905. The three were, according to one witness, "swinging." But like most New Orleans musicians of the day, Bolden did not regularly attend church once he began working steadily, especially on Saturday nights. Nevertheless, he would not have forgotten what he heard as a child. As Armstrong famously observed, it all started in the Sanctified Church.

Then as now, black musicians raised in the church were entirely capable of singing and playing the dirty blues. Unlike the characters in films like *Green Pastures* (1936) and *Cabin in the Sky* (1943), black musicians were not caught in a Manichaean struggle between the dance hall and the church. Few would have drawn a sharp line between the bawdy music of the one and the sacred songs of the other. There is a revealing scene in *Ray*, the biographical film about Ray Charles released in 2004. Early in his career, when Charles and his band are playing a hot dance number based on a gospel tune, several members of the audience and at least one of the musicians walk out, warning Charles and the rest of his band that they are on the fast track to hell. Charles tells the remaining audience to say "Amen" if they like his music. They do, and the band gets back to business.

The musical careers of several eminent black composers were also based in the combination of gospel and the blues. W. C. Handy composed hymns for churchgoers as well as secular songs about loose women and hard-drinking men. Thomas Andrew Dorsey, known as the "Father of Gospel Music" for his anthems of the black church, including Martin Luther King Jr.'s favorite, "Precious Lord," was also capable of writing that bawdy gem of sexual double entendre "It's Tight Like That" even after his "second conversion" to Christianity.[17] This is not to say that Handy and Dorsey were always of one mind about their separate careers as composers. The long, painful history of successful black artists struggling with religious parents and even with their own convictions stretches from Mahalia Jackson and the Staples Singers to Sam Cooke and Al Green. Even in the scene from *Ray*, a few of the listeners *do* leave when Charles is charged with abusing religious traditions.

INVENTING JAZZ

Preaching the blues—imitating the cadences and the improvisatory spirit of the preacher—helped Bolden prevail in the cutthroat contests among New Orleans musicians, where innovation was the surest way to defeat the competition. This is not to say that no one before Bolden had taken liberties with rhythm and melody. As early as 1885, even white bands were "ragging" the tunes in parades, giving them syncopation and a rhythmic bounce their composers never imagined. In the string bands, there had been cornetists who enchanted audiences with delicate filigrees behind a solo violin, not unlike the way Harry Edison would make short, piquant statements with his muted trumpet behind the vocals of Frank Sinatra. But Bolden made the cornet the main attraction, loudly taking over the role of the violin and essentially ending its dominance in turn-of-the-century dance bands.

Bolden delighted crowds by imitating human speech and even animal sounds. To this day, African American jazz instrumentalists are more likely than whites to deploy a sound that recalls vocal inflections. Bolden could make his cornet moan and growl. He also departed from the "legitimate" technique to shake or smear his notes. As an African American in the South, Bolden had the "advantage" of being excluded from conservatory training. He may not have been sufficiently accomplished to make the lightning-fast runs up and down the horn that would become Louis Armstrong's trademark, but he was able to make up countermelodies to familiar songs on the spot. He may have been one of those improvisers who engaged in a dialogue with the song as written, often coming up with a variation that was as beautiful or as well structured as the original.

As an improviser, Bolden stood between two traditions. On the one side were the New Orleans Creoles with their conservatory training, their symphony orchestras, and their pride in playing difficult music exactly as written. On the other side were musicians in the rural South who could not read music but could play by ear and in some way re-create what they had heard. A few decades later, Duke Ellington would call the nonreading musicians "ear cats." These players had been performing simple improvisations on church music and popular songs for several years before Bolden's appearance. But the skilled professionals in the brass bands and string orchestras of New Orleans had little respect for such musicians and scorned their improvisations. Bolden did not. Listening to them as carefully as he had listened to the marching bands, the string bands, and the preachers, he took their improvisatory techniques to a new level.

Mixing the blues with the emotional intensity of the Holy Roller church, Bolden also took a more aggressive approach to syncopation. His band may have been among the first to take the raggy rhythmic feel of the older brass bands and loosen it up a bit so that dancers could let themselves go. Bolden could also play soft, even for dancers. On some numbers, he told the members of his band that he wanted to be able to hear the dancers' feet. When he stepped back from playing at the higher decibels, Bolden may even have been involved in the wholesale transformation of the group interaction in dance bands. Although his cornet was the dominating voice, Bolden could play the melody at a delicate volume while the clarinet bobbed and weaved around him and the trombone slid in and out with long notes. This is still the style of the front line in a Dixieland band, and it almost surely began with Bolden.

Some who heard Bolden referred to the "heartbreaking warmth" of his tone. They may have been responding to Bolden's talent for imitating the human voice. Whether vocalists sang opera, the blues, or saloon ditties, they could create a powerful emotional effect by using vibrato and dramatic changes in dynamics. Growing up in the vast musical culture of New Orleans, Bolden could have learned the art of an emotional vibrato almost anywhere. In one of the stories in the Bolden cycle, he endowed "Home Sweet Home" with so much nostalgic feeling that black sailors who were about to sail out of a nearby harbor to fight in the Spanish-American War suddenly jumped ship.[18]

By 1905, the popularity of Bolden's band in New Orleans was matched by only one other organization, John Robichaux's orchestra. Although most Creoles lived Downtown and scorned the blacks who lived Uptown, Robichaux was a recent immigrant to New Orleans and actually lived Uptown with blacks. He was, however, classically trained and made a vigorous attempt to appeal to listeners from higher social strata. He liked to call his band "a society orchestra." For many whites, there was no difference between a Creole like Robichaux and an African American, and shortly after Bolden's day, Southern legislatures created a raft of Jim Crow laws that consigned both groups to the same level of disenfranchisement. But there were major musical, religious, and political differences between the two groups. By the 1920s, there were bands in New Orleans that combined blacks and Creoles and even Italians and Latinos. Nevertheless, in the early years of the century, in spite of the widely accepted notion that one drop of black blood could turn anyone black, most "Creoles of Color" looked down their noses at African Americans and avoided their company.

John Robichaux still had violins in his orchestra, and all of his musicians were skilled in the art of reading music. They played the polite dance tunes of the day with finesse and authority, and they drew crowds when they performed for free in the parks. Many witnesses recalled the moment when Robichaux was playing in Lincoln Park and Bolden was performing in Johnson Park, just a few blocks away. Playing at full volume, Bolden called the children home, spurring a mass migration from Robichaux's audience. In the dance halls too, patrons began to prefer Bolden's more exciting music to the smoother, more sedate sounds of Robichaux. There is no question, however, that Bolden learned a thing or two from Robichaux, and vice versa. Some of the same musicians actually worked for both bandleaders, surreptitiously violating the de facto musical segregation of the period.

DECLINE AND FALL

In 1906, after he had become King Bolden, Buddy began to fall apart. The first sign of trouble was an attack of headaches. Then he began seeing things. He said he was afraid of his cornet. After a serious bout with pains in his head, Bolden took to his bed, where he was attended by his mother, his wife, and his mother-in-law. But he was not bedridden for long. He jumped up and became so violent that the police were called in. Marquis has found a newspaper story from March 1906 reporting that Bolden was arrested for striking his mother-in-law with a water pitcher. He told police that his mother was trying to drug him, which does not explain why he struck his mother-in-law. Soon afterward, his wife Nora left him.

For the next year, Bolden's behavior and playing continued to deteriorate. He fired members of his band, even those who had been with him for several years and had helped make the band a success. In later years, many New Orleans musicians would proudly claim that they had played with Bolden, but most of them passed through his band during the chaotic year when he was hiring and firing almost at random. He began showing up late for performances or not at all, and on at least one occasion he refused to pay his bandsmen. After he hired Frankie Dusen, a trombonist with a gift for managing a business, Dusen began finding regular bookings for the band. He also made sure that another cornet player could be counted on to show up when Bolden did not. Eventually Dusen took over the band and fired Bolden.

For the next few months, Bolden worked sporadically when and where he could. In March 1907, almost exactly a year after the newspaper account of his attack on his mother-in-law, Bolden was arrested again. According to Marquis, there is a note in his first arrest record that reads, "Read or write: yes." In his arrest record the following year, Bolden is listed as illiterate, surely an indication of how disabling his illness had become. His age was estimated at thirty-six; he was actually twenty-nine.

Bolden spent a month in a jail cell, a horrifying experience for a man already so delusional that he could no longer read and write. In some ways Bolden was fortunate that the mayor of New Orleans was engaged in a campaign to move mentally ill prisoners out of prisons and into mental institutions with empty beds. The East Louisiana State Hospital in Jackson was a long way from New Orleans, and it provided Bolden with the peace and quiet he probably needed. The doctors and orderlies at the state hospital seem to have been humane if not especially attentive. Although he had been drinking heavily prior to his troubles and alcoholism may have contributed to his breakdown, the official diagnosis was "dementia praecox," an obsolete term used to describe seriously delusional patients. Bolden was almost certainly a paranoid schizophrenic who might have been treated successfully with drugs had he been born several decades later.

During his first days in the sanitarium, Bolden had a series of incoherent and violent outbursts, but his rage gradually subsided. One member of the staff recalled that he spoke in some detail about his sexual conquests. He occasionally performed with the institution's orchestra of inmates, but mostly he kept to himself, muttering incoherently. The asylum's doctors reported a gradual decline during his twenty-four years in the facility. In 1920, after thirteen years of confinement, he was no longer able to recognize his mother and sister when they paid him a visit. Bolden was fifty-four when he died of a stroke in 1931. Although his sister saw to it that he had a funeral, there was no brass band to play hymns on the way to the Holt Cemetery or to play joyous New Orleans music on the way home. Two years after his burial, his sister was no longer able to keep up the payments to the cemetery for the care of his grave. His remains were dug up and buried deeper so that another body could be buried on top of them. No one knows the exact location of his remains in an old cemetery that was overgrown with weeds even before Hurricane Katrina.

As the oral histories indicate, Bolden was remembered by a small coterie of musicians who admired his showmanship and his innovative approach to the cornet. Otherwise, he was almost completely forgotten, at least until the late 1930s when historians began taking the first steps toward writing a jazz history. But whereas historians had to resurrect Bolden for posterity, his widow was doing her best to forget him. The life of Bolden's wife after his institutionalization ends his story with special pathos. Like Bolden's mother, Alice, Nora Bass was a devout Baptist from a conservative home. When he began courting her, Buddy Bolden took Nora to the First Street Baptist Church along with her sister Dora. In 1902 Buddy and Nora moved into an apartment together, probably to get away from family members who did not approve of their common-law marriage and a child born out of wedlock. Nora must have made her peace with Bolden's late-night schedule as well as with his habit of spending entire nights at his old home, with or without female companionship.

Nora moved out in 1906 when Bolden became too erratic even for a woman accustomed to life with an eccentric musician. At some point, she left New Orleans for Los Angeles and then moved to Chicago. She remarried and settled with her husband in Iowa. When William Russell tracked her down in 1942, Nora was puzzled by the arrival of a white man with a necktie and a notebook. Once she learned that he wanted to talk about Bolden, she asserted that she had never heard of him. Eventually she admitted that she had lived with him but expressed disapproval of his life and of the people with whom she associated. She also told Russell that her current husband did not know that she once kept house with a man to whom she was not married, and she worried aloud that he might come home at any minute and demand an explanation. As a courtesy, Russell left early.

INVENTING BLACK MASCULINITY

Buddy Bolden may not have been a great musician. Peter Bocage, a cornetist and violinist who was born the same year as Bolden, told interviewers that Bolden played everything in B-flat, the easiest key for improvisers on the cornet and trumpet.[19] Others would praise Bolden but then declare that they preferred the playing of some other cornetist. Sidney Bechet implied that Bolden was a semitalented show-off, more of an entertainer than a musician, and that he "faked" his way through a solo when his knowledge of the tune faltered. "It didn't matter to him whether it was especially fitting or not what he made up, he'd just go ahead and do it, and he'd make you forget all about whatever it was *he* had forgotten."[20] Bechet was too young to have had much direct experience of Bolden, and he was probably holding him to a higher standard than was fair for a man who was flying by the seat of his pants while creating a brand-new music.

Bechet may also have known, if only from hearsay, that Bolden's popularity was based on his readiness to titillate his audience with dirty words and sexy lyrics. But in this sense, Bolden stands in a great tradition. Like many of the most famous trumpeters—Louis Armstrong, Bunny Berigan, Louis Prima, Dizzy Gillespie, Clark Terry—Bolden sang when he needed a rest from playing. Trumpeters need periods of rest after just a few minutes of intense blowing on this most difficult of instruments. Bolden was surely not the first to discover that singing gave him a break from the pressure of metal on his lips. Nor was he the first to hear his audience cheer loudest when he sang about sex and bathroom humor. Bolden's popularity may have been based more on his innovations than on his execution of those innovations. But how successful would a brilliant musician like Louis Armstrong have been had *he* not expanded his stage act with suggestive lyrics and bawdy humor?

Marquis is surely on target when he points out that Bolden, born more than a decade after the Emancipation Proclamation, faced a world full of possibilities that few black men could have imagined even a few years earlier. As a young man, he would have seen the men in brass bands with their flashy uniforms marching majestically in the parades. And he must have noticed how the eyes of women lit up when they saw tall, uniformed men gracefully brandishing their polished brass instruments. Although he never played in the marching bands, the uniformed men surely inspired Bolden both as a musician and as a man.

The American cornet virtuosi of the late nineteenth century were like no one else.[21] These men found time after their jobs in shops, factories, and offices to master their instruments. They belonged to none of the guilds and court organizations to which the European trumpet masters had belonged centuries earlier. Towns that might have had a brass band or two were not likely to have a community theater, so there were no virtuoso actors who lived and worked in the vicinity. And even if the town did have an admired amateur actor, or an accomplished singer in the church choir, neither would have felt the need to invest the hours and years needed to master the cornet repertoire.

The local cornet master surely had the respect of a large portion of his community, especially if he was white and a respectable tradesman. But what if the cornet virtuoso was black? Obviously, in a Southern town like New Orleans, no black musician, no matter how talented, could have the stature of the white musicians who were nevertheless his peers. Even before Bolden, a handful of black cornet virtuosi became professionals and traveled the world giving concerts and astounding audiences. Francis Johnson, born in Philadelphia in 1792, was one such professional. He taught students, both black and white, and conducted orchestras. He was the first African American to publish his own musical compositions as sheet music. In England, Queen Victoria presented Johnson with a silver bugle after a command performance.[22]

Francis Johnson, however, applied his technical abilities to the exact same repertoire that white artists of the time were playing. Before Bolden, no black cornet virtuoso became famous for appropriating rhythmically exciting African-inflected sounds in so assertive a fashion. We can probably add to the list of Bolden's achievements the discovery of a new way for a black American to express himself as a man.

Ralph Ellison, who once made the essential observation that American culture is jazz shaped, helps us understand Bolden's transformations of African American masculinity. An avid student of jazz and a trumpet player in his own right, Ellison knew about Bolden and even quotes from "Buddy Bolden's Blues" in the final pages of his masterpiece, *Invisible Man*. In 1964, Ellison reviewed *Blues People*, an ambitious and provocative book by Amiri Baraka, then known as LeRoi Jones, who described how black music spoke to black Americans and emerged from their lives. Ellison took issue with much of what Baraka had to say, especially his assertion that American blacks had been so oppressed that they were without hope. For Ellison, even a young slave was not likely to say, "I want to be a slave when I grow up." Ellison saw too many other possibilities for black men, even under slavery. He argued that a young black slave would have said he wanted to grow up to be "a coachman, a teamster, a cook, the best damned steward on the Mississippi, the best jockey in Kentucky, a butler, a farmer, a stud, or, hopefully, a free man!"[23]

Given his great admiration for Louis Armstrong, even during the years when many blacks regarded the trumpeter as an Uncle Tom, Ellison might have put "trumpet master" on his list. For me, the crucial word is *stud*. Today, a man who is hip or stylish may be called a stud, but in the nineteenth century, and surely in Ellison's list, a stud was a man known for his sexual prowess with women. Even if someone like Buddy Bolden had to step aside when a white person approached him on the sidewalk, and even if he was regularly referred to as "boy," he knew that he possessed everything it took to be a man, including sexual power. As Michael Ondaatje understood many years later, Bolden's sexuality and masculinity were inseparable from his cornet playing. His command over the instrument made women desire him and men envy him. His cornet artistry was driven by his ability to make it sound sexy, to "jazz" it. He was a stud *and* a cornetist extraordinaire.

In the American South that Bolden knew, a black man was either agreeable and eager to please around white people, or he was strange fruit hanging from a poplar tree. Between 1895 and 1907, when Bolden was a working musician in New Orleans, more than fifteen hundred black men were lynched in the United States. Photographs taken at lynchings were often turned into postcards and circulated freely throughout the country. If the faces of the black victims in the photographs are horrifying, so are the expressions—both of execration and of complacency—on the white faces.

Playing his horn at extreme volume, ragging the melodies with sexual innuendo, and singing the dirty blues, Bolden was as audacious as any black man in the South. He had found a way to assert himself as a man without experiencing the fate of those proud black men who refused to yield to white racism and paid for it with their lives. Because he expressed himself with music, and because whites have always been more fascinated than repelled by black music, he was not punished for his self-expression.

We know that Bolden played for white audiences on at least a few occasions. He must have taken delight as he lofted lyrics and musical ideas unique to black culture over the heads of his white audiences. There are no records of trouble or police action, so we can assume that whites in New Orleans responded well to Bolden's intense performance style. White cornetists were surely listening carefully to Bolden and borrowing his ideas. And many of these white musicians, whether they thought about it or not, were borrowing styles of masculine expression from Bolden along with the music.

At least since the 1830s, white men at the minstrel shows applied burnt cork to their faces and ridiculed black men. But the shows also offered whites an opportunity to enjoy the transgressiveness, sexuality, joie de vivre, and unfettered masculinity they attributed to black men.[24] And in one sense the white men got it right. A manly style of walking and talking is most essential when your manliness is least likely to be acknowledged. The minstrel performers regularly sang songs about sexual antics as they played variations on the masculine deportment that black men had so scrupulously cultivated. The white suburban youth with a loping walk, baggy shorts, turned-around baseball cap, and hip-hop songs on his iPod is the direct descendant of the white audiences at the minstrel show of 150 years ago. So is the white rocker with his thrusting pelvis and the gravel of authenticity in his voice. And so is the slam-dunking, high-fiving, trash-talking white athlete on the court.

As far back as the 1840s, advertisements for minstrel shows featured a caricatured black man holding a banjo out in front of his crotch, just like the white rocker today brandishes his phallic guitar. Indeed, with the arrival of rock 'n' roll and teen culture in the 1950s, the guitar became the instrument of choice for any young man striving to act out his masculinity. But because of people like Buddy Bolden, Louis Armstrong, and the other early black masters, men who wanted to express powerful masculinity with music turned to the trumpet for the first half of the twentieth century. Unlike boxing champion Jack Johnson, who infuriated whites by defeating white opponents with his fists, many whites applauded the black trumpeters, even when they were outplaying their pigmentally deprived opponents.

Buddy Bolden did more than invent jazz. He took hold of the royal, ceremonial, and military aspects of the trumpet and remade them for black culture. He invented a new breed of masculinity, essentially teaching subsequent generations of black men how to strut their stuff as men while delighting the same whites who might otherwise have brutally punished their expressions of black masculinity.

chapter 2

From the Pyramids to New Orleans:
The Trumpet Before Jazz

uddy Bolden worked his magic in many ways, but perhaps the most salient among them, as witnesses regularly observed, was that he played loud—louder than anyone had ever played anything in New Orleans. Whether he knew it or not, Bolden was part of a long history of pumping up the volume that goes back at least to ninth-century China, when gunpowder in fireworks made for earsplitting public entertainments. Throughout the Renaissance and the baroque period, European royalty regularly increased the number of trumpeters and kettledrummers in their court ensembles, and symphony orchestras grew bigger and louder throughout the nineteenth century. Tchaikovsky upped the ante by supplementing his orchestra with cannons for his 1812 Overture. And ever since the 1960s, rock bands have blown the minds and eardrums of their audiences by plugging into potent amplifiers and gargantuan speakers. In the mock documentary film *This Is Spinal Tap* (1984), Christopher

Guest's Nigel Tufnel proudly points to the volume control on an amplifier that goes up to eleven.

Recent evidence suggests that people were already seeking out high levels of volume for reasons of their own more than seventeen thousand years ago. The cave of Lascaux was discovered when some teenage boys playing with their dog on a hill in the Dordogne region of France in 1940 stumbled upon what seemed like a bottomless pit. When they came back with a lantern, they saw a huge cave lying beneath their feet. They returned with one of their schoolteachers, who quickly called in the archaeologists. As the world soon found out, the walls of the cave of Lascaux were painted sometime between 15,000 and 13,000 B.C.E. Often regarded as the world's oldest surviving works of art, the colorful paintings of cows, bulls, bison, and stags are vivid and naturalistic. Art historians believe, however, that the hunters who produced the pictures were *not* creating works of art. More likely they were attempting to capture the life force of the animals, preparing themselves for the hunt on which their community depended for survival.

Even though the Lascaux cave was thoroughly explored immediately after 1940, a new discovery was made in 1988. A group of French researchers took sound equipment into the cave and tested each of its several caverns. The animal paintings, they discovered, are located exactly where acoustical resonance is most intense.[1] The Lascaux tribes painted the animals at precisely the place where they could make the most racket. Perhaps the paintings were incidental to a larger goal of increasing communal power and bolstering the prowess of the hunters through noise. The tribes may have chanted, shouted, sung, banged on drums, or blown on flutelike instruments. Did they also make trumpetlike sounds by blowing into horns and thighbones of animals they had hunted, killed, and eaten?

The story of the trumpet may not go back that far, but the instrument's history has always revolved around its ability to rack the environment with sound. Writing in the eighth century B.C.E. about events that may have taken place much earlier, Homer inserts a trumpet into one of the similes that were essential to his epic style. When a Greek warrior cries out in battle, Homer compares his voice to a trumpet sounding the alarm when the enemy is at the gate of a city.

The trumpet's direct association with masculinity also dates back at least to ancient Greece. The geographer Pausanias wrote in the second century C.E. that the trumpet was invented by Tyrsenus, a son of Heracles. The trumpet, in other words, begins only one degree of separation from the single figure in Greek myth most associated with unreconstructed masculinity. There is also a trumpet story involving Achilles, a character only slightly less hypermasculine than Heracles. In the second century B.C.E., the mythographer Apollodorus wrote that Achilles' mother, the goddess Thetis, knew that her son would die if he went to Troy.[2] Attempting to hide him from the Greek captains, Thetis dressed Achilles as a girl and concealed him among the daughters of King Lycomedes on the island of Scyros. Already a boy warrior, Achilles was uncomfortable living among women, but he decided to endure the cross-dressing when he fell in love with one of the king's daughters. The prophet Calchas, however, divined where Achilles was staying and told the Greek captains, including Odysseus. Always portrayed in Greek literature as crafty if not devious, Odysseus arrived at Scyros with cases of gold trinkets and stylish clothing. He displayed the gifts on several tables, making sure that he also put out a sword and a shield. When the king's daughters arrived at the tables to swoon over the gifts, Odysseus arranged for a trumpet to sound a call to battle. Achilles quickly threw off his woman's clothing, seized the sword and shield, and ran in the direction of the trumpet call. His ruse exposed, Achilles was soon on his way to Troy. The tale of how a trumpet provoked an instant reaction in the young Achilles and definitively reestablished his maleness combines two of the central elements in trumpet history. But even before Homer, war and masculinity were essential to the story of the trumpet.

PLAYING IT BACKWARD

The first trumpets were conches, elephant tusks, antelope horns, thighbones, and various types of hollowed-out tree trunks such as the Australian didgeridoo. Prehistoric people discovered that buzzing the lips at the end of these naturally occurring objects could make a distinctive sound. Putting metal to use for an even more potent sound must have been a natural thought as the first civilizations moved from stone to bronze. Trumpet historians, however, are frustrated by how little we actually know about ancient instruments. For example, the distinguished brass scholar Anthony Baines has noticed that inscriptions on Macedonian coins suggest that Alexander the Great had relatively short trumpets in the armies he led in the fourth century B.C.E. But since no trumpet survives from the days of Alexander, Baines wonders if the trumpets were made to look short so that they could fit onto the coins.[3]

If we had more information, we could surely write a better history of the trumpet. But even if we knew more about trumpets from ancient Macedonia and elsewhere, we would still have to contend with the fact that, as Thomas Kuhn and others have convincingly argued, history is written backward. In other words, we understand the past best if we can see its fulfillment in the present. If an event has no real impact on the present, it is not likely to be written up as history. A simple, coherent story that ends with—but in fact begins with—the modern trumpet would go back to Egyptian relief sculptures from the end of the fifteenth century B.C.E. These are the first known representations of metal trumpets. The sculptures depict men blowing into tubular instruments with flared bells at the end. More often than not, the man with the horn is at the front of an advancing army. The trumpets in these representations bear an unmistakable resemblance to two trumpets buried with King Tutankhamen in approximately 1350 B.C.E. These oldest surviving metal trumpets were among the treasures when King Tut's tomb was famously excavated in 1922. One trumpet was made of silver, the other of bronze with touches of gold (figure 3).

The horns rested quietly until 1939, when a producer at the British Broadcasting Company decided to record the sound of the instruments. Long before a madman named Laszlo Toth got close enough to Michelangelo's *Pietà* in the Vatican to strike it fifteen times with a ball-peen hammer, museums were wide open in ways we can barely imagine today. With the consent of the nervous curators at the Cairo Museum—who were, after all, British subjects at that time—a British soldier was sent to try out the horns. When he inserted a modern mouthpiece into the sleek, silver tube with the flare at the end, he gave it an extra push, resulting in a split down the side of the instrument.

Fortunately, the silver trumpet was quickly repaired and restored. In the early years of the twenty-first century, it was included in the traveling exhibit of treasures from Tutankhamen's tomb. A few years after the disaster with the silver trumpet, a more cautious Egyptologist and brass specialist named Hans Hickmann put his lips to the still-intact bronze trumpet. Carefully adopting what he assumed to be the appropriate embouchure for a thirty-five-hundred-year-old trumpet, he produced a few powerful if unpleasant tones. The sound was consistent with writings from about 100 C.E. by the Greek philosopher and biographer Plutarch, who said that the Egyptians despised the sound of the trumpet because it was so much like the braying of an ass. Plutarch said that many Egyptians had such hate for the monstrous god Typhon, usually portrayed with the features of an ass, that even hearing a trumpet was considered a sin.[4] If it was associated with a despised god and despised animal, the Egyptian trumpet could not have possessed a melodious sound, at least not in the time of Plutarch.

The trumpet was more useful for rousing armies to battle and for intimidating the enemy, as the relief sculptures suggest. Ancient Egyptian instrument makers had mastered the art of metallurgy, combining different metals to produce an alloy, softening it with intense heat, hammering it into a sheet, and then bending it into a cylinder. These smiths and craftsmen discovered that they could hammer together a device that could produce a uniquely powerful sound, especially when the right player buzzed his lips at the narrow end of the tube. They also knew how important it was to attach a flare at the end of the cylinder to make the sound even louder.

The Egyptian trumpets were approximately twenty inches long, very short by historical standards. Trumpets with greater length were eventually produced all over the ancient world. A standard B-flat trumpet today would measure about fifty-one inches uncoiled. The dung, a copper trumpet still played in Tibet on religious occasions, measures more than fifteen feet, so long that it must be rested on the ground when played. In the Renaissance, Europeans built long trumpets with unusually large flared bells and then fastened them into circular coils. These were the first hunting horns. Later, with the addition of valves, the hunting horn became the modern French horn.

Homer called the trumpet a "salpinx," the word for tube, which is basically what the trumpet has always been. The oldest surviving Greek trumpet dates to the middle of the fifth century B.C.E. and sits in the Museum of Fine Arts in Boston (see figure 4). Although the Greeks had metal trumpets, this salpinx is made primarily of ivory and measures a little more than five feet. We know that the trumpet was played at the Olympic Games and at the drama festivals. The Greek tragedian Aeschylus wrote that the sound of the salpinx was piercing, like a woman screaming. The Romans called their trumpet a "tuba," adopting, like the Greeks, the word for tube. In spite of its name, the Roman tuba bears no resemblance to the modern tuba or Sousaphone. Sometime before 550 B.C.E., when the book of Numbers took its present form, the Israelites created a metal trumpet about four feet long called a chatzotzrah. The Hebrew Bible distinguishes between the chatzotzrah and the shofar, a much shorter instrument made from the horn of a sheep or goat killed in ritual (see figure 5). Although these two types of trumpets were often used on the same occasions, the chatzotzrah was used more in secular events, while the shofar was more likely to be used on specifically religious occasions. It is the chatzotzrah, however, that Jehovah orders Moses to build in Numbers. Moses was told to make two trumpets from hammered silver and to entrust them to priests to play on specific occasions, such as summoning the community, breaking camp, and rousing soldiers at war.

In approximately 500 B.C.E., the Etruscans may have been the first to make trumpets out of brass, an alloy of about 70 percent copper and 30 percent zinc. It was easy to forge when hot, but firm and responsive when cool. By the Middle Ages, however, metal trumpets were rare in Europe, but they continued to be made in Asia and the Middle East. Crusaders returning to Europe around 1100 brought back long cylindrical trumpets with pommels or knobs at crucial junctures, allowing the instrument to be disassembled. These Arab trumpets strongly influenced medieval instrument makers in Europe, if only because the Arab—or "Saracen"—armies were so successful at terrifying their enemies with noise. In the eleventh century, one chronicler wrote that the Saracen trumpets and kettledrums created such a din that the Christian invaders had to stop up the ears of their horses. At about the same time, long metal trumpets begin to appear in European art, usually as the instrument announcing the Last Judgment. Those trumpets were there to wake the dead, more evidence that the early trumpet was intended for something other than lovely music.

The presence of the word *buisine* in the *Song of Roland* has raised questions for scholars. The word suggests an instrument similar to the bucina, a short metal horn used by Roman armies for signaling. None of these instruments exists anymore, and we know them only from ancient gravestones that give the buried man's occupation as buccinator, roughly the equivalent of a camp bugler. But it would be strange if the author of the *Song of Roland* knew about the instrument. Written around 1100 by an unknown author, the *Song of Roland* has long been an inevitable reading assignment for graduate students specializing in French literature. This lengthy epic poem appeared just as Arab trumpets were being introduced into Europe, but *buisine* is used to describe the horn with which the heroic Roland summons the armies of Charlemagne. Roland is in a desperate battle with the Saracens, but he refuses to call for help. Only when it's too late and most of his troops have died does Roland blow his horn, believing that once the emperor sees what has happened, he will wreak vengeance on the enemy. Like many subsequent trumpeters who suffered from the stern demands of the instrument, Roland's temples burst when he plays the loudest note. In spite of the sin of severe overblowing, he dies a martyr's death, and saints take his soul straight to paradise.

The appearance of the buisine in this tale is confusing, since Charlemagne's armies almost certainly did not have metal trumpets. One clue is that the *Song of Roland* says that the trumpet was hung around Roland's neck. Scholars have speculated that the instrument was a smaller horn, probably made from ivory, commonly known as an oliphant since it resembles the tusk of an elephant. In fact, many translators have used *oliphant* when rendering the text's *buisine* into another language.

In the late twelfth century, more than a century after the literary

Roland blew his brains out, Richard the Lionheart was in Sicily en route to Palestine. There he heard an instrument that resembled a Roman tuba. The Sicilians, however, referred to it as a "trumpa." Like most of the battle trumpets the Christians were then encountering, the trumpa probably came from the Arab world. In fact, the Saracens had only recently left their colony in Sicily. Regardless, *tromba*, *Trompeta*, *trompette*, and *trumpet* are the names that have stuck in Italian, German, French, and English. The root word originally referred to an animal's horn.

Once the Renaissance was under way, instrument makers discovered a new technique, perhaps inspired by the Arab trumpets brought back by Crusaders.[5] Around 1375, they learned how to bend a hot metal tube to specification. Instruments that were more than simple tubes had previously been made by casting the halves of a metal instrument in molds and then soldering them together. Because copper, the major ingredient in brass and the first metal trumpets, melts at a much higher temperature than lead, a copper tube will maintain its shape when filled with molten lead. When the lead cools until it is pliable but firm, the tube can be bent without kinking or losing its cylindrical form. Renaissance smiths surely worked with a wooden hammer of some sort to help shape the tube. Once the tube attained its desired shape, the lead could be heated again so that it flowed out of the tube. Trumpet makers today use a similar process, using a tar-like substance or even ice to fill a brass tube before bending it.

THE NATURAL TRUMPET

The raucous, high-pitched sound of a trumpet could be heard above the clamor of war, but if soldiers were to understand the exact commands blaring out from the trumpet, each signal had to be markedly different from the others. During the Civil War, infantrymen in combat had to recognize more than twenty bugle calls, including "fix bayonets," "deploy as skirmishers," "commence fire," "change directions to the right," "change directions to the left," "lie down," "rally by fours," "rally by sections," "rally by platoons," and so on. Because longer horns can produce more notes and hence more distinct signals, some of the first battle trumpets may have been as long as seven feet. Once these trumpets were folded on themselves twice, they were much more manageable and less likely to be smashed against trees or run over by retreating soldiers. By 1400, most trumpets were folded twice with a mouthpiece at one end and a flared bell at the other. This device is now known as a natural trumpet, a brass instrument similar to a stretched-out version of a Boy Scout's bugle (see figure 6).

Although court trumpeters were playing dance music for royalty as early as 1430, it was not until the early 1600s that the natural trumpet began to assume a significant role in European art music. The valveless trumpet continued to be an important orchestral instrument until well into the nineteenth century, but the natural trumpet was essential to the music of Bach, Vivaldi, and Purcell. When audiences first heard the chorus sing "A Trumpet Shall Sound" in Handel's *Messiah*, they heard a natural trumpet. The same instrument first played the solo that later become famous for announcing the weekly television broadcast of *Masterpiece Theatre*. That piece of bravura trumpet work is a fanfare from the first *Suites de Symphonies* by Jean-Joseph Mouret (1682–1738), a French composer of the baroque period who might otherwise be completely forgotten.

Like the bugle, however, the natural trumpet could play only a few notes in the lower register. Think of a modern B-flat trumpet played without valves. The lowest note a trained player can manage is a middle C, the note at the bottom of the treble clef. The next note that can be played open or without pressing any of the valves is G, a fifth higher in the middle of the staff. The next note is a C, a fourth above the G and one octave above middle C. As the player proceeds upward, the laws of physics make more notes or "partials" available. These partial notes are already present in the lower notes when they are played loud, a harmonic effect of a vibrating column of air within a tube. In the next octave, a player not using the valves can hit an E, only a major third above the previous C. After that, the partials that come out most effortlessly are the G at the top of the staff, the B-flat above that, and then the next C, usually known as high C, only a step above the previous note. (See figure 7.)

Once the trumpeter reaches the highest extremes, where only the most accomplished masters can play comfortably, almost any note is possible. In other words, the higher the pitch, the more partials are available to the player of the natural trumpet. Those trumpeters today who command the stratospheric upper reaches essentially have no need of valves at a certain point, just as the eighteenth-century masters who played the appallingly high notes in Bach's second *Brandenburg* Concerto could do it all on a valveless natural trumpet.

For the less advanced musician, the natural trumpet had limited use because the player could not hit all the notes in the lower and middle registers that are readily available to violinists, flutists, and most of the other instrumentalists in the orchestra. A most unlikely predecessor of the modern trumpet presented a solution to this problem. A cornetto, also known, confusingly, as a cornett, is a curved wooden instrument about two feet long, often wrapped in leather (see figure 8). In Germany, the instrument is called *der Zink*.

When Monteverdi wrote his beautiful Vespers of 1610, he wrote the lower horn parts for posaune, the brass predecessor of the trombone. But for horns in the upper register, he wrote for the cornetto. Although it can sound somewhat like a trumpet, the cornetto has holes instead of keys or valves. At first glance, it resembles a large, gently curving recorder. Its distinctive, trumpetlike sound is produced by the type of cupped mouthpiece found on most brass instruments.

In much of the majestic sacred music that the Italian composers Giovanni Gabrieli and Claudio Monteverdi wrote in the early seventeenth century, wooden cornetti soar into the upper register, producing sounds meant to suggest an ascent into heaven.

The cornetto was not, however, a brass instrument, and many composers in the Renaissance sought the unique sound that only a well-crafted metal tube can produce. One solution to the problem of how to get a natural trumpet to produce more notes on the chromatic scale was hand stopping. A surviving portrait of the eighteenth-century trumpeter Gottfried Reiche (figure 9) shows him holding a trumpet with numerous coils, an instrument that would have allowed the player to put his hand into the bell. (Some scholars have argued, however, that the actual practice of hand stopping did not begin until the classical period.)

The conventional natural trumpet with two folds is too long to allow such a maneuver. Just as contemporary players of the coiled French horn place their hands in the large bell of their instrument to change the pitch, hand stopping was more feasible when a natural trumpet was coiled. To create another solution, some trumpet makers drilled holes in crucial places along the length of the natural trumpet so that the pitch could be altered by moving a finger on or off the hole, as is done with woodwind instruments and the cornetto. Musicians who play baroque music on "original" instruments today are likely to play a modified copy of an old natural trumpet with holes along its tubes, but some aficionados believe that this technique destroys the stirring sound of the instrument.

Some baroque composers took advantage of another adjustment developed by industrious trumpet makers. Since the pitch of a trumpet could easily be changed by altering the length of the instrument, craftsmen were finding ways to fit a slide onto the horn as early as the fifteenth century. The first slide trumpets were essentially natural trumpets with long mouthpieces that could be pushed in or pulled out of the slightly larger tubing at the front end of the horn. Later instrument makers found ways to put slides at the crooks where the tubes were folded back on themselves. Thus, with one hand the player could keep his instrument stable at his lips while the other hand worked a slide back and forth. This type of slide trumpet was still in use in many English orchestras at the end of the nineteenth century. More recently, jazz musicians Maynard Ferguson and Steven Bernstein have found ways to work slide trumpets into their music. Otherwise, the instrument became obsolete after it grew a few feet and became the trombone.

As early as the 1760s, some manufacturers were adding keys to trumpets, for the first time providing an efficient system for making every note in the chromatic scale available to the player. As with the modern saxophone, the performer pushed down a key to uncover a hole. This was a more advanced version of the old system of covering and uncovering holes along the tubing with fingers. In 1796, Franz Joseph Haydn wrote his trumpet concerto, still an essential part of the trumpeter's repertoire today, for his friend Anton Weidinger, a master of the keyed trumpet. Weidinger also played the concerto that Johann Nepomuk Hummel wrote for a keyed trumpet in 1803. (See figure 10.)

THE MODERN TRUMPET IS BORN

The most essential breakthrough was, of course, the valved trumpet. The lead pipe of the horn could be connected to a series of tubes of different lengths. A valve of some type would open up a tube to the airflow so that the length of the trumpet was immediately changed. The bell then emerged from the other end of the system of tubes. Rotary valves, still in use on French horns, were invented in 1835. In parts of Eastern Europe, trumpets with rotary valves are still preferred today. Basically, a cylinder with holes is rotated either to open or bypass the tube attached to the valve. (See figure 11.) The piston valve, however, eventually became standard equipment on virtually all trumpets, cornets, baritone horns, and tubas. Invented in about 1815, it used the same principle of accessing or bypassing a series of tubes, but the holes were on a piston that could be quickly pressed and released. (See figure 12.)

By the 1840s, the Périnet valve that is now standard equipment on modern trumpets had been perfected. Instrument makers added tuning slides and the water key or spit valve. Although manufacturers continued to experiment with configurations throughout the nineteenth century, the modern trumpet was essentially invented at this time. The oldest trumpets we are likely to recognize, however, were manufactured at the Besson factory in Paris in the 1880s. Surely the most important makers of brass instruments in the late nineteenth and early twentieth centuries, the Besson engineers designed a trumpet with an arrangement of tubes, valves, and tuning slides that is now universally accepted as the most efficient (see figure 13). If it looks familiar today, it is because it was carefully copied by major American manufacturers such as C. G. Conn and Vincent Bach.

The addition of valves was not, however, an entirely satisfactory solution to the limitations of the natural trumpet. It certainly did not catch on immediately. A singular figure in the history of musical instruments, Adolphe Sax, gave his name to an entire family of brass instruments. The saxhorns, valved instruments ranging from contrabass to soprano, were all built on the model of the ophicleide, a long, slowly tapering metal tube folded once in the middle. Unlike the natural trumpet, which was folded twice so that the mouthpiece was at one end and the bell at the other, the first few inches of the ophicleide's lead pipe were bent at a 90-degree angle to the rest of the tube. The ophicleidist could hold the horn vertically, its bell pointed upward. With a number of keys placed along its length, the ophicleide was essentially a lower-voiced version of a keyed bugle. By replacing the cupped mouthpiece of the ophicleide with a reed, Sax made his most significant contribution to musical culture—the saxophone.

Compared with some of the other instruments that emerged from Sax's factory, the saxhorns were mundane. Others were so bizarre that they could have been invented by Dr. Seuss. One of the most distinctive was a contraption with seven valves and thirteen small bells. It resembled nothing so much as the multiheaded Hydra of Greek myth. And what kind of a carrying case did it require? Sax's instruments also show highly creative approaches to the arrangements of tubes. The saxhorns were produced in a multitude of shapes and sizes, always with long, tapered bells that pointed directly upward and inevitably collected water on rainy parade days. But Sax was not the only one who had his own ideas about how to put together a trumpet. The great music museums, such as the Cité de la Musique in Paris and the National Music Museum in Vermillion, South Dakota, are full of trumpets from the nineteenth and early twentieth centuries with one, two, four, or six valves (see figure 14). The museums also feature individual trumpets with valves *and* keys, horns that present elaborate and bewildering systems of tubing, and trumpetlike instruments that could be completely de- and reassembled with a variety of interchangeable parts.

Even after Besson had perfected the valved trumpet, there were still audiences and musicians who regarded the sound of the natural trumpet as fuller and richer. More important, some of the lower notes on the modern trumpet—especially the D above middle C that requires the use of the first and third valves—play out of tune. One solution came in the 1880s, when slides were added to the tubes on the first and third valves so that they could be extended with a small movement of the player's fingers, thus adjusting the pitch of a note that might otherwise be sharp. Schooled trumpeters have also learned the art of lipping a note up or down so that it plays in tune.

Indeed, the great natural trumpeters were so accomplished at lipping that they could create notes that were not supposed to be possible on the horn. Many composers resisted the encroachment of the valved trumpet because it seemed an unnecessary solution to a problem that existed only for those who had not mastered the natural trumpet. This sentiment resurfaced in the second half of the twentieth century with a new passion for playing early music on original instruments. Purists asked why the music of Bach, Handel, and Vivaldi should be performed on the instruments of Tchaikovsky. Manufacturers filled special orders for natural trumpets, striving to re-create as precisely as possible the horns manufactured in the seventeenth and eighteenth centuries.

Today, the most adept players have so mastered the natural trumpet that many audiences hearing baroque music on original instruments have no desire to listen to the awkward sounds produced by contemporary horns that would have been unknown to the composers. Jean-François Madeuf, one of the most accomplished masters of the natural trumpet today, even scorns the notion of lipping, explaining that proper execution involves much more than embouchure. He speaks of the importance of combining the proper re-creation of the natural trumpet with a musical discipline in which the entire body becomes one with the instrument. When I first heard Madeuf talk about his approach to the valveless trumpet, I thought I was listening to a tall tale, but hearing him play Handel's Music for the Royal Fireworks made me a believer.[6]

THE SHORT, HAPPY LIFE OF THE CORNET

The history of the trumpet I have just sketched is based primarily on the design of the instrument, what specialists call organology. Written as a series of logical steps leading up to the instrument in its contemporary form, my history suggests a clear evolution from 1350 B.C.E. to the present. But it is written backward, acknowledging only those instruments that anticipated the modern trumpet.

Another way of thinking about trumpet history is through the biological concept of evolution or natural selection. Evolutionary processes are driven by what Darwin called "selection pressure," the conditions that preserve various mutations as they emerge randomly over the history of a species. When the first mammals walked on land, good vision was necessary if the creature was to survive attacks by predators and other mishaps. If a genetic mutation gave a mammal better vision, it survived to give birth to more sharp-eyed animals while myopic siblings were gobbled up before they could reproduce. In the case of the trumpet, selection pressure was driven first by the need to create an extremely noisy instrument and then by the need to make it the peer of instruments that could play every note in the scale. Niles Eldredge, an evolutionary biologist who is a curator at the American Museum of Natural History in New York City, is also a collector of brass instruments. He has filled the walls of his house with a vast collection of cornets and trumpets and has applied the principles of Darwinian natural selection to the histories of the instruments, scrupulously theorizing on the similarities between biological evolution and cultural evolution.

Eldredge's theories are appealing because they account for the many evolutionary changes that had limited or no success. They flesh out my narrow history built on the idea that an instrument is part of the story only if it anticipates the three-valved trumpets of today. In fact, Eldredge has written extensively on how the humble cornet can be seen as a mutant species that once threatened the rise of the modern trumpet. Today we think of the trumpet and cornet as interchangeable. In school bands, the two instruments are regularly mixed indiscriminately depending on what each child brings to school. This was even more so in the middle years of the twentieth century, when schoolchildren were more likely to play the cornet than the trumpet. Nevertheless, the cornet has an entirely different history, one that begins with a mutation called the post horn.

In the fifteenth century, mail service was taken over by the state, first in France and Venice, later in most European countries. Postal couriers were supplied with horses and small horns to announce the arrival of the day's mail. In Nuremberg, Germany—long established as the city where the best natural trumpets were made—apprentices were employed to build smaller instruments that a postman could easily hold in one hand while keeping his other hand on a horses's reins. Well into the nineteenth century, post horns were coiled instruments, resembling modern French horns but much smaller (see figure 15). Post horns were no longer than four feet if straightened, much shorter than the seven-foot-long natural trumpets. Surely people loved the sound of the post horn, the Renaissance equivalent of "You've got mail." Mozart even made use of the instrument in one of his most memorable serenades, directing a horn player to switch to the post horn at a crucial moment in the Menuetto. It must have been a delightful surprise for an audience that knew the sound well.

A few decades after Mozart, in 1834, one manufacturer had the idea of adding the newly developed system of valves to the post horn. This may have been the first cornet, also known for some time in the nineteenth century as a cornopean.[7] The first cornets had deep mouthpieces that allowed for a mellower sound, what we might expect from an instrument associated with the happy arrival of the postman rather than with the battle sounds of the natural trumpet. A group of players took to the instrument immediately, primarily because of the sound, but also because it was easier to play. They may also have liked the appeal of a novel instrument that was not steeped in the long and pompous traditions of the natural trumpet. And compared to the trumpet, the cornet was less exhausting to play for long periods of time and was therefore taken up by brass bands and even symphony orchestras. The essential technical manual by Arban, still in use today by both amateur and professional trumpeters, was written entirely for the cornet.

In the early years of the twentieth century, the cornet had become so popular that it almost completely replaced the trumpet. Few composers were writing symphonic music specifically for the trumpet. Although the natural trumpet was still part of French orchestras as late as the end of the nineteenth century, most symphony musicians in France were playing the cornet. In the United States, the cornet was favored, for both its compactness and its sound. Herbert L. Clarke (figure 16) was internationally known as the principal cornet soloist with John Philip Sousa's orchestra and then as the leader of his own band, but no one playing the trumpet at that time was nearly as famous.

In 1921, Clarke himself discouraged a friend from taking up the trumpet, declaring that it was simply "a foreign fad," that he knew no one who played trumpet solos in public, and that the instrument "pollutes the art of music."[8] Clarke may have been trying to stop the move toward valved trumpets among jazz musicians in New Orleans and New York. The louder, more piercing sound of the trumpet was suddenly what jazz players were seeking. Indeed, in Germany at this time, piston-valved trumpets were often referred to as "jazz trumpets." But symphony players soon embraced the trumpet as well. Eldredge has extensively documented the trend toward the look and sound of the trumpet during the second decade of the twentieth century, when manufacturers began to build cornets that were longer, sleeker, and musically brighter, essentially more like a trumpet (see figure 17).

Photographs of New Orleans musicians in the first decades of the twentieth century are collected in a wonderful book called *New Orleans Jazz: A Family Album.*[9] The pictures show how quickly and completely the trumpet replaced the cornet. Almost without exception, in photographs dated before 1920, the musicians are holding cornets. After 1920, again almost without exception, the players are holding trumpets. The mellower cornet had been the instrument of the pioneering Buddy Bolden and the old dance music. But the valved trumpet, with a sharply focused sound that could pierce through all other musical and nonmusical sounds, was the instrument of the new Jazz Age. Surprisingly, one of the last New Orleans musicians to make the switch was Louis Armstrong. In the early 1920s he was playing with his mentor and father-surrogate Joe "King" Oliver, an older, more conservative musician who was slow to accept change. Armstrong remained as loyal to the cornet as he was to Oliver. Not until 1924, when he left Oliver behind in Chicago and joined Fletcher Henderson's groundbreaking jazz orchestra in New York, did he switch over. The trumpet had become the premier instrument of urban life, hot dance music, and burgeoning sexuality. At the time that Armstrong embraced the trumpet, the cornet was on its way to extinction. Setting up parallels between natural and cultural evolution, Eldredge has written that the cornet went the way of the dinosaur, just like the cornetto and the ophicleide.

Of course, there are still musicians today who prefer the cornet, not all of them antiquarians. There is also a significant element that the cornet passed on to the trumpet before the longer instrument prevailed, a bit of what Eldredge would call the cultural evolution of the trumpet. Unlike biological evolution, cultural evolution involves copying and imitation as the "species" changes over time. In the middle of the nineteenth century, when the cornet was spreading to a variety of venues, the prestige of the natural trumpet inhibited many musicians and composers from accepting the valved trumpet as a valid replacement. Unlike the natural trumpet and the first valved trumpets, cornets were almost always tuned to the key of B-flat. Although there was a wide variation in tuning, most natural trumpets were in D or F. During the decades when the cornet was filling the gap left by the decline of the natural trumpet and ambivalence toward the new valved trumpet, composers wrote for soprano brass instruments in B-flat. When trumpets began to replace cornets, the need for B-flat trumpets grew. Eventually, the B-flat trumpet evolved as the standard instrument, almost entirely because of the earlier dominance of the cornet.

THE TRUMPET IN CONTEXT

There is still more to the trumpet story than how it outlasted instruments that suffered extinction. Also missing from my backward history is information about who played the horns, where they played them, and why they played them. In order to fully understand the trumpet, as well as what men like Buddy Bolden and Louis Armstrong did with it, we need a richer sense of the instrument's cultural history.

The trumpet, with an overbearing sound that can evoke awe and wonder, has long been connected with worship. The Egyptians said that their trumpet was invented by the god Osiris, who reigned over the underworld. This was not the last time that the trumpet would be associated with death (see Chapter 5). In Vergil's *Aeneid*, however, a trumpet blast comes not from the underworld but from the heavens. A trumpet rings out when Aphrodite, the mother of Aeneas, parts the heavens to give enchanted armor to her son just as he is about to begin the battle that will determine the fate of the Roman people. For the Israelites, Jehovah himself orders the manufacture of two silver chatzotzrahs. The Old Testament also tells us that it took only seven priests with seven shofars to bring down the walls of Jericho. The archangel Gabriel, connected to the trumpet only through the elaborate "higher criticism" by biblical scholars, appears in the New Testament and tells the Virgin Mary of the impending birth of Christ. And in the first chapter of Revelation, the voice of God is specifically compared to a trumpet.

No doubt gods and trumpets were linked in other religions. And those gods were almost surely male, just as the trumpet has almost always been put to masculine use, whether as an accessory in battle or an accoutrement to a king's ego. The German anthropologist Alexander von Humboldt wrote of a tribe living on the banks of the Orinoco River in Venezuela in the early nineteenth century that worshipped a "holy trumpet." The tribesmen hid it away in a remote place where the "Great Spirit" would someday appear and play it. Those who were initiated into the trumpet's mysteries and were thus prepared to hear the Great Spirit play his divine tunes were, like medieval flagellants, expected to remain celibate and to scourge their bodies. Any woman who somehow managed to see the holy trumpet was immediately killed.[10] In the more demure culture of seventeenth-century Scandinavia, specially made trumpets were considered sufficiently sacred (or suggestive) to be kept out of sight. The instruments were brought out once a year for Advent ceremonies and then hidden away for the rest of the year. A woman who accidentally laid eyes on it, however, was allowed to live out the rest of her life.

An especially masculine image of the trumpet goes back to legends of the old West with a soldier on horseback blowing a bugle. An entire genre of American movies inevitably includes a scene of cavalry arriving to rescue helpless settlers from murderous Indians, always with the stirring sound of a bugler riding vigorously at the head of the army. The director John Ford gave special significance to the bugler in his 1948 Western *Fort Apache*. As the cavalry rides into battle with the Indians, a bugler repeatedly sounds the charge. The assiduous man with the horn, however, is shot and falls off his horse. Ford's camera cuts several times to the riderless horse, still racing forward with a bugle attached to its saddle.[11] Significantly, the cavalry suffers a major defeat at the hands of the Native American warriors. Even before they were claimed for the mythology of the American West, battle trumpeters were romantic figures. In addition to rousing the armies and sending them in the right direction, European trumpeters frequently had the dangerous assignment of taking messages across enemy lines. They had to be fearless as well as skilled in dealing with hostile parties. Some must have developed substantial diplomatic abilities. Nevertheless, in 1472, a trumpeter for Charles the Bold was killed after he entered a besieged French city and told the inhabitants to surrender. After capturing the city, the duke took retribution by cutting off the hands of a group of prisoners. Because the battle trumpeter was such a symbolic part of his army, the duke was not acting entirely out of random cruelty.

FROM THE BATTLEFIELD TO THE COURT

For several centuries the battle trumpeters were, like the man in Charles the Bold's entourage, of real importance to warlords, kings, and princes. The trumpeters were well paid, well dressed, and well respected. Because of their high status, trumpeters could move back and forth between the battlefield and the court. Even though a trumpet was not as essential at court as it was in wartime, there were many reasons for its courtly presence. The prestige of displaying trumpets at court was part of the gradual rise of metal, especially among the ruling classes that could announce their authority with startling noises but also splurged on metal trinkets and weapons. Indeed, trumpeters were usually the first musicians to be hired by aristocrats throughout the late Middle Ages and Renaissance.

The players hired immediately after the trumpeters were drummers. At least since the early fourteenth century, trumpets and kettledrums were on hand to announce a king whenever he appeared in public. Johann Ernst Altenburg, who wrote an essential treatise on the trumpet in 1795, put it best. He said that trumpets were essential to "princely pomp," and not just because the instrument stood out "more solemnly and magnificently" than any other instrument, especially in the open air. In addition, wrote Altenburg, a monarch "creates a great sensation if he can display one or two choirs of trumpeters and kettledrummers, clothed in sumptuous livery, and playing silver trumpets."[12]

As in ancient cultures, the trumpeters of the Middle Ages and early Renaissance were anything but musical. If the battle trumpeters knew how to play a precise figure that any simpleton in the army could understand, they probably did not play anything more complicated at court. They may have had much in common with musicians in ancient and prehistoric ages, who played low, droning sounds on their didgeridoos, conchs, and animal horns. Brass historians have wondered if the first trumpet music was similar to the droning of bagpipes. It's also possible that the mantralike sounds could become hypnotic, easily associated with magical powers—still another reason for a king or a warlord to include trumpeters in his retinue.

Brass historians have also remarked upon the many Renaissance paintings and sculptures that show trumpeters with their cheeks puffed out. The marble relief sculpture by Luca Della Robbia on a Florentine choir loft from the 1430s is one of the most famous. The striking resemblance of the players to Dizzy Gillespie has been noted. In the case of Gillespie, the arrangement of the muscles and tendons in his face is responsible for the huge swelling of his cheeks. An obsessive might urge him to change his embouchure, but no one who has heard Gillespie perform would argue that there is something wrong with how he plays. However, the old images of swelling cheeks on trumpeters point to a different mode of playing. If the idea was to make a loud noise—for battle, the arrival of the king, or celebrations at court—musicians may have been told to take a big breath and let it out as forcefully as possible. The power of this kind of blowing would surely have puffed out the cheeks of the player. In all those late medieval and Renaissance paintings of angels with bulging cheeks playing trumpets, the sound could hardly have been angelic.

Eventually, however, the trumpet did arrive as a musical instrument, at least in part because of its presence at the courts of emperors, kings, and dukes. Court musicians regularly played table music for the sovereign and his guests, and we can assume that the trumpeters tried to blend in. The addition of the slide to the trumpet was a further incentive. In 1430, an unidentified painter depicted several aristocrats dancing stiffly with the accompaniment of a group of musicians, one with a slide trumpet.

THE MEN ON THE WALLS

In addition to announcing the arrival of important people, calling the troops to battle, and scaring the hell out of the enemy, trumpeters contributed to the sense of community in cities and villages. Men with trumpets were stationed on walls surrounding medieval cities. Everyone inside the walls knew what time of day it was when the trumpeters played their easily identifiable flourishes. People also knew that a fire was raging nearby or that an enemy attack was imminent when the appropriate signal was played. Similarly, in the late nineteenth century, anthropologists found that in some South African villages, everyone lived within range of sound of an antelope horn that a retainer for the chief regularly played at important moments.

The first medieval trumpeters were itinerant entertainers, not unlike jugglers, minstrels, and other nomads. Held in contempt because of their wandering ways, they were not even allowed into the church to receive the sacraments. Nevertheless, many communities saw the need for municipal trumpeters and hired the disreputable fellows. There is evidence that men with high-pitched brass instruments were situated on city walls as early as the twelfth century. They would announce sunrise, lunch breaks, and various evening events. In Bologna, the city trumpeters were admired for their polished silver horns decorated with pennants. In Germany and elsewhere in Italy, the city paid to provide the players with splendid uniforms. By the fourteenth century, tower musicians were playing tunes and engaging in primitive harmony. In the fifteenth century, city trumpeters began to form guilds and brotherhoods to protect their positions and to increase their social status. Once they had gained as much status as the members of the better-established guilds, trumpeters were even allowed to receive the sacraments.

If the prestige of the municipal trumpeters was increasing, they were still very different from the court trumpeters. The musicians at court forcefully policed a sharp divide, often with the help of royal and imperial decrees. In 1653, in Hanover, Germany, court trumpeters broke into house of a tower watchman while he was practicing. They used his own instrument to knock out his teeth. Then they smashed his trumpet. When the issue was taken before magistrates, the court trumpeters insisted that they were simply looking after their own interests, expressly protected by decree of the Elector of Saxony. The court trumpeters were acquitted.

THE AGE OF THE VIRTUOSO

Nevertheless, when the instrument finally made its way into art music in the early years of the seventeenth century, it was the town trumpeters who got the jobs. We might expect the court trumpeters to take over this function, but they were primarily in the business of making noise for the king. Municipal trumpeters were more likely to be available for the kind of freelance work that composers and kapellmeisters needed for their performances, especially in church. One of the most honored of the city trumpeters was Gottfried Reiche (see figure 9), for whom Bach may have written the trumpet solo that is the glory of the second *Brandenburg* Concerto. The second *Brandenburg* is an especially difficult piece that has long been feared by trumpeters, and not just because of high notes. The trumpeters must also play extremely soft so as not to overpower the concerto's three other solo instruments—a recorder, an oboe, and a violin. Even worse, in many passages the trumpeter must continue playing for long stretches without rests. It's no surprise that many of the modern recordings of the second *Brandenburg* feature piccolo trumpets with easy access to the upper registers, and that recording engineers have used the magic of the mixing board to let the trumpeters play as loud as necessary without overwhelming the other solo instruments.

Gottfried Reiche was a cherished city musician in Leipzig, Germany. He must have been up to the task, because Bach continued writing extremely difficult passages in the upper register. In 1734, the trumpeter collapsed after playing an especially challenging solo in one of Bach's many cantatas. He died the next day. Bach must not have been especially sympathetic to the plight of the trumpeter because he soon made Ulrich Ruhe his principal trumpet soloist and continued to write music that would have taxed the heart, lungs, lips, and spinal cord of any musician.

Several decades before Bach, a few accomplished trumpeters were writing method books. Not surprisingly, these books began appearing in 1614, just as the trumpet was finding its way into art music. The system of trumpet guilds would have created a caste of masters who wished to pass the tricks of the trade along to their apprentices. The oldest surviving method book is *Tutta l'arte della trombetta* by Cesare Bendinelli, who also wrote a number of trumpet sonatas. His compositions are among the earliest that call upon the trumpeter to make pleasing music in the upper registers—what came to be known as clarino playing. As with the subsequent compositions of Bach, Bendinelli placed great strain on his musicians. In fact, one of Bendinelli's compositions appears to be a drinking song that not only celebrates the act of imbibing but actually directs the player to take regular sips from a large glass of wine while performing.[13] The piece was so strenuous that the trumpeter could make it through only by regularly stopping for strong drink. Nevertheless, in spite of his passion for the clarino register, Bendinelli's method book devotes only a few pages to it at the end.

Most historians of brass instruments have reason to celebrate the period of musical history known as the baroque. Edward Tarr, one of the most eminent of these scholars, calls the period 1600–1750 the "Golden Age of the Natural Trumpet." Composers throughout Europe wrote thrilling music that allowed the best natural trumpeters to show off their mastery of the clarino style. Among the earliest surviving natural trumpets, the best were made in the fifteenth century in Nuremberg, Germany, long a center of trumpet manufacturing. Some of the surviving Nuremberg trumpets are gorgeous instruments with elaborate engravings on the bells and even at the ferrules, those small cylindrical pieces where the curving tubes are connected to the longer tubes.

The natural trumpet's golden age came to an end in the late eighteenth century. At least in part because of the French Revolution, an instrument that had been linked to the court and the aristocracy became unfashionable. Even those who still lived under monarchy were intrigued by humanism and representative government, and many believed that the trumpet symbolized an opposite set of values. The instrument did, however, remain a powerful presence in the military, where pomp and hierarchy were still enforced.

In the late eighteenth century, in the symphonic works of Haydn and Mozart, the trumpet enjoyed none of the prominence it experienced during the baroque period. Symphonies of the classical period used the trumpet only for the occasional climax, often hitting a few notes along with the timpani. Later on, in the romantic period, it would regain some of its stature, especially in the hurly-burly symphonies of Gustav Mahler and Anton Bruckner, not to mention the works of Richard Wagner, who ordered special trumpets for his opera orchestra. Giuseppe Verdi demanded that six long trumpets be built especially for *Aïda*. If you have seen a full-scale production of Verdi's opera, you know just how impressive the trumpet can be, both musically and visually.

CUSTER'S LAST BAND

Meanwhile, in the United States, a new golden age was under way, but for the cornet rather than the natural trumpet. Brass bands had always been important in the American military, but after the Civil War, as instruments began to be mass produced and priced more reasonably, every regiment had its own brass band. Community groups outside the military began acquiring the same instruments as the army bandsmen, but they performed a wider range of music on them. A good example of the role of brass music in late-nineteenth-century America is the story of the band that accompanied General George Armstrong Custer to his last stand.

In the early 1870s, President Ulysses S. Grant sent Custer to the Black Hills of the Dakota Territory. During an extraordinary blizzard in April 1873, Custer and his army were camped several hundred miles east of the Black Hills in Yankton, then the capital of the Dakota Territory. After the blizzard, the city fathers held a ball to honor Custer, his officers, and their wives. A group of local musicians played stirring marches, patriotic songs, polkas, and sentimental ballads, the kind of music that could then be heard in concert halls and gazebos throughout most of middle America. Custer was greatly impressed by the arrangements he heard in Yankton, virtually all of them by Felix Vinatieri, an Italian immigrant bandsman who had come to the United States in 1859. Custer invited Vinatieri to join his regiment as chief musician, and the bandsman accepted.

In 1876, when Custer was on his way to Little Bighorn under orders to see that the people of the Sioux Nation were returned to their reservation, Vinatieri and his bandsmen were still part of Custer's army. Custer had presidential ambitions and may have hoped that a stunning rout of Indian braves would add luster to his heroic image. His attack on the warriors of Sitting Bull did not, of course, bring him the presidency. Fortunately for the bandsmen, they were safely stationed on a steamboat not far from the site of Sitting Bull's devastating defeat of Custer. Like many American musicians who traveled with the military in the late nineteenth century, Vinatieri's men doubled as medics, even the cornettists. On June 25, the musicians were much more involved with treating wounded soldiers than with playing music. Vinatieri honored his deceased patron by composing "General Custer, Last Indians Campagne March." But Vinatieri may not have been completely enamored with Custer. He also composed a march for Sitting Bull.[14]

AMERICAN BRASS

The American heartland continued to be home to brass bands well into the twentieth century. As more and more people moved from agrarian communities to cities and towns, communities were brought closer with fraternal organizations, city governments, and schools. All of these organizations were likely to have their own bands. Even factory owners sponsored brass bands for their workers.

A major figure in the brass band movement was "Colonel" C. G. Conn, whose first achievement was the creation of a rubber-rimmed mouthpiece designed to ease the pressure on the lips of hard-blowing cornetists. A legend that he invented the device after a member of his band split Conn's lip in a fistfight has been questioned by Conn's biographer, Margaret Banks.[15] Regardless, the rubber-rimmed mouthpiece never caught on. Undaunted, the entrepreneurial Conn was soon patenting processes for silver-plating brass mouthpieces. By 1876 he had begun working with a French instrument maker to produce brass instruments in a factory in Elkhart, Indiana. Within a few years, he was mass-producing a variety of instruments, most famously his series of Conn Wonder cornets, modeled closely on cornets manufactured in France at the Courtois factory. After years of importing instruments from France and England, Americans suddenly had ready access to high-quality, inexpensive instruments manufactured in the United States.

Conn sold his factory to Carl Greenleaf in 1915 and died penniless a few years later. It was Greenleaf who went to work aggressively promoting brass instruments to schools, community groups, and various musical organizations. When the African American jazz artist Andy Kirk toured with his big band in the 1930s, for example, they unfurled a sign that read, ANDY KIRK AND HIS 12 CLOUDS OF JOY USING CONN INSTRUMENTS. Although C. G. Conn Ltd. long ago became part of various international conglomerates, a large portion of the trumpets played by musicians throughout the world still come from Elkhart. The Bach Stradivius trumpet, surely the industry standard today, has been made in the old Conn factory in Elkhart since 1963.

It's difficult to say exactly what black musicians were playing in New Orleans prior to the arrival of Conn's cornets. A superior French import would have been out of their reach. Even the Boston 3-Star that Herbert L. Clarke played went for $55 and up. No wonder we hear about early jazz and ragtime musicians building their own horns. They were probably tinkering together a functional cornet from discarded ones. But at least a few of the more successful cornetists were able to get their hands on a Conn Wonder, which cost as little as $40 in 1896.[16] Buddy Bolden was so attached to his Conn that he scoffed at a patron who offered to let him play his cheaper cornet at a dance when Bolden's was out of commission.

Perhaps the late nineteenth century saw at least one version of an American dream come true. Jazz, as well as the achievements of Buddy Bolden, represents the fulfillment of a democratic ideal that meshed perfectly with both the financial projects of C. G. Conn Ltd. and the American appropriation of a majestic instrument that once served only gods, kings, and generals.

But what about the women's dreams?

"I WAS WEANED ON THE HORN"

For more than thirty-five hundred years, the trumpet has served its purpose in male-centered activities such as war, religious ceremony, and royal pageantry. In the early twentieth century, African American men made brilliant use of the trumpet to assert that they were men and not boys. Many of these black men were single-mindedly devoted to making great music, but they may also have found the trumpet to be the ideal instrument for telling the world that they were not merely manly but *extremely* manly. By reappropriating and remaking the instrument, black trumpeters inspired white musicians looking for their own means of masculine expression. Even before the term *alpha male* had been coined, a certain breed of white man was attracted to the trumpet and its power to astound. Many of these men were listening carefully to black trumpeters. Whether they knew it or not, African American trumpet masters figured prominently in the long history of whites looking to blacks for models of masculinity. Although I would not celebrate every aspect of this tradition, it is nevertheless at the heart of jazz, the music that I love.

By no means, however, does this history of the trumpet mean that women cannot play it. Or that women cannot play it as well as men. For one thing, there is nothing in a man's lips, lungs, tongue, or spinal cord that makes him uniquely equipped to make music on the instrument. Women can be every bit as adept at buzzing lips, pushing down valves, and delivering large gusts of air into a metal tube. I asked Ingrid Monson about the long association of trumpets with all things masculine. In addition to being a first-rate trumpeter and jazz scholar, Ingrid has the hippest job title of anyone I know—she's the Quincy Jones Professor of African American Music at Harvard. When we spoke, we mused about the strange way that musical instruments have been categorized as male and female. Are women supposed to play the cello because it's shaped like a woman? And are women *not* supposed to play the trumpet because it's "unladylike" to be loud and brassy? Then, with a wry laugh, she said, "You know, in some ways, the trumpet *ought* to be a woman's instrument. It is, after all, a soprano horn, pitched in the same range as a woman's singing voice and thus more compatible with a woman's body."[17] I think of Ingrid's observation every time a male trumpeter demonstrates a particular passage written for the trumpet by singing it in a delicate, falsetto voice.

So, why, even today, does it seem that so few women play the trumpet? The easiest answer is that women have always been discouraged from entering professions that seem too masculine. The word has come down from fathers as well as from teachers, preachers, and band directors. The word can also come from certain mothers and other guardians of the carefully constructed boundaries around what is supposedly feminine. Still, in the twenty-first century, we are not surprised when a women becomes a general, a Supreme Court justice, a soccer player, an astronaut, or even a race car driver. And yet a female trumpeter still seems like an anomaly.

WHO WERE THE TRUMPET QUEENS?

In fact, there are many women who play the trumpet, but for a variety of reasons they have been ignored. In the 1990s, for example, the Bravo television network ran a pair of programs about famous jazz soloists. Clarinetists and saxophone players were celebrated in a program called *Reed Royalty*, a category that might have included women even though none were shown in the program. The program on trumpeters also excluded women. But it was called *Trumpet Kings*, assigning a gender to the instrument from the outset.

A women's history of brass instruments might begin with the numerous medieval representations of female angels with natural trumpets. There is also a secular illustration from Germany in the sixteenth century that clearly shows an elegantly dressed woman playing a trombone. In the early eighteenth century, Antonio Vivaldi was a violin tutor at the Conservatorio dell'Ospedale della Pietà in Venice, an institution for girls who had been abandoned or orphaned. Vivaldi wrote a great deal of music for the women, including many who never married and remained at the *ospedale* for most of their lives. When they performed the music, the women played all the instruments, including brass. It was surely not the first all-female orchestra.

Susan Slaughter, for many years principal trumpet with the St. Louis Symphony, formed the International Women's Brass Conference to bring together what she knew to be a large population of women brass players. A 1990 survey turned up more than fourteen hundred women who made their living playing the trumpet, the trombone, the tuba, or the French horn. The IWBC meets regularly to give these women an opportunity to play together, to share their stories, and to encourage younger women entering the profession. The organization makes special efforts to honor "Pioneers," women like Marie Speziale, who became the first woman ever to play first-chair trumpet in a major orchestra when she took that position with the Cincinnati Symphony; Leona May Smith, who sat first chair with the Brooklyn Symphony and was the first woman to play a trumpet solo at Radio City Music Hall; and Bette Eilers, who was only seventeen when she became principal trumpet in the Chicago Civic Orchestra. All of these women overcame prejudice and harassment to become principal trumpet players and distinguished soloists long before there was anything like affirmative action.

A significant number of women have played jazz on the trumpet, particularly in the 1940s, when they were needed to staff the big bands after so many men went off to war. Sherrie Tucker has exhaustively researched the subject for her eye-opening study, *Swing Shift: "All-Girl" Bands of the 1940s*. Long lists of female brass players and jazz orchestras appear in her book, many of whom have simply been written out of jazz history. One is Ann Cooper, who worked regularly in the 1930s and '40s, playing with various territory bands. In her interviews, she used the memorable phrase "I was weaned on the horn." In Cooper's telling of her own story, the trumpet is associated not with phallic symbols but with the mother's breast.

Tucker has coined the term *brass ceiling* to describe what women face when they take up the trumpet. A man who believes that proficiency with the trumpet is proof of his manliness can be profoundly threatened when a woman plays as well as he does. Like many jazz musicians, jazz critics also tend to form a boys' club. There are noticeable and even heroic exceptions, but most of these writers are highly suspicious of any female artist who does something other than sing or play the piano, and they have colluded in writing women out of jazz history. The result is a vicious circle—because women's names do not appear in the histories, women are more likely to believe that they do not belong in the trumpet section.

Ingrid Monson has a telling anecdote about the business-as-usual prejudice women trumpeters are likely to encounter. As a grade-school student she was among a large group of girls who played trumpet in the band. At least at that stage there was nothing unusual about a girl with a trumpet. Ingrid, however, was better than the many girls *and* boys in the band, and the director recommended that she take private lessons. Her teacher, a young man in his twenties, was also impressed and brought Ingrid along to a rehearsal when the Doc Severinsen orchestra was in town. Ingrid was excited when the teacher promised that she would have an opportunity to meet the famous trumpet master. She was fourteen years old, blond, and beautiful. When her teacher introduced her as one of his best students, Severinsen took a look at her and said, "Yeah, sure."

In her own research, Sherrie Tucker has been sensitive to the strategies female players have devised to counter these kinds of attitudes. Valaida Snow, for example, bypassed the ordeal of playing in an orchestra and coming up against men by becoming an all-around entertainer. She appeared in films, toured Europe, and made several recordings in the 1920s and '30s. Always dressed in highly feminine clothes—evening gowns as well as skimpy chorus girl outfits—she presented herself as a singer/dancer who worked the trumpet into her act. She was careful to lift the trumpet to her mouth in a graceful, alluring fashion. Then she would play stirring jazz solos in the style of Louis Armstrong.

Maxine Sullivan, the great jazz singer who was one of only three women to appear in the famous "Great Day in Harlem" photograph of fifty-seven jazz musicians posed in front of a brownstone, added valve trombone, flügelhorn, and pocket trumpet to her act. Just as Armstrong and many other male trumpeters sang to give themselves a rest between trumpet solos, Sullivan played the trumpet so that she could take a break from singing. Then there is Carole Dawn Reinhart, who won beauty pageants as a teenager even as she was perfecting her craft as a trumpeter. By the 1960s and '70s she was appearing regularly on television programs, most memorably on a Richard Rodgers program where she played "Bewitched" on her trumpet as she descended from the rafters in a large glass bubble. She literally rose above the brass ceiling, setting herself off from the men in the trumpet section as well as from earthbound humanity. Reinhart eventually settled in Austria, where she took a professorship at the Academy of Music in Vienna.

Female jazz artists have always been aware of the extent to which their music, especially trumpet jazz, has been developed primarily by black men. If a woman tried to make the instrument her own, someone would surely say that she was no longer playing jazz. Clora Bryant, who began working regularly in the 1950s, was an astoundingly talented woman who could keep up even with the be-boppers. She made it seem easy as she nailed notes in the upper reaches of the high register, often gesturing skyward with her left hand while holding the trumpet with her right. She later developed a solo act that took her to Ed Sullivan's television program in the 1960s. Bryant found a way around the notion that the trumpet was exclusively masculine by calling herself a *trumpetiste*.[18] Although the word is not exactly French, the final *e* gives it a feminine connotation. More important, the word is unique. Bryant played in the great jazz tradition, but, as Tucker has argued, she insulated herself from comparisons to men by saying she was not a female trumpet player but a *trumpetiste*.

In the early twenty-first century, Ingrid Jensen (figure 18) is among the few contemporary trumpet soloists to have broken through the brass ceiling in jazz. Although she is tall, slim, and attractive, Jensen is all business when she plays. She does not engage in the girly antics that were once a necessity for performers like Valaida Snow. When Jensen plays, she devotes her energy to the music and not to making herself an erotic object. She too has had to deal with preju-dice, and she has spoken of how surprised she was on a European tour when the subject of being a woman in a man's world never came up. They liked what she did, and that was that.

Jensen plays regularly in the superb jazz orchestra led by the com-poser Maria Schneider. One of her section mates in the Schneider orchestra is an older trumpeter named Laurie Frink, who has played with a variety of bands in her career and is now widely regarded as the best trumpet teacher in New York. I wondered how Frink felt about gender stereotypes when she arrived in New York in the 1970s. She told me that at first she thought that she would play classical music. Her teachers had all agreed that she had excellent technique and real talent as a sight reader. But then she met Jimmy Maxwell, who had played trumpet with Benny Goodman and many other Swing Era bandleaders. Extremely supportive of promising trumpeters regardless of gender, Maxwell had just learned that Gerry Mulligan was looking for a lead trumpeter. After winning great praise for his Concert Jazz Band in the 1960s, Mulligan was putting together a new edition in the 1970s. Frink got the audition at least in part because Mulligan had just heard the Cincinnati Symphony and watched Marie Speziale take a solo. Suddenly aware that women really *can* play the trumpet, Mulligan invited Frink to audition and listened to her without prejudice. She nailed the audition, and he hired her to be his lead trumpet player.

Frink told me that Mulligan and the other members of the band—all of them male—treated her well, inflicting none of the hazing rituals that other female trumpet players have reported. What hurt was being excluded from the bandstand. When a member of the band was about to be married, Frink was the only person in the band not invited to the party the night before the wedding. She understood about stag parties, so she was not insulted. But then she wasn't invited to the wedding itself. That hurt.

Long after she had left Mulligan, a male friend told Frink how much he had enjoyed playing in a boys' band when he was in grade school. He then told her that his school now let girls into the band. "It's just not the same," he said. "I really liked playing in a boys' band." Frink said nothing at the time, but it was another example of how oblivious male musicians can be, especially to someone who is trying to make a living in the grown-up equivalent of a boys' band. As Frink put it, many men have the same attitude toward playing music that they have toward watching the Super Bowl.

Frink has not sat silently through all of this, however. One night she had a rare opportunity to respond to the boys' club mentality. As the only female in a band that was about to begin a performance, she listened to the bandleader make a typically sexist remark as he exhorted his musicians: "All right, guys, tonight we're going to go out there and play our dicks off." Without missing a beat, Laurie replied, "Oh, I did that years ago."

chapter 3

Louis Armstrong's Beam of Lyrical Sound

et's begin with the tributes. Duke Ellington, the only artist of Armstrong's generation who can be considered his peer, was eloquent and concise: "Nobody had ever heard anything like it, and his impact cannot be put into words." Miles Davis denounced Armstrong in his autobiography for grinning too much, but he once told an interviewer, "You know you can't play anything on a horn that Louis hasn't played—I mean even modern."[1]

In 1923, a young Bix Beiderbecke brought his friends Hoagy Carmichael and Bob Gillette to the Lincoln Gardens, a huge dance hall on the Near South Side of Chicago, to hear Armstrong play with King Oliver's band. In his autobiography, Carmichael wrote, "I dropped my cigarette and gulped my drink. Bix was on his feet, his eyes popping. For taking the first chorus was that second trumpeter, Louis Armstrong [figure 19]. Louis taking it fast. Gillette slid off his chair and under the table. He was excitable that way. 'Why,' I moaned, 'why isn't everyone in the world here to hear this?' "[2]

The French novelist Marie Cardinal did more than slide off her chair. In her memoir she writes about hearing Armstrong perform in the late 1940s:

> I was nineteen or twenty. Armstrong was going to improvise with his trumpet, to build a whole composition in which each note would be important and would contain within itself the essence of the whole. I was not disappointed: the atmosphere warmed up very fast. The scaffolding and flying buttresses of the jazz instrument supported Armstrong's trumpet, creating spaces which were adequate enough for it to climb higher, establish itself, and take off again. The sounds of the trumpet sometimes piled up together, fusing a new musical base, a sort of matrix which gave birth to one precise, unique note, tracing a sound whose path was almost painful, so absolutely necessary had its equilibrium and duration become; it tore at the nerves of those who followed it. My heart began to accelerate, becoming more important than the music, shaking the bars of my rib cage, compressing my lungs so the air could no longer enter them. Gripped by panic at the idea of dying there in the middle of spasms, stomping feet, and the crowd howling, I ran into the street like someone possessed.[3]

Toni Morrison's reaction to the passage is the same as mine: "What on earth was Louis playing that night?"[4]

In the first pages of his Great American Novel, *Invisible Man*, Ralph Ellison's unnamed narrator marvels at the range of what Armstrong could achieve. The Invisible Man has withdrawn from public life, hiding in a basement he has illuminated extravagantly with electricity stolen from "Monopolated Light & Power." And like Armstrong, the narrator is thoroughly American, prepared to improvise and hope for the best. "I'd like to hear five recordings of Louis Armstrong playing and singing 'What Did I Do to Be So Black and

Blue'—all at the same time. Sometimes now I listen to Louis while I have my favorite dessert of vanilla ice cream and sloe gin. I pour the red liquid over the white mound, watching it glisten and the vapor rising as Louis bends that military instrument into a beam of lyrical sound."[5] The red and white of the dessert is joined by the blue of Armstrong's lyric. Ellison always believed that being American meant being a little bit African American. We're all red, white, and blue, but also black. And with a musical score by Louis Armstrong.

Writing a half century after Ellison, Roddy Doyle arrived at a similar view of Armstrong in his novel *Oh, Play That Thing*. The book begins in the 1920s after Henry Smart has escaped a violent past in Ireland and landed in New York. About a third of the way into the novel, Smart wanders to Chicago, where he encounters Armstrong, befriends him, and becomes his de facto manager. Having carefully researched Armstrong's life, Doyle surgically inserts Henry Smart into Armstrong's story without changing any of the facts. Surely knowing that critics cannot agree on the identity of the singer, Doyle has Smart claim that he provided the brief falsetto voice on Armstrong's 1928 recording of "Tight Like This." In the novel Armstrong emerges as a psychologically complex character with a vivid linguistic imagination. Doyle has him calling the Irish hero "O'Pops."

In *Oh, Play That Thing*, Henry Smart is immediately transformed when he first hears Armstrong. Like Ellison, he recognizes something profoundly American about what Armstrong is playing.

At last. I wasn't Irish any more. The first time I heard it, before I was properly listening, I knew for absolute sure. It took me by the ears and spat on my forehead, baptised me. There was a whole band of men on the bandstand, and a little woman at the piano, all thumping and blowing their lives away. Two horns, a trombone, tuba, banjo, drums, filling the world with their glorious torment. There were two trumpets blowing but the spit on my forehead from only

one man's. I looked at him through the human steam—it was too hot
for sweat—and I knew it.

I was a Yank.

At last.[6]

As these tributes demonstrate, and as David Yaffe has elegantly
demonstrated, we can learn as much about jazz from fiction as we
can from the critics.[7] While novelists like Ellison and Doyle riff on
the many narratives of Armstrong's life, jazz writers have tried to
make sense of Armstrong by casting him as a giant guarding the gates
of jazz history. He is *the* canonical figure of jazz, or, in the words of
musicologist Gunther Schuller, "the first great soloist."[8]

Emerging from dire poverty at a time when African Americans
were violently suppressed, Armstrong somehow managed almost
single-handedly to remake the trumpet. He even changed the way
symphony players performed. When Armstrong was making his extraordinary recordings in the 1920s and '30s, most of the men who
played trumpet in American symphony orchestras were either European expatriates or American-born products of a Eurocentric conservatory system, all of them with deep prejudices against popular
music. But the symphony players eventually came around. Few today
express anything except admiration for Armstrong, and many are inspired by his improvisations and his complete command of the instrument. Symphony musicians today play with a wider vibrato than
their predecessors, a definite influence from Armstrong.

OUT OF THE CRADLE OF JAZZ

Even if Armstrong is in fact *the* giant of jazz, there were surely giants
before him. Like Buddy Bolden, Armstrong absorbed and expanded
upon a thriving New Orleans tradition that we know only from surviving oral histories. Many of the great New Orleans brass men who pre-

ceded him either never recorded or arrived in a recording studio late in life after they had lost their sparkle. Freddie Keppard, for example, replaced Bolden in the band that Frankie Dusen had taken over and renamed the Eagle Band. Less charismatic than Bolden, Keppard was widely praised for his articulation and rhythmic zeal. He should have made the first jazz records in 1916, but, at least according to legend, he turned down the opportunity, fearing that competing cornetists would listen to his records and steal his ideas. The Italian American Nick LaRocca and the white members of the Original Dixieland Jazz Band got the job instead.

Joe "King" Oliver, Punch Miller, Kid Rena, and Bunk Johnson were also there when Armstrong was an apprentice, but like Keppard, they did not record until several years later. In fact, Johnson and Rena did not record until the 1940s, when they were shadows of their former gladiatorial selves. The cornet masters who never recorded include Chris Kelly, Buddy Petit, "Big Eye" Louis Nelson, and Edward Clem. Kelly was admired as a "freak" player. Witnesses say that he made his horn growl like a dog, crow like a rooster, and cry like a baby. The *vox humana* wah-wah sounds that King Oliver creates in his 1923 recordings with Armstrong were probably inspired by Kelly. Either that, or both Oliver and Kelly were inspired by an even earlier freak specialist.

Although the young Armstrong impressed the competition with his high notes, some said that Kid Rena could play even higher when he and Armstrong were teenagers in New Orleans. In fact, they were already in competition when they were both children in the Colored Waifs' Home. It was Kid Rena who famously filed down his mouthpiece so that it was shallower, making it easier to hit the high notes. But this trick made the low notes more difficult. According to Punch Miller, Rena eventually found a man in Chicago who could make a mouthpiece with two different screw-on cups so that he could switch back and forth. Buddy Petit, known as one of the first great improvisers, created beautiful melodies on the spot that were much more than decorated versions of a familiar tune. But like so many other jazz trumpeters, Petit died young. He was gone at the age of thirty-three after years of ferocious alcoholism. Armstrong returned to New Orleans to serve as a pallbearer at his funeral in 1931.[9]

Luckily for us, Armstrong was not prone to self-destruction. He loved the trumpet, and he knew what it could do for him. Like Bolden, he saw the trumpet as a way to enhance his masculinity, asserting his power with volume and showing off his ability to "get it up" with the high notes. It could win him the attention of women and increase his stature among men. Actually, Armstrong did not have to steal any of this from Bolden. Several thousand years of history made the trumpet ripe for masculine appropriation by the sons and grandsons of slaves.

Before they transformed the trumpet, both Bolden and Armstrong were themselves transformed by music they heard in church. As Armstrong once wrote, "It all came from the Old Sanctified Churches." Much of what makes jazz unique was already present in what preachers and congregations were doing at the turn of the century. But what Armstrong meant by "Old Sanctified Churches" must be distinguished from virtually all the other churches in the South, including New Orleans. In the late nineteenth century, Baptist missionaries had successfully reached out to a large group of freed slaves and their families. Inspired by the emotional power of these missionaries, many blacks formed their own Baptist churches, employing preachers with no seminary training but with great skill in inciting parishioners to vigorous worship. In Bolden's day, many black Baptists believed that ecstatic singing and dancing was the only proper way to worship.

In the early years of the twentieth century, however, a new wave of missionaries from the North came to preach the rewards of respectable behavior and assimilation. By the 1910s, many congregations had given up group singing. Instead they sat sedately and listened to a choir and soloists perform carefully rehearsed songs. But the unassimilated, poverty-stricken blacks rejected the new Baptist rituals and preserved ecstatic, in-the-moment worship by forming the Sanctified Churches. The church of Bolden, Armstrong, and many poor blacks was held in contempt even by middle-class African Americans. Nevertheless, it is where Armstrong acquired his first musical experience.

In his essential book, *Louis Armstrong's New Orleans*, Thomas Brothers emphasizes the importance of Armstrong's upbringing in the Sanctified Churches. There he found his identity as a black man in an earthy, robust culture that had little in common with New Orleans white culture. Although Armstrong was eager to earn a good living, and although he knew that he had to please white people in order to accomplish this goal, he had no desire to assimilate into a higher or whiter class of society. He was always devoted to a way of life we now call vernacular. The word—taken from the Latin *verna* meaning "from slaves"—describes language as it's spoken and culture as it's lived rather than the literary and the "refined."

Not for Armstrong the pretensions of "dicty" blacks who carried themselves like upper-class whites, spoke about uplift, and attended the reformed Baptist churches. Armstrong loved to tell dirty jokes, laugh from his belly, and speak openly about sex and defecation. Even when he had become a millionaire and was famous throughout the world, he continued publicly to sing the praises of his favorite laxatives. In the 1950s, when he was granted an audience with Pope Pius XII, the pontiff asked him if he and his wife had children. "No," he said. "But we're still wailin.'" Ralph Ellison characterized Armstrong's wit as Shakespearean, suggesting a comparison to bawdy, transgressive characters such as Touchstone in *As You Like It* and the Fool in *King Lear*.[10] But the author whose writings most strongly resemble Armstrong's style is Rabelais.

With its French heritage, its thriving culture of prostitution, and its intoxicating traditions of music and dance, there was something Rabelaisian about New Orleans itself. Whether or not it is true that a six-year-old Louis peeked through the cracks in the dilapidated walls of Funky Butt Hall to watch Bolden perform, we *can* believe him when he describes what he saw when a band—any band—played a tune like "The Bucket's Got a Hole in It." Armstrong wrote that the women "would get way down, shake everything, slapping themselves on the cheek of their behind. Yeah!"

In the second of two autobiographies published during his lifetime, Armstrong vividly recalls the days when he was still "Little Louie" playing the blues for the women in brothels with other members of a "kid band." He was probably about fourteen and already proficient at playing the blues. As soon as he put down his horn, he wrote, the prostitutes would want to fondle him. "Come here you cute little son of a bitch, and sit on my knee." These were the rewards awaiting a cornet player who knew his way around the blues. A few years later, Armstrong would marry a prostitute. In total, he was married four times and would carry on with numerous women both in and out of wedlock. He would even enjoy the occasional reunion with an ex-wife. Lucille Wilson, to whom he was married for the last three decades of his life, had to make her peace with a husband who was constantly on the road, surrounded by adoring fans, spending his nights in hotel rooms alone or with an invited guest.

RESISTING RACISM

The pleasures of the flesh must have been especially appealing to an African American male who was regularly told that he was not a man and was punished for any assertion to the contrary. Growing up in New Orleans in the early twentieth century, Armstrong had to deal with a racist culture even more virulent than what Bolden had endured. Two events are central to New Orleans racial history during the infancy of jazz. In 1900, a black man named Robert Charles was so incensed at the unprovoked abuse he received from a white policeman that he shot and killed two and wounded a third. He eventually barricaded himself in a building and held off an angry mob of whites with a Winchester rifle. He killed several more and wounded nineteen before he was fatally shot by a Tulane medical student who had voluntarily loaned his services to the police. Not satisfied with the death of one black man, several thousand white New Orleanians rained bloody hell throughout black neighborhoods in New Orleans, burning, beating, and killing at random.

Ten years after the Robert Charles riots, when the flamboyant black pugilist Jack Johnson defeated the Great White Hope, Jim Jeffries, whites went on murderous rampages not just in New Orleans but throughout the United States. A nine-year-old Armstrong hid in his house to avoid the roving gangs. In the years between these two riots, the Louisiana state legislature dreamed up increasingly punitive Jim Crow laws to disempower and intimidate the black population. The number of black voters in Louisiana decreased dramatically during this first decade of the new century.

There was very little that blacks could do to stop the violence and institutionalized racism. But a few gestures of resistance were available. Ecstatic worship in the Sanctified Churches was one. Playing the blues was another. It was, after all, the music of an oral, vernacular culture that flourished outside the schools and conservatories of white society and refused to accept the established musical hierarchies. The blues singer would bend notes, cry, moan, and grunt, always in a voice completely unlike any white singer's. Even if blues artists delighted white audiences, the music was a cry of self-affirmation in the face of white racism.

The blues was also a heartfelt expression of the singer's humanity and feelings. Buddy Bolden may not have been the first man to play the blues on a wind instrument, but he was certainly the first to be-

1. Buddy Bolden (back row, holding cornet) with his band, circa 1905. (*Courtesy William Ransom Hogan Jazz Archive, Tulane University*)

2. Art Farmer in the 1970s. (*Courtesy of Frederick Warren*)

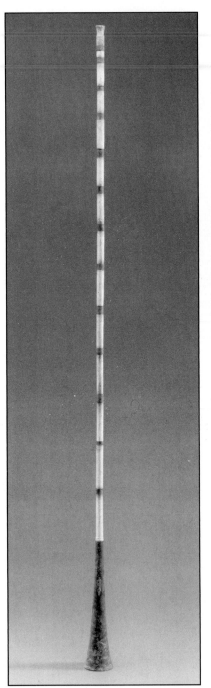

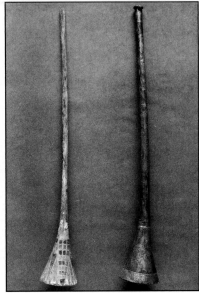

3. Silver trumpet buried with Tutankhamen with device designed to help trumpet hold its shape when not in use. (*The Metropolitan Museum of Art*)

4. Greek salpinx. (*Photograph copyright © 2008 Museum of Fine Arts, Boston*)

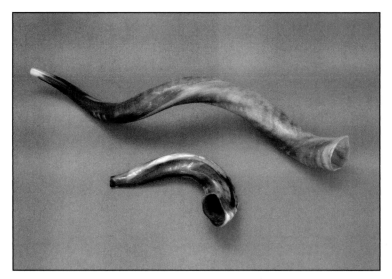

5. Sephardic (Spanish, African tradition, top) and Ashkenazic (German, Eastern European tradition, bottom) shofars. (*National Music Museum, University of South Dakota. Joe and Joella Utley Collection. Photograph by Mark Olencki*)

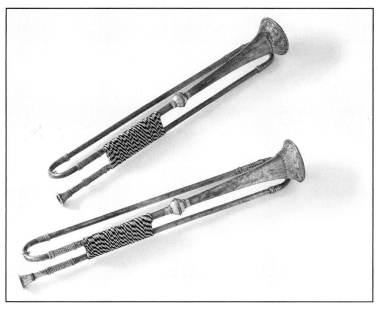

6. Natural trumpets from 1578, manufactured in Basel, Switzerland, by Jacob Steiger. (*Historiches Museum, Basel*)

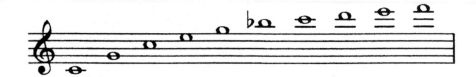

7. Musical example: partials available on a modern trumpet played without valves.

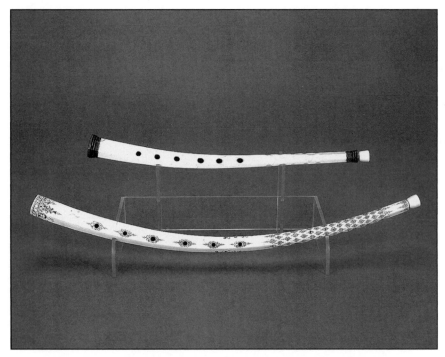

8. Cornetto and cornettino of ivory, presumably made in south Germany in the sixteenth or seventeenth century. (*National Music Museum, University of South Dakota. Joe and Joella Utley Collection. Photograph by Simon Spicer*)

9. Painting of Gottfried Reiche (1667–1734) by Elias Gottlob Haussmann. (*Bridgeman Art Library, Wetherby, UK*)

10. Keyed bugle in B-flat, circa 1840. (*Hal Oringer Collection. Photograph by the author*)

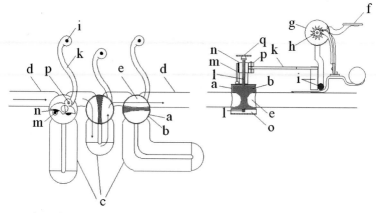

a = valve casing	i = articulated crank
b = rotor	k = push rod
c = valve loop with slide	l = rotor spindle or shaft bearing
d = main tubing	m = pin stop
e = port	n = stop cork
f = touch piece	o = valve cap
g = spring box with coiled clock spring inside	p = reciprocal driver pivot
h = gear	q = screw to hold rotor in place

11. Rotary valves. Drawings by Sabine K. Klaus. (*Courtesy of National Music Museum, University of South Dakota*)

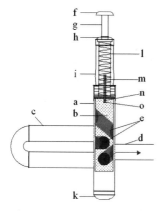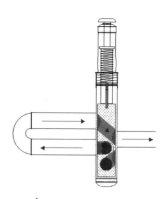

a = valve casing	h = top valve cap
b = piston	i = baluster
c = valve loop with slide	k = lower valve cap
d = main tubing	l = return spring
e = port	m = guiding slot in stem/piston
f = touch piece, finger tip, lever	n = key
g = valve system	o = keyway for piston valve guide in casing

12. Piston valves. Drawings by Sabine K. Klaus. (*Courtesy of National Music Museum, University of South Dakota*)

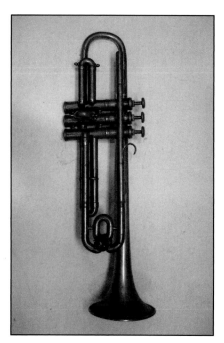

13. B-flat trumpet, manufactured in the 1880s at the Besson factory. (*Niles Eldredge Collection. Photograph by the author*)

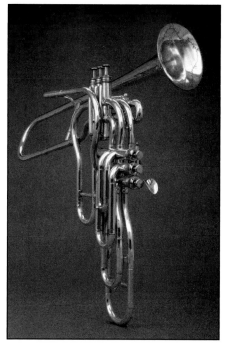

14. Trumpet with six independent valves, manufactured by Adolphe Sax, Paris, 1868. (*National Music Museum, University of South Dakota. Joe and Joella Utley Collection. Photograph by Mark Olencki*)

15. Post horn, dated 1866, used for the postal service in Brünn, the capital of Moravia at the time. (*National Music Museum, University of South Dakota. Joe and Joella Utley Collection. Photograph by Mark Olencki*)

16. Herbert L. Clarke (1867–1945). (*Courtesy of Library and Archives Canada*)

come famous for it. Because blues musicians have little use for precise intonation and musical execution, the music was perfect for the makeshift instruments that blacks could afford to buy or invent. Bolden could have been reminded of the blues at some point when he heard the sound of a cheap or damaged horn. Although Bolden would eventually acquire a first-rate cornet, it wasn't always necessary to invest serious money in a horn when emotional expression was the goal. And of course the blues has always been an erotic music. Although many think of the blues as simply the expression of suffering, what W.E.B. Du Bois called "sorrow songs," it can also be seductive. Both Bolden and Armstrong sang the blues as much as they played it. If nothing else, it gave them something to do while they rested their lips between solos. The singing was always a great delight for audiences, especially when it was the dirty blues. We don't know if Bolden relished the opportunity to sing about sex and the body as much as Armstrong did, but we do know that Bolden sang lyrics such as "If you don't rock you get no cock" and "Kiss My Funky Ass."

Also like Bolden, Armstrong relished the opportunity to compete. If you won a trumpet battle, you won public recognition and the respect of other musicians. Armstrong had the additional advantage of winning over audiences with his recordings. When he was still an obscure sideman in 1924 and 1925, people were more likely to buy a record by Fletcher Henderson or Bessie Smith if they could hear Armstrong's piercing trumpet sound (and by this time it was a trumpet and not the mellower cornet).

There were, however, crucial differences between Bolden and Armstrong. Armstrong was not a drunk; his drug of choice was cannabis. Not long after he left New Orleans, he fell in love with the feeling he got from marijuana—or "gage," as he called it—and he smoked it every day of his life. Although we remember Armstrong as an exuberant jester, early in his career he was extremely nervous about performing. When he got a job playing with a brass band on a riverboat in 1919, he had to read music on every number. By this time he had picked up a bit of reading ability, but he had previously been playing almost exclusively with ear cats. His first day on the job, he was so intimidated by the idea of reading music that he drank himself sick with wine. Later, he found that marijuana soothed his nerves and made him less shy. This was surely another way he asserted his independence in a society that enforced laws against a substance that made him feel less intimidated by racism.

While both Bolden and Armstrong had devoted mothers, Bolden's saw to it that her young son had access to a trumpet teacher. Armstrong's mother, May Ann, couldn't provide the same for Louis. In contrast to the devoutly religious and self-sacrificing Alice Bolden, Armstrong's mother worked as a prostitute. Although she and her son were close, and although she would have given him more if she had it in her power, she seldom had much to offer. The judge who sent Louis to the Colored Waifs' Home in 1913 could have sent him back to his mother, but without his father at home, the boy was clearly not getting enough supervision, so the judge sent him off to the home.

Armstrong ended up at the Colored Waifs' Home after he fired off a pistol on New Year's Eve during the last seconds of 1912. He fired the pistol in the air to celebrate the New Year, not unlike several generations of New Orleanians before and after. He was unfortunate to get caught, but he was extremely fortunate to be sent to the home. The time Louis spent there was, in the words of Armstrong researcher Tad Jones, "the best thing that could have happened to him." Peter Davis, a music teacher in the Colored Waifs' Home whose dedication to students has won him a special place in jazz history, first gave a tambourine to the eleven-year-old Louis after the boy persistently asked to join the brass band. When Davis saw that Louis had a real talent for rhythm, he gave him a snare drum. Davis further tested the boy's talent by giving him first an alto horn, then a bugle, and finally a cornet. When the boy showed dedication as well as ability, Davis gave him private lessons. He would even bring Louis to his home, where his daughter Ida played piano and Louis soloed on cornet. When Louis reluctantly left the home after a year and a half, he was ready to take his place in the thriving New Orleans music scene.

MATRIARCHAL BEGINNINGS

Peter Davis was as close as Armstrong had come to having a father. His natural father, who never married May Ann, left when Louis was still an infant. William Armstrong soon found another woman, married her, and raised two children. Although Armstrong visited his father periodically, there was never much of a connection between the two. Essentially he was raised by women. We know that his paternal grandmother, a Catholic, baptized him and was primarily responsible for his welfare during the first months of his life. He was then raised by May Ann and his older sister, whom he called Mama Lucy. Various women in the neighborhood who looked after him are mentioned affectionately in his autobiographical writings. But none of them kept the boy on a tight leash, and he had plenty of time on his own, singing on the streets and hustling for pennies.

Another woman who figures prominently in Armstrong's boyhood was a Jewish immigrant from Lithuania whose first name does not even appear in the biographies. As a teenager, Louis worked for Tillie Karnosfsky's husband and sons riding on a coal cart. Only slightly less poor than the black residents of New Orleans, the Karnofsky family made a living selling coal to prostitutes in the red-light district. Like many Eastern European Jews who emigrated in the nineteenth century, the Karnofskys settled in the Southern United States, in a poor section of New Orleans near Storyville. Armstrong made better money assisting the Karnofskys than he did with his informal vocal quartet or selling discarded potatoes and onions to restaurants. The Karnofsky family took special interest in young Louis, admiring his ability to sing and complimenting him on his good intonation. They knew enough about music to realize that the child had perfect pitch. The family was so taken with Armstrong that they regularly invited him home in the evenings for meals and even allowed him to spend the night. He must have told the Karnofskys about his success as a cornetist in the Colored Waifs' Home because one day, when Louis was transfixed by a used cornet in the window of a pawnshop, the Karnofsky boys knew what to do. By this time Armstrong surely knew that the instrument could masculinize even an abject street waif, especially if he played it loud and with the kind of authority he was beginning to learn with Peter Davis. He asked his employers to advance him the money to buy the horn for $5, and at the rate of fifty cents a month, he paid back the debt. Armstrong wrote that the horn was black with age, but that the Karnofskys used brass polish on the outside and some kind of liquid to clean out the interior. And they encouraged him when he played the tunes he had learned in the home.

The Karnofskys' efforts to provide food, fellowship, and encouragement to a black teenager went well beyond what most employers would have done for anyone, anywhere. They may have been won over by Louis's charm, much like Peter Davis, who said yes to an insistent, enthusiastic boy who wanted to join the band in the Colored Waifs' Home. Regardless, the family's generosity toward Armstrong left a profound impression. In a long autobiographical essay he wrote in 1969, two years before his death, he devoted several pages to how much he loved the Jewish people in general and the Karnofskys in particular. Armstrong began writing the essay in New York's Beth Israel Hospital, where he was recovering from surgery and where, by coincidence, his beloved Jewish manager, Joe Glaser, was dying in another room. Already in a reflective mood and knowing that his own death was not far away, he heard a doctor singing "A Russian Lullaby," a song that was in fact written by Irving Berlin but that Armstrong confused with a song he had learned many years before from

Tillie Karnofsky (Louis called her "Mother Karnofsky"). It may have been the song she sang when she put Louis to bed on the nights he stayed over, or when she cooked hot meals for the family and their guest. But Armstrong surely heard more than lullabies at the Karnofskys'. He must also have been listening carefully when they talked about their love of classical music and opera.

Late in life, when asked about his religion, Armstrong would say that he was raised a Baptist, always wore a Star of David around his neck, and was friends with the pope. The Star of David was his lasting tribute to the Karnofskys. He could have added that he was baptized a Catholic, but he probably was not aware that he had received the sacrament. He also did not know that he was born on August 4, 1901, rather than on July 4, 1900, which is the epochal date he always gave when asked. We know the facts now only because Tad Jones found Armstrong's certificate of baptism at the Sacred Heart of Jesus Church on Lopez Street in New Orleans several years after Armstrong's death. Armstrong's mother was unmarried and no more than sixteen years old when her only son was born, so she may have had good reason not to tell him the exact circumstances of his birth.

Louis was correct, however, when he said that his mother was a Baptist. In spite of—or because of—the fact that she was also a prostitute, May Ann took young Louis to church on a few occasions. It's also likely that the boy wandered into services on his own now and then, perhaps to hear the music. For all practical purposes, however, Armstrong had little formal instruction in Christianity, and although his early experiences in the Sanctified Church were essential to the entertainer he became, he had little use for religion after he reached maturity. Hence his evasive remark about the Baptist church, a Star of David, and friendship with a pope.

Consistent with his bawdy humor and his disdain for those who feigned virtue, Armstrong joked freely about religion. In general, he believed that clergymen were more interested in money than in saving souls. Listen, for example, to the mock sermons on his 1931 recording of "Lonesome Road," where he tells a preacher not to pocket the money in the collection plate. Much later, in 1967, Armstrong received a letter from a marine stationed in Vietnam who mentioned his love for jazz. A devoted correspondent, even with strangers, Armstrong wrote back with some words about the importance of music, tracing it back, not surprisingly, to the Sanctified Churches. He reminisced about his own experiences in church and then told a joke about a large, imposing fellow who was forced into the baptizing waters by even larger, more imposing deacons. The story is reproduced in Thomas Brothers's collection of Armstrong's writings, complete with Louis's inimitable orthography:

> "*Brother* do you Believe?" The Guy didn't say anything—Just looked at them. So they Ducked him down into that River again, only they held him down there a few minutes Longer. So when the Deacons looked in the guy's *eye* and said to him—"Do you Believe?" This Guy finally answered—he said "*Yes*—I Believe you *Son of Bitches trying* to *drown me*."[11]

At the end of the letter, Armstrong gives the marine some words of consolation to help him through his ordeal in Vietnam. He quotes sixteen lines of lyrics, not from an old spiritual but from "You'll Never Walk Alone," a song from the Broadway musical *Carousel*, words and music by Rodgers and Hammerstein.

AN APPRENTICESHIP LIKE NO OTHER

When Louis was out of the Waifs' Home, he worked on the Karnofskys' coal cart and took several unpleasant jobs as a day laborer in New Orleans. He did not always have time for playing music, but he listened whenever he could. There were plenty of cornet masters in the intensely active musical city, but Armstrong thought Joe "King" Oliver was the best in town. Louis was probably about fifteen when Oliver was playing with Kid Ory's band, and for whatever reasons, the older cornettist took a liking to the teenager. Oliver may have been another man who responded to Louis's charm and exuberance. Armstrong wrote that he would tag along after Oliver in parades and ask to carry his horn. Young Louis could be shy about performing, but he was not at all reluctant to approach a musician he idolized.

Oliver was hardly the traditional figure of masculinity that a boy would take as a role model. For one thing, one of his eyes had been damaged and tended to wander, provoking some of his associates to complain that they never knew when he was actually looking at them. Oliver was, however, a tall man with substantial girth at the waist. And like Buddy Bolden, he wore a red undershirt that he would rakishly display by unbuttoning the top of his shirt. In his years as a freak player, Oliver would amaze audiences with bizarre effects and sounds that could be strange or uncomfortably familiar. Armstrong says he can remember Oliver effortlessly nailing the high notes, but Oliver probably gravitated toward freak playing after gum and tooth problems made it difficult or painful to hit the high notes. Brothers wrote that Oliver's performing inventory included "beer buckets, toilet plungers, glasses, derby hats, coconuts, and kazoos combined with half valving, flutter tonguing, fake fingering, vibratos, growls, and subtle changes of tension in the lips to produce a creative array of vocalized effects."[12]

Oliver gave regular lessons to Armstrong and even brought him to his house, where he introduced him to his wife and her heaping plates of red beans and rice with ham hocks. When Oliver replaced his cornet with a new one, he gave the old horn to Armstrong, who later wrote, "I prized that horn and guarded it with my life. I blew on it for a long, long time before I was fortunate enough to get another one." One school of psychoanalysis has theorized that boys grow up wanting the father's phallus, the symbol of his power. If they are right, then this primal fantasy came true at only one remove for young Louis Armstrong. But even if the shrinks are wrong and sometimes a cornet is just a cornet, Louis knew how much masculine symbolism a horn can carry. No wonder this incident sticks out in his memories of his surrogate father.

With his growling, talking cornet, King Oliver was an important influence on a large group of early jazz players, especially the men in Duke Ellington's brass section. The trombonists Charlie Irvis and "Tricky Sam" Nanton and the trumpeters Bubber Miley and Cootie Williams were first, but Ellington employed at least one brass man who specialized in an Oliveresque sound throughout his nearly fifty years as an orchestra leader. Oliver was also a fine blues player who could project emotion, even when his powers were fading. When he formed his own band in Chicago in 1920, he began to perfect the contrapuntal style that had been taking shape a few years earlier when Buddy Bolden was flourishing.

Oliver moved on to greener pastures in 1918. Like many eminent New Orleans musicians, he could make a better living up north or in California, especially after the momentous closing of Storyville in 1917 and the reduction in venues for black musicians. Soon after Oliver had formed his own band, he was touring the country and making a name for himself. Back in New Orleans, Armstrong was busy filling Oliver's shoes in the band of Kid Ory. The trombonist Ory and most of the musicians in his circle played by ear, so Armstrong had his work cut out for him in his late teens when he joined the reading bands on Mississippi riverboats. The experience also gave Armstrong an opportunity to travel and meet people he never would have encountered in New Orleans. The riverboats took him as far north as Davenport, Iowa, and it may even be true that there he met a local boy named Bix Beiderbecke. It's probably an apocryphal story, but it adds a delicious synchronicity to the history of the jazz trumpet.

Regardless, Armstrong was becoming a professional, polished performer with a growing knowledge of the world outside of New Orleans—even of Iowa. He was also developing the thick, wide, majestic sound that became his trademark and that almost every jazz trumpeter since has tried to emulate.

Meanwhile, in Chicago, King Oliver was having even more trouble with his teeth and gums. By 1927, he would be completely toothless. In 1922, he knew that his continued success as a band leader required someone to hit those sexy high notes and keep the audience interested, so he sent Armstrong a telegram that August. By this time, Armstrong was making good money playing in New Orleans's clubs and tonks, but he was ready to move on and make even better money with his old idol.

When Louis was fresh out of the Waifs' Home and begging to carry Oliver's horn, the older man must have seen something of himself in the teenage boy. Although they didn't see each other during the four years after Oliver left New Orleans, there was still a connection. Both came from poverty, and both were dark-skinned blacks in a musical culture where light-skinned Creole musicians took the best-paying jobs. And both were stout men who loved to eat. Take a look at the picture of Oliver and Armstrong from 1923 (figure 20). With the same complexion, round face, and dour countenance, they actually could be father and son. Louis has none of that sly, insouciant look we see on the face of Buddy Bolden in his one photograph. At this stage, Armstrong may have still been shy and uncertain, but Stanley Crouch claims there is more here than meets the eye: "We see an arrogant, surly young man who seemed to think himself handsome and was not to be fucked with."[13]

If Crouch is right about young Armstrong's attitude, he was about to meet his match in Chicago. Lil Hardin (figure 21) came from a black bourgeois family in Memphis. Although her parents hated jazz and blues, Lil was a free spirit who developed a passion for the blues once she ventured far enough outside her family's house. She contin-ued learning to play the classics on the piano and even attended Fisk University for two years. After moving from Tennessee to Chicago, she took a job playing piano in a music store, plugging songs for peo-ple who might buy the sheet music. Musicians who stopped by the store noticed that she had a talent for blues and ragtime in spite of her conservatory training. Beginning in 1918, she played in several groups that included Oliver as cornetist. When Oliver formed his own group shortly before Armstrong joined in 1922, Hardin became the regular pianist with King Oliver's Creole Jazz Band. Although at first she paid little attention to the chubby country boy on second cor-net, she eventually took a serious interest in Armstrong, both roman-tically and professionally. They played classical music together, and Lil gave Louis some instruction in music theory. Armstrong had never met anyone like her—a beautiful, talented, aggressive woman who drove her own car. Armstrong did not even know how to drive when he got to Chicago. His first marriage had gone sour some years earlier, and conveniently, Hardin was estranged from her husband. It was she who did the paperwork so that both could get divorces. They were married in February 1924.

Lil first began paying attention to Louis when Oliver himself told her, "That boy plays better than me." If you listen to the recordings that Oliver, Armstrong, and Hardin made in 1923, you can hear that he's right. Oliver plays with authority, and he has that striking ability to make his cornet talk and growl. Armstrong was never able to get those same effects, but he could do much more. In spite of the prim-itive recording conditions for Oliver's band—the first time any of them had been in a studio—Armstrong's fat sound comes through. So do his fluid, assertive, and rhythmically sure solos. And like Bolden, he played loud—so loud that he had to stand in the back of the stu-dio, much farther away from the recording horn than the rest of the band.

Having become Louis's tutor and his lover, Lil made up her mind that he could do better than play second cornet to a musician who was already past his prime. She managed to find various ways to drive a wedge between Armstrong and his mentor. Her work became easier when the members of the band discovered that Oliver had been holding back part of their pay. About the time that Armstrong began looking around for a better job, he received another momentous invitation, this time from Fletcher Henderson to join his orchestra in New York.

BECOMING A STAR

Henderson was a college-educated African American from Georgia who had come to New York to earn a master's degree in chemistry at Columbia University. In order to make ends meet, he went to work as the house pianist at Black Swan Records, one of the first black-owned businesses in the United States. One of his earliest jobs was providing accompaniment for a twenty-five-year-old "cake-walking baby" singer named Ethel Waters. As the record label's business grew, and as Henderson had the opportunity to work with larger groups of musicians, he began playing in clubs. Within a few years he had given up graduate school, but he had effectively invented big-band jazz as we now know it. He was not, however, a good businessman. His first band fell apart in 1934, as did the band he put together the next year. In 1935, however, Benny Goodman had the good sense to buy some of the arrangements that Henderson had written for his own band in the early 1930s. The Goodman band entered its period of enormous success only after it began playing Henderson's music.

Armstrong had already become a showstopper in Chicago, revising everyone's notions of the cornet's limitations. More established cornetists such as Johnny Dunn and Freddie Keppard dropped by the enormous Lincoln Gardens dance joint with hopes of outplaying him. Like everyone else who tried, they went home humiliated, especially on those nights when Armstrong hit one hundred high Cs in a row while his band counted them off. Audiences loved his singing, his patter, and his unique body language. He had perfected his gladiatorial skills in the tonks and parks of New Orleans, and he had honed his performance style on the riverboats and in the clubs of Chicago. By the time he arrived in New York, he was ready to show the world what he could do.

Tenor saxophonist Coleman Hawkins was a key figure in the Henderson orchestra, both before and after Armstrong arrived. Before Armstrong, Hawkins was playing a novelty instrument with slap-tongue articulation and flat-footed timing. After Armstrong, he was playing an important jazz instrument with fluid improvisation and deftly swinging rhythm. Much the same can be said for many of the musicians in the Henderson band, who were never the same after they played alongside Armstrong for several months. It must have been agonizing for Henderson's urbane, elegant New Yorkers to accept the reality that an awkwardly dressed Southern boy was the best musician they knew.

In New York, Louis continued to grow as an improviser and as an entertainer. He also recorded with blues singers, most notably Bessie Smith, and with New Orleans musicians who were living in New York, including Sidney Bechet. He bought himself a new Conn trumpet, too. (Later he would buy LeBlanc and Selmer trumpets in France, a practice he kept up even after the major factories for both companies were relocated to Kenosha, Wisconsin, and Elkhart, Indiana. Who can blame him if he preferred shopping in Paris?) In New York, the trumpet had already become the instrument of modernity, jazz, and the Roaring Twenties. Armstrong had been essential to this transformation, even when he was playing the cornet. But once he got his hands on a trumpet, the real Jazz Age began!

Henderson, however, did not take well to Armstrong's style. The

New York musicians who made up Fletcher Henderson's band were used to playing for whiter and politer audiences than were the vernacular artists Armstrong grew up with. Henderson was especially contemptuous of Armstrong's singing. Everybody loved his bawdy, exuberant vocals and the gravel in his gutbucket voice. One musician said that other singers would stick their heads out of windows in the middle of winter hoping to catch whatever it was that gave Armstrong that sound. Henderson, however, discouraged Armstrong from breaking the studious decorum of his band with his raucous vocals. Armstrong takes trumpet solos on more than fifty of the songs he recorded with Henderson, but his voice can be heard on only one. On "Everybody Loves My Baby," recorded in November 1924, he speaks a few words as the tune ends. He regularly sang with Henderson in clubs, but never on record.

Armstrong may have quit Henderson's band not because he wasn't allowed to sing but because he was not given the first trumpet chair. Historically, the trumpeter who does the most soloing sits in the third or fourth chair, playing less challenging parts so that he is not exhausted when he stands up to solo. Armstrong, however, knew that he could play higher and louder—and better—than anyone else in the section and asked to be moved up to first after Henderson consigned him to third chair. His request was denied. And when Lil arrived in New York for a visit, she was appalled to discover that advertisements for Henderson's orchestra made no mention of Armstrong's presence. As soon as she was back in Chicago, she found a promoter who would pay him more than he was making with Henderson. After fourteen months in New York, Louis was back in Chicago with Lil in the fall of 1925.

In Chicago, Armstrong began the most important years of his musical career. Between 1925 and 1928, with his Hot Five and Hot Seven bands, he recorded one extraordinary solo after another. Had he died in 1928, his reputation would be intact. "West End Blues," "Struttin' with Some Barbecue," "Potato Head Blues," "Weatherbird," "Hotter Than That"—these are still among the most admired recordings in jazz history. The trumpet would never be the same.

How did he do it?

GENIUS AT WORK

The jazz historian Thomas Brothers has written that Armstrong and the players of his generation were always looking for ways to move beyond their predecessors. Buddy Bolden brought in the blues, and King Oliver perfected the art of the trick player. Younger musicians like Armstrong (and some would add the unrecorded Buddy Petit) found ways to add melodic complexity to the established style. As Brothers explains, the blues was still central, but it was "more nimble and fancy, no longer quite so lush."[14] With his trumpet, Armstrong made the blues more urban. In Harlem, Armstrong saw elegant black Americans like Henderson every day, well educated, always immaculately dressed, always articulate "New Negroes." Even if he remained the Rabelaisian character from a poor neighborhood in the South, he was discovering ways of making his trumpet sound like it belonged in the more sophisticated cities of the North. When Louis recorded with Bessie Smith in 1925, he embroidered her singing with elaborate lines that, for many listeners, were a perfect counterpoint. Smith, however, did not like what Armstrong was doing, finding his work too complex. She was country. Louis had become truly cosmopolitan, if only to compete with the musicians around Henderson.

In an extremely useful study, "The Early Musical Development of Louis Armstrong, 1901–1928," Brian Harker notices a bit of synchronicity that helps explain how Armstrong perceived his instrument.[15] In 1922, just after Armstrong had moved to Chicago, he went to see Bill "Bojangles" Robinson dance. Armstrong later wrote that Robinson "was the greatest comedian and dancer in my race. Better than Bert Williams."[16] The comparison is intriguing. Bert Williams was an extremely popular black singer and actor. W. C. Fields said that Williams was the funniest man he ever knew as well as the saddest. Very much rooted in the old minstrel tradition, Williams wore a tattered top hat and tails with pants cut off below the knees. Although his songs and his stage routines were very much about the hopeless situations in which blacks found themselves, he never really left behind the minstrel stereotypes. He even appeared on stage in blackface. Not Bill Robinson. He never wore blackface, and his clothes were always stylish and carefully tailored. His dancing was graceful, elegant, and precise. Bert Williams died in 1922, the same year that Armstrong arrived in Chicago and first saw Robinson. It was truly the end of an era.

Harker argues that Armstrong was to Robinson what an older cornet master like King Oliver was to Bert Williams. Having developed his style in a vaudeville/minstrel tradition, King Oliver fell back on freak sounds to win easy laughs from his audience. In the breaks—those moments in New Orleans music when the rest of the band lays out so that one player can take a quick solo—Oliver would take a hat or a bottle and produce the dependable freak sounds. Armstrong, however, found another way. We know that as a teenager he had been listening carefully to clarinet players, especially Sidney Bechet, who took advantage of the relative effortlessness of playing the clarinet to create fast, leaping solos. At some point, instead of hitting a few ratty notes in the breaks, young Armstrong began playing breakneck runs and arpeggios with the kind of care and precision he had learned from listening to Bechet and the clarinetists. He danced through his solos like the agile Bill Robinson. As much as we may admire the older trumpet master, Oliver had more in common with the blacked-up joker, Bert Williams.

In his breaks and solos, Armstrong also incorporated bits of the classical music he learned to love with the Karnofskys as well as anything he could pick up from the innumerable virtuosos who appeared every weekend in New Orleans parks. He perfected his skills in the many competitions that were rites of initiation for young New Orleans musicians. For Armstrong it may have begun as early as his days in the Colored Waifs' Home, where Kid Rena was also confined. Rena was a Downtown Creole with light skin. His people were likely to look down their noses at Armstrong and other dark-skinned blacks from Uptown. This kind of prejudice added an extra level of intensity to the competition between Armstrong and Rena. In fact, Kid Rena made an especially revealing set of comments on Armstrong's early style: "He is not playing cornet on that horn; he is imitating a clarinet. He is showing off and he's gonna bust a vein in his neck screaming on that horn."[17] Although he was wrong about exactly what was going to happen to Louis, he understood perfectly what Armstrong was trying to do with what he had learned from the clarinetists.

Regardless of what instrument they play, classically trained musicians learn to play arpeggios quickly and cleanly. In Armstrong's day, very few jazz musicians bothered with these kinds of exercises. Louis saw an opening. He realized that he could stand out with arpeggios, sounding fleet and darting while the competition was still playing old blues licks and freak sounds. And what has impressed the more classically inclined critics like Gunther Schuller is the logic and architecture with which Armstrong built his solos. Listening to classical music, he must have become sensitive to patterns of repetition, peaks and valleys, dynamic variation. Unlike virtually all other New Orleans musicians, he found ways to make these patterns work for him, to make the music *dramatic*.

As Gary Giddins has pointed out in his superb account of Armstrong's achievement, injecting drama into his solos was the trumpeter's greatest and most influential achievement.[18] Much of the drama came from his ability to expand the range of the trumpet upward. With the high notes as well as with timbre, vibrato, volume, and phrasing, Armstrong built climaxes into his solos and greatly expanded the instrument's emotional range. Listen to records by any of the trumpet masters who preceded Armstrong, such as Oliver and Keppard from New Orleans, or Joe Smith and Howard Scott, who soloed with Henderson's bands pre-Armstrong. You'll hear a music that floats along monochromatically without much variation from phrase to phrase. Classical opera and the melodramatic performances of singers like Enrico Caruso surely helped Armstrong figure out how to build those climaxes. The journalist and jazz musician Terry Teachout has suggested that Armstrong's cadenzas—elaborate pocket dramas all to themselves—might have been inspired by the fancy cornet cadenzas of men like Herbert L. Clarke, the premier cornet soloist with John Philip Sousa's brass band. Clarke's recordings from the first two decades of the 1900s are now available on CD, just as they were available to young Louis on 78s. Clarke's unaccompanied solo cadenzas reveal a careful study of arias from operas, and they may have inspired Armstrong when he was constructing his own unaccompanied solos. Armstrong's most memorable cadenza is surely the one that opens the 1928 recording of "West End Blues." His old friend and mentor King Oliver was among the many who were flabbergasted by the solo. A mere six months after Armstrong made his recording, a band led by Oliver recorded the same tune with trumpeter Louis Metcalf attempting a note-for-note re-creation of Armstrong's improvised cadenza. A few weeks after that, a band called Zack Whyte's Chocolate Beau Brummels released its own version of "West End Blues" with two trumpeters playing the same solo in unison.

Armstrong's trumpet drama did not come only from opera, the classics, and their appropriations by someone like Herbert Clarke. There was definitely drama in the sexual interactions he saw in brothels and in his own "wailings" with women, not to mention his dramatic juggling of wives and mistresses. Part of his genius was the ability to import whatever he felt in these situations into his musical style. In Armstrong's recordings, there are even passages where he playfully delays a climax, a kind of musical foreplay. Members of his band in the 1930s referred to the tempo Armstrong adopted for "Star Dust" as "the fucking rhythm."

TECHNO-POPS

Just as Armstrong was in the right place at the right time to absorb a degree of urban sophistication when he arrived in Harlem in 1924, he was also fortunate to grow up with the beginnings of modern recording technology. After making the first real jazz records with Oliver and then making regular forays into studios with Fletcher Henderson, Bessie Smith, and Sidney Bechet in New York, Armstrong knew what to do when he was back in Chicago with his Hot Five and Hot Seven bands. These bands were not designed to play in clubs. They were primarily recording units. Armstrong had figured out which instruments sounded best on record, where each musician should stand in the studio, and how the members of the band could play off one another without losing the balance that was essential for the crude recording process. Several decades later, Miles Davis would change the trumpet again with technological sophistication. Davis would stick a Harmon mute into the bell of his trumpet, pull out the stem, and place the mute's empty hole right on top of the microphone. He let the engineer control the volume, knowing that no one in the booth would let the drummer drown out his trumpet. The result was a sound that was muffled and metallic but also keening and emotionally rich. It became Davis's trademark.

Armstrong not only understood the new technologies; he was fascinated with gadgets his entire life. He always traveled with a record player. When he knew that a hotel was going to refuse laundry services to black guests, he would pack a small washing machine to clean the more than fifty handkerchiefs he used each day to wipe his brow and the rest of his body. He acquired a typewriter in 1922, just after he arrived in Chicago, and added it to his regular baggage. He eventually owned a long succession of typewriters on which he pecked out reams of letters. Whenever a technological device came on the market, Armstrong was among the first to purchase it. He was especially fond of tape recorders, often making tapes of himself playing along with his favorite records. He also made tapes of conversations and even staged readings with his friends, whether they knew that they were being recorded or not. Among the treasure trove of tapes available for listening at the Louis Armstrong House and Archives in Corona, Queens, is one on which Armstrong and friends take turns reading aloud from a pornographic novel. On another tape, Louis can be heard arguing with his wife, Lucille, who at one point blurts out, "Is that damn thing still on?"

Earlier, when he was earning enough to buy records in New Orleans, Armstrong purchased the first recordings by the Original Dixieland Jazz Band, but he also bought the music of Caruso, the Italian soprano Luisa Tetrazzini, and the Irish tenor John McCormack. With entrepreneurial spirit, Armstrong combined this exotic material with everything else he was absorbing. By 1930, in his recording of "Dinah," Armstrong would play a solo that lasted only two choruses but that borrowed short, easily recognizable phrases from Verdi's *Rigoletto*, "My Hero" from Oscar Strauss's *The Chocolate Soldier*, Gershwin's "Lady Be Good," Edwin Eugene Bagley's "National Emblem March," Sigmund Romberg's "Lover Come Back to Me," and that hoochie-koochie dance to which schoolchildren used to sing, "Oh, oh, down in France, where the naked women dance." Armstrong's solos were "high art" combined with "low art" combined with Americana. Or more simply, Americana. As Ralph Ellison and Roddy Doyle both knew, America is the place where high and low, honor and ridicule, urbane and homespun comfortably coexist. No one did it more expertly than African American musicians in general and Louis Armstrong in particular.

Kid Rena was right about one thing. Armstrong was wearing himself out with his intense style of playing. By the 1930s he was having serious problems with his lip. Blood would run from his mouth at the end of performances. When he had a blister, he would pick at his lips in ways that horrified onlookers. Little by little, he backed off from his take-no-prisoners gladiatorial style. If his playing became less adventuresome, it also became more economical, more structured, and, some would say, more mature. In 1930, Armstrong gave up on the old contrapuntal, New Orleans style of jazz with a trumpet, a clarinet, and a trombone out in front of a rhythm section. Like many other musical stars of the 1930s, he began performing with a big band. Standing alone in front of his orchestra, Armstrong was now indisputably the main attraction. When he hired a fellow Crescent City trumpeter, Henry "Red" Allen, considered by many to be a major artist in his own right, Armstrong made sure that Allen never soloed with the band.

THE GENIUS BECOMES AN ENTERTAINER

For many purists, Armstrong's decline began when he formed the big band. He had sold out. Worse, he told interviewers that his favorite bandleader was a cornball named Guy Lombardo. Today we remember Lombardo as a corpselike figure with a baton, brought out on New Year's Eve to play his signature song, "Auld Lang Syne." But in the late 1920s and early '30s, Lombardo was extremely popular, even with young audiences. Although there were exceptions, most whites preferred "sweet" bands like Lombardo's to the "hot" bands of Henderson and Ellington. As a soloist, Armstrong continued to play at a more advanced level than anyone else in the business, but his band sounded like the ones the largest audiences most appreciated. After growing up in poverty and enduring several episodes of failure in his early career, Armstrong was finally able to earn a good living. At no point would he have thought that he was selling out. And he certainly did not turn his back on his roots. He still ate red beans and rice, told dirty stories, and bragged about what he could do with his sphincters and his genitals.

In 1935, after years of working together on and off, Armstrong hired Joe Glaser as his manager. Actually, it's more accurate to say that Glaser hired Armstrong. Glaser was a deeply unsavory character, possibly a murderer and a rapist but definitely a gangster who had worked for Al Capone in the 1920s. Glaser, though, knew how to deal with many characters who were even more unsavory and who could make life miserable for Armstrong. In the early 1930s, Armstrong found himself in a desperate situation, threatened by two different sets of gangsters in Chicago and New York. Both groups had made offers he could not refuse. For several years, he appeared in neither New York nor Chicago, performing only in the South, California, or Europe. Glaser knew how to deal with the tough guys who were menacing Armstrong, and he quickly won his client's everlasting loyalty. Glaser paid Armstrong a salary that was much less than he might have earned on his own, but he also handled the payroll for the band, arranged all bookings, dealt with the IRS, and even sent checks to Armstrong's girlfriends. He left Armstrong free to provide exuberant entertainment to adoring audiences and to live the good life. By the time of Glaser's death in 1969, there is every indication that the two men had developed genuine affection for each other.

Glaser found Armstrong a wide variety of acting gigs in their years together, including a starring role in a 1939 Broadway show, a musical adaptation of Shakespeare's *A Midsummer Night's Dream* called *Swingin' the Dream*. In a mostly African American cast, Armstrong received rave reviews as Puck. But the show was not a hit and closed after a few performances. Even before Glaser came on as his manager,

Armstrong had acted in several movies. Although many admire the surrealist, subversive humor of the Fleischer Brothers and their series of Betty Boop cartoons, not everyone admired the casting of Armstrong as a cannibal out to consume Ms. Boop in a 1932 cartoon. In *Going Places* (1938), Armstrong sings "Jeepers Creepers" to a horse. In *Pennies From Heaven* (1936), he steals chickens, and in *Every Day's a Holiday* (1937), he is a street cleaner.

When Glaser took over, he did little to upgrade the kind of work that Armstrong was getting in Hollywood. At least not at first. Armstrong's greatest film role may be the beloved elder statesman of jazz he plays in Martin Ritt's 1961 film *Paris Blues*. But in 1947, Glaser could do little to stop the gradual downgrading of the roles that Armstrong and Billie Holiday (whom he was also managing) were hired to play in the 1947 film *New Orleans*. Initially written as a love story about two jazz artists who leave New Orleans after the closing of Storyville, the prominence of Armstrong and Holiday declined with each new version of the script. Ultimately, Armstrong became a musician performing for the pleasure of the film's hero, a casino owner played by the profoundly forgettable Arturo De Córdova. Holiday had an even smaller role, playing a maid for the film's leading lady, the equally unmemorable Dorothy Patrick. At the film's horrifying finale, Patrick stands in front of an enormous symphony orchestra and struggles her way through "Do You Know What It Means to Miss New Orleans." Earlier, however, when Armstrong and Holiday sing and play a magnificent rendition of "The Blues Are Brewing," all is forgiven.

The film *New Orleans* supposedly takes place in 1917. In spite of a host of anachronisms—such as when, in the opening of the film Armstrong plays the "West End Blues" cadenza that he would record ten years later—the film's producers got it right by uniting Armstrong with a front line and a rhythm section of New Orleans musicians. The big-band era was ending, and a new fascination with the "classic" jazz of New Orleans was building. The experience on the set of *New Orleans* inspired Armstrong to lead new, smaller groups that returned to the front line of trumpet, clarinet, and trombone that began in Buddy Bolden's era. He would continue to play with this lineup for the rest of his life, and although he had many hits and was always trying out new material, his act never really changed for the next twenty-four years. He was still the star of the band, singing, clowning, and telling bawdy stories.

OUT OF FAVOR

For many blacks, however, he was also playing the Uncle Tom. By the late 1940s, the old minstrel stereotypes were anathema to young African Americans, many of whom had just returned from fighting fascists and racists in Europe and the Pacific. If Armstrong had been a hero in the black community for several decades, he lost a large portion of this audience when he played the King of the Zulus in New Orleans in 1949. When pictures of the trumpeter in blackface and a grass skirt were widely published, many African Americans were deeply offended. And his enthusiastic performance persona began to seem like an obsequious zeal to please, especially the whites in his audiences.

Armstrong, however, loved being King of the Zulus. As a New Orleanian, he knew that it was a special honor reserved for the community's most distinguished personalities, who rode majestically through town on one of the Mardi Gras floats. He also saw nothing wrong with his theme song, "When It's Sleepy Time Down South," with its references to "darkies" and "Old Mammy" falling on her knees. He first performed the song in 1931 and continued to feature it at every performance right up until the end of his life, in spite of pleas from civil rights groups. Ironically, the tune was written by three black songwriters.

Even Armstrong's widely publicized denunciations of President Dwight Eisenhower and Arkansas governor Orval Faubus during the struggle to integrate Little Rock's public schools in 1957 did not entirely change his image. After watching black children turned away from schools by armed troops, Armstrong told a reporter that the American government could "go to hell" and that Eisenhower had "no guts." Fifty years after the incident, the reporter who interviewed Armstrong wrote that Louis was angry enough to sing a version of "The Star-Spangled Banner" that began with "Oh, say can you see, by the dawn's motherfucking light," and continued in that vein for several minutes. Even when the sanitized version of his interview was published, Armstrong was attacked by Sammy Davis Jr. for appearing before segregated audiences. In a notorious article following the fracas, the columnist Jim Bishop suggested that Armstrong's subsequent apology to Eisenhower may have been the result of a drop in ticket sales and "some empty tables at the Copacabana."[19] Bishop did not acknowledge, however, that Armstrong apologized only *after* Eisenhower found his guts and sent federal troops to Little Rock to enforce court-ordered desegregation. Although Charles Mingus gave Orval Faubus a permanent role in jazz history with his 1959 evisceration, "Fables of Faubus," Mingus was one of many boppers and postboppers who did not bother to stand beside Armstrong when he publicly denounced official racism. Armstrong did, however, receive public support from Lena Horne, Jackie Robinson, Marian Anderson, and several other eminent African Americans.[20]

Strangely enough, Armstrong was united with Sammy Davis Jr. a few years later when both starred in the 1966 film A *Man Called Adam* (see figure 22). Loosely inspired by the life of Miles Davis and produced by Sammy Davis's own production company, the film cast Armstrong as a relic from jazz history brought to New York by an enterprising club owner, Nelson (Ossie Davis). Armstrong's character, "Sweet Daddy" Willie Ferguson, is so impoverished that Nelson arranges to have him bunk with Adam (Davis). At one point, Ferguson sulks alone in the corner of a roomful of partying people, as out of touch with contemporary society as with contemporary jazz. Seeing the old trumpeter sitting alone, Adam rebukes Nelson, telling him that when the novelty of hearing Ferguson wears off, "that nice old man's gonna be bumming drinks at bars up in Harlem." A *Man Called Adam* contrasts the lost soul played by Armstrong with Davis's Adam, who represents not just modern jazz but modern racial politics. Adam takes no guff from white policemen and his white manager, ultimately to his peril. At the film's conclusion, he is another casualty of racism and the jazz life.

Although the Sweet Daddy Ferguson of *A Man Called Adam* gazes mournfully at a world that no longer has a place for him, Armstrong's working band performs exuberantly on several occasions in the film. Suddenly Louis is no longer Sweet Daddy. He is himself. He delivers a bravura performance full of stirring trumpet solos and racy side remarks. Today, the film is downright incoherent, suggesting that a seasoned performer like Armstrong, the same recording star who had just knocked the Beatles out of first place on the record charts with "Hello, Dolly!" in 1965, was somehow a tragic figure from a forgotten past.

There is no question, however, that many people—both black and white—never forgave Armstrong for his excessive clowning and grinning. In 2005, at a workshop for secondary school teachers interested in adding jazz to their schools' curricula, I showed a video clip from the 1932 short film *Rhapsody in Black and Blue*. Dressed in a leopard skin and standing in a sea of soap bubbles, Armstrong sings the minstrel song "Shine" ("Just because because I always wear a smile, that's why they call me Shine"). His eyes bulge, his mouth gapes open, and he flaps his arms like a bird struggling to take flight. His body language can easily be interpreted as an eagerness to please. He almost bows as he sings. But once he has finished mugging his way through the song, he puts the trumpet to his lips and ceases to be the epicene jester. He is now a proud black man. His exposed biceps swell as he stands erect to give sexually provocative body language to an important note. His solo is full of crystal-clear high Cs, delicately bent notes, and floor-to-ceiling glissandi. Toward the end of his solo, he develops a playful, teasing motion with his shoulders, his body as well as his music contributing to the foreplay before the climax.

At the workshop, the video clip from *Rhapsody in Black and Blue* had barely begun when two African American teachers walked out. Upon returning, they told me that they had seen this demeaning image before and had no intention of showing it to students. They were insulted that I would show it in public. I tried to make the case that Armstrong the trumpeter had to be separated from Armstrong the obsequious clown, that the scene was coded masculine display at its most advanced, so advanced that the garden-variety white racist of 1932 probably did not regard the powerfully masculine Armstrong as in any way "uppity." This in itself, I argued, was a major achievement by a uniquely talented musical genius. The resisting teachers were not convinced. One asked, "Why are you making excuses for it?"

I have since thought long and hard about the wisdom of showing early film footage of Louis Armstrong to students. The codes of masculinity that he so cleverly deployed in the 1930s have outlived their usefulness, and now they are simply offensive. Fewer people, I now realize, will be offended if I show clips of the dignified, affectless Miles Davis. Or if I simply play Louis's records without the video. I have also rethought the argument that Armstrong the trumpeter can be separated from Armstrong the highly mannered stage performer. In a brilliant essay, Brent Hayes Edwards argues that we must see Armstrong's grinning and mugging as much more consistent with his exuberant playing and singing.[21] Edwards finds the same spirit of excess in Armstrong's writing. He quotes an especially revealing letter in which Armstrong connects his bowels to his trumpet as well as to his penis. Recalling his mother's careful attention to the health of her children, he quotes her advice on the importance of laxatives:

> She said—"Son—Always keep your bowels open, and nothing can harm you." . . . I always remember what my mother said where ever or when ever somebody would die with gas or indigestion . . . And still uses the phrase—"They didn't *shit enough*." . . . it all derives— from negligence of the bowels . . . I am about to be fifty nine years old . . . And I have to say it myself, I am blowing better and twice as strong as I was when I was in my twenties . . . Well I won't mention my sex sessions these days, because I hate to be called a braggadosha . . . Wow . . . Did that come *outa Mee* . . .[22]

What came out? Was it the sexual boasting or was it the music that he was blowing better than ever? Or was he talking about what came out of his ass? Or his penis? The ambiguity is consistent with Armstrong's humor and his gift for Rabelaisian excess.

Armstrong's innumerable letters exhibit his unique style of punctuation, his bathroom humor, and his self-mockery. In this same spirit of verbal play, he permanently changed the style of jazz and popular music with his use of scat and nonsense syllables. He may not be, as some historians have claimed, the inventor of scat singing. But he taught singers how scat could be an effective means of emotional expression beyond words. And not just for pure jazz singers like Ella Fitzgerald and Betty Carter. Frank Sinatra and Bing Crosby were also using nonsense syllables after Armstrong's example. The novelist and critic Nathaniel Mackey hears Armstrong's scat as a continuation of a blues tradition in which everyday speech is mangled and replaced by moans and cries. Mackey has invented the invaluable phrase a "telling inarticulacy," to describe this kind of performance. He sees it as the result of an "unspeakable history" of racial violence that included lynching and castration. The inarticulacy represents the singer's "willful dismantling of the gag-rule amenities which normally pass for coherence."[23]

The inarticulacy in Armstrong's scat singing, his bizarre writing style, and his complex body language may be a unique form of communication as legitimate as his elegant trumpet solos, which also surpass anything that can be put into words. For Brent Edwards, Armstrong forces his audiences to come to terms with "a swinging incommensurability." The singing, the mugging, the body language, the lyrics, the asides, *and* the trumpet playing "all seem to be saying all too much at once." Think of the vast range of songs and arias that Armstrong inserted into his 1930 solo on "Dinah." How do we reconcile Verdi, Gershwin, and the hoochie-koochie dance all crowded into the same enchanted space? Edwards goes so far as to compare Armstrong's wildly meaningful communications to the novels of James Joyce.[24] Armstrong gives little offense to people who close their eyes and listen only to the trumpet solos. But is it really possible to hear only the trumpet? Would Armstrong have been as popular— or as despised—if all we had were the trumpet solos? Edwards is probably right. We'll never know, because the trumpet solos are inconceivable without the mugging, the dirty jokes, and the tellingly inarticulate scatting.

What about Armstrong? Did he see himself as an artist, possibly even as a high modernist brandishing contradictory meanings as fearlessly as James Joyce? An interviewer once spoke to him about his great relationship with audiences and then asked how he would describe himself. Armstrong responded quickly: "As one of them. I'm just the same as one of those people out there in the audience."[25] I wonder, however, if Armstrong the audience member could have decoded all those messages that came tumbling out, one on top of another, from Armstrong the performer. One thing is certain: only a performer as promiscuously talented as Armstrong could have so completely changed the history of the trumpet.

chapter 4

Bending Brass: The Art of the Trumpet Maker and My Romance with the Equipment

The first note I played in the year 2004 might have drawn a belly laugh from Satchmo. It sounded like it came from my ass, not from my horn. I had not picked up that cornet since 1967, when I was a sophomore in college. Long before that moment I had played in the grade school band, starting out in the fourth grade with an old nickel-plated cornet passed down from my grandfather. I have no idea what became of that heirloom after my parents bought me a new horn a few years later. With my current passion for the equipment, I'd do anything to get my hands on it now. In 1960, however, I was delighted when my parents presented me with a brand-new York Custom cornet. It came in a slick maroon case, much admired by my twelve-year-old peers in the cornet section.

After playing that York cornet throughout junior and senior high school, I took it with me to the University of Chicago in 1966. It was not just the ferocious Chicago winters that made college life more intimidating than I had anticipated. It was, after all, the late sixties.

Nevertheless, I still found a few spare moments to play my cornet. I was especially intrigued when Jim Wesley, the physics major who lived down the hall, asked if I wanted to play in a brass quartet. He knew a composer who wrote for a group that played on Sundays at a Swedish Lutheran church near the university. Jim was one of those whiz kids who played the French horn when they weren't theorizing about astrophysics or creaming me at bridge. He told me that the brass group needed a second trumpeter (or in a pinch, a cornetist). When I showed up for rehearsal, the other trumpeter was brandishing a shiny, gold-plated King trumpet. I was embarrassed by my "student" instrument, acquired when schoolchildren were given shorter, mellower cornets and before the trumpet became the instrument of choice, even for twelve-year-olds. In fact, when my parents ordered the York cornet from a local dealer, all he had on hand was a trumpet. It was also a York Custom, and the price was the same. The dealer let me use it for a few days before the cornet arrived. I was completely enchanted by the longer, sleeker horn and would have told my parents that I wanted to keep it had not the band director been adamant about grade schoolers playing cornets. A few years later, band directors all over the country would stop squelching prepubescent boys' attraction to the trumpet's length and power to penetrate. Trumpets eventually became ubiquitous, even in grade schools.

The composer at the Swedish Lutheran church wrote mildly atonal, mildly uplifting music for the brass quartet. For several months, we rehearsed once a week and played every other Sunday for services. The members of the congregation, delighted to see so many young people in church, made us feel extremely welcome even though most of us looked less like well-scrubbed churchgoers and more like the scruffy agnostics we were. The sound of two trumpets, a French horn, and a trombone filling the cavernous sanctuary of the old church was pleasant, but it was the last time I would make music for many years.

I might have kept on playing had I been in some kind of a jazz group. But in the 1960s, jazz was no longer the music of youthful hipness. For virtually all of the young men in my dormitory, jazz hardly existed. Frank Zappa and the Jefferson Airplane were much more essential to their lives. One was a serious guitar player and a devotee of urban blues, so I thought he might be susceptible to jazz. I played my Dizzy Gillespie records for him, but he left my room mumbling about everything happening too fast. There were in fact a few jazzers on campus, but they weren't inviting me to sit in. And I was a miserable failure when I answered an open call to sit in with a group led by a "man from the Chicago community" named Joseph Jarman. He was entirely charming as he handed out incredibly difficult music by a composer named Richard Abrams. The music was well beyond my abilities, and I wasn't invited back. A few years later, Joseph Jarman would become a mainstay of the Art Ensemble of Chicago, and Muhal Richard Abrams would be recognized as one of the finest American composers of the twentieth and twenty-first centuries. For what it's worth, I knew them when.

The brass quartet and the Swedish Lutherans were fine, but the music did not give me the charge I got from playing jazz. Maybe I quit because so many people in the dormitory were sternly suggesting that I go somewhere else to practice. I liked to play in my room, where I could go back and forth between my books and my horn. People banging on my door and demanding quiet did not inspire me to continue my practice regimen. And anyway, several band directors going back to grade school had told me that my embouchure was no good and that I would never improve. The coup de grâce was delivered by the trumpeter in the brass quartet. He told me that the way my neck swelled up when I played indicated a serious medical condition and that I would probably need surgery someday. He was a medical student, so I believed him. And I quit playing.

MIDDLE C AND ME

Shortly before the end of those thirty-seven cornetless years, my dentist finally convinced me to see an orthodontist. In adolescence I had avoided getting my teeth straightened because, ironically, I was told that it would put an end to my trumpet playing. But when I stopped playing a few years later, I decided against wearing braces, telling myself that crooked teeth gave my face character. This did not prevent me from never smiling for photographs. My teeth were, in dentistspeak, "severely malposed." They overlapped in multiple places, and my front teeth stuck out too much. They called that an overjet. But at age fifty-two I was getting cavities in places where my crowded teeth made normal brushing impossible. Shortly after my dentist explained about the cavities, I bit into a cashew and a large piece of a molar fell off. Back in the dentist's chair, I was told that the broken tooth could be repaired with $800 worth of gold, not to mention the dentist's fee. As an alternative, the dentist could yank the damaged molar out of my head along with a molar on the other side of my mouth. The remaining teeth could then be rearranged into a single orderly row by an orthodontist. My time had come. I was the oldest person at the orthodontist's, and I was not a good patient. I regularly accused my orthodontist of being a brutal sadist. But two and a half years later, the braces came off, and I was suddenly smiling for photographs.

When I began to play the trumpet again, this time without the overjet, my fantasy was that the horn would extend out directly perpendicular to my erect body. This was the posture of the heroic trumpeter, an ideal of which I had always fallen short when my protruding front teeth forced me to play with my cornet drooping downward. In high school on the football field, when the highly unmusical marching band tried to attract the attention of the highly unmusical spectators in the stands, I used to do backbends trying to get the horn pointed straight ahead.

Now, in my midfifties, I was ready to start from scratch, building an entirely new embouchure with my freshly rearranged teeth. I decided that I would not touch the horn to my lips until I had enlisted a good teacher, one who would steer me away from my old bad habits. My imperfect embouchure had once prevented me from becoming a skillful jazz trumpeter, even a high-note specialist. Or so I told myself.

I was surprised to learn that I was not the first person to pick up the trumpet after several decades of inactivity. In fact, there are many "comeback players," older gentlemen, usually retired, who have returned to youthful pleasures. I spoke with one fellow in his eighties who played trumpet in a big band in Houston, Texas. He had played in swing bands before and just after World War II, but he hung up his trumpet in 1948 to go to law school. Fifty years later he picked it up again. The members of his big band played only for themselves, and most were, like him, retired professionals. But they chipped in enough money to hire a professional lead trumpeter and a professional lead alto saxophone player who would rehearse with the band once a week and provide inspiration. As soon as the words were out of his mouth, I knew that I would give anything to play in such a band. By this time I was living in New York City, and I was certain that I could find—or maybe even start—such a band whenever I was ready.

At the recommendation of several friends in the jazz world, I hired a trumpet teacher named Eddie Allen, a first-rate jazzman, a composer, and the leader of his own big band. Sitting in a small rehearsal room in Harlem for my first lesson, I asked Eddie where I should place the mouthpiece. I was convinced that I used to keep the mouthpiece too low on my lips, constricting the ability of the upper lip to vibrate properly. I was amazed when Eddie told me it didn't really matter. It had more to do with what was comfortable for me. He said that if I looked at pictures of the best jazz trumpet players, I would see that some had very little of the mouthpiece on their upper lips. The trumpeter Jimmy Owens later told me that the great Gillespie once developed a severe ulcer in the center of his upper lip but continued playing with the horn at the corner of his mouth while the ulcer healed. No one could tell the difference.

So I put the mouthpiece where it seemed to feel right. Emboldened by the feel of fresh metal on my lips, I asked Eddie if he had any requests. He said, "Why don't we start with middle C?" That's the lowest note on the horn that can be played "open," without pressing down any of the three valves. It's home base on the trumpet, the place where the C scale begins, where the least effort can be expended to make a note.

Before I began buzzing my lips into the mouthpiece, I asked Eddie how much of my lips should go inside. Again he told me that the main thing was to feel comfortable. I told him that my grade school band director had instructed me to keep at least half of the mouthpiece on my upper lip. The director told everyone in the cornet section that this was the only way to do it. Eddie, who is African American, then told me what a white band director had said to him when he first began playing trumpet in grade school. Although that was in the mid-1960s, when racial myths were constantly being debunked, and although several generations of black trumpeters had already risen to the highest level of performance on the instrument, the white band director said that black people should not play the trumpet. Their lips were too big for the small trumpet mouthpiece. They would be better off playing trombones and tubas, he said. Wow. All the more reason to reject the notion that there's a right way and a wrong way to put your mouth on the horn.

As a beginner, however, the tricky part about doing what feels most comfortable is that I had not been doing it long enough to know if *anything* felt comfortable. Nevertheless, I began buzzing into the mouthpiece. After hearing nothing but air working its way through tubing, I finally succeeded in producing that farting sound. That was the best I could do. To make matters worse, breath was coming out of the corners of my mouth, perfectly good air that should have been going into the horn. I asked Eddie how I could prevent all that air from escaping outside the mouthpiece. He told me to place a finger on my cheek, just beyond the corner of my mouth. "Now flex," he said. I felt no difference. "Now put your finger here," he said, pointing to the corresponding spot on his face. When he flexed, it felt like a biceps. After four years of playing, I now have a muscle about the size of a pea, and although I have little to brag about, those small muscles on either side of my lips have helped me keep the corners of my mouth tight so that most of the air goes into the mouthpiece.

After that first lesson, Eddie told me that I should spend all of the next week concentrating exclusively on middle C. He also urged me to practice no longer than ten minutes at a stretch. For several days, I spent most of those ten minutes trying to get my mouth in and around the mouthpiece. Then I would buzz into it. In those highly abbreviated practice sessions, I began to hear that middle C take shape. I was beginning to sound the way I did when I was in fourth grade. By the end of the week, I was bold enough to try a C major scale.

At the next lesson, Eddie told me to buy a book of trumpet lessons by someone named Robinson. I went to a music store and asked where I could find the elementary trumpet books. And there it was. Exactly the same book I had used in the fourth grade. *The Rubank Elementary Method for Cornet and Trumpet* even had the exact same cover it did fifty years earlier. I had a Proustian moment holding that book. I could smell the valve oil and slide grease in the old band room where I had played as a child. I looked inside the book to discover that it was copyrighted in 1934. It would have looked the same if I'd started *seventy* years earlier. Later, I would be even more amazed that Arban's essential book of exercises—which almost every professional trumpeter constantly works with—is largely unchanged since it was published in the 1860s. Traditional values may be dying everywhere, but not for trumpeters.

After I had spent about two months slowly squeezing out half notes and whole notes, never very far apart from one another, Eddie assigned a series of lip slurs. The idea was to glide from one note to a higher one without using valves, only breath and the muscles in the embouchure. Although I should have been far enough along to manage an octave slur, I kept hitting notes in between that were not part of the music. Eddie diagnosed the problem. My old cornet was holding me back, he said. It was strictly a student horn, and I had already outgrown it. Eddie told me about what he faces when parents ask him what they should buy for a child starting out on an instrument. If children are going to make progress and perhaps even enjoy playing, they should start with the best instrument possible. It doesn't just sound better; it should also be easier to play. But since the child is fully capable of losing interest, it also makes sense to buy an inexpensive instrument. Since I was not a parent, and since I knew that I was going to stick with it, I was delighted to have an excuse to buy a better trumpet. Indeed, I had been paying special attention to the beautiful, shining trumpets I saw in the hands of musicians when I went to jazz clubs. I had already decided that I wanted a silver one. A silver finish on a trumpet has become more chic than brass in recent years.

Eddie recommended that I try out trumpets at Sam Ash, a busy music store in midtown Manhattan. He even suggested a buying strategy. I was to begin by playing as many horns as possible (at Sam Ash, that's quite a few). When I found the brand that felt right, I should try out all the different models from that manufacturer. After I found the model I liked most, I should ask to play as many trumpets of that precise model as the store had in stock. Except for some cheap models mass-produced in Asia, virtually every trumpet is hand-made. The best manufacturers turn out horns that look the same, but there are always slight differences. An instrument will have a different sound if cold air suddenly blows into the factory and changes the physical qualities of the hot brass at a crucial stage in the annealing process. Or there may be a small error in how parts of the horn are soldered together. Any number of tiny anomalies during the many man-hours it takes to make a trumpet can result in turbulence and interference. Furthermore, every trumpet manufacturer makes horns with slight variations in weight and bell size. And they all make trumpets with different "bores," or diameter of tubing. Bigger bores require more air but produce a darker, richer sound. Trumpets with smaller bores are less labor-intensive and deliver a brighter sound. And then there is the mouthpiece, more essential than the horn itself in the minds of most trumpeters. There are literally a million different possibilities available to the buyer of a mouthpiece. How wide is the rim? How narrow is the bore? How deep is the cup? Exactly how does the cup taper as it gives way to the throat? Is the cup funnel shaped or bowl shaped? A tiny difference in any one of these measurements can change the way a trumpet plays and the way trumpeters feel when they play. Eddie even told me that I should make several trips to the store over several days to try out the same horns more than once and that I should not make a purchase until I had slept on it.

With the delicious license to indulge my desire for a new horn now authorized by my teacher himself, I eagerly planned a trip to Sam Ash the next day. But that night I had arranged to play in a band just put together by my friend Will Friedwald. He has a C melody saxophone, an instrument that virtually no one has played since the 1920s. Except for Will. He loves the horn even though he can barely get a few notes out. He simply likes to use his substantial skills as an organizer to bring together a few musicians to blow. He even had a name for our band—the Sad-Asssed Gypsies. The night I joined him, he invited along a clarinetist and a guitarist, both of them at the same early stages as Will and me. He also invited an experienced bassist to keep us on our toes rhythmically.

At this stage, I was just beginning to develop some chops with my old cornet, and I had not lost the ability to sight-read. Our band of rank amateurs played "I'm in the Mood for Love" and "If Dreams Come True." I loved it. No one expected perfection, least of all Will. We played the songs over and over again for almost an hour. It was the first time I had played in a group since the brass quartet at the Swedish Lutheran church in 1967. I was grinning ear to ear as I walked home, knowing that once again there was music in my life. I was also smiling because I was about to become the owner of a shiny new silver trumpet.

Eddie had warned me about playing too much in the early stages. He was right, of course. The morning after multiple choruses of "If Dreams Come True," I woke to a nightmare. I could not produce a single note. No matter how I put the mouthpiece to my lips and no matter how many different ways I tried to blow, the best I could do was a blatting sound. Eddie did not need to scold me when I called him to report my situation. He simply assured me that this kind of thing happens all the time. I had strained the delicate muscles in my lips and cheeks, and I'd be back to normal in a day or two. Actually, it was three days before I could produce a decent note, and I spent most of those three days hating myself for delaying the acquisition of a new trumpet.

MY NEW BACH

Finally, at Sam Ash, a salesman opened the huge display cases and began carrying trumpets to a practice room at the back of the store. I was especially interested in a few well-established brands in spite of the fact that Eddie insisted it didn't matter. When I first asked him what make of a trumpet he played, he responded, "Why do you ask?" In other words, it's not the horn, it's what you do with it. This is another paradox at the heart of the trumpeter's craft. Players fuss over every aspect of design and many remain true to a particular make. Or to one particular horn. Doc Cheatham once said that he never found a suitable replacement after someone stole the Giardinelli trumpet and mouthpiece he had used for many years in his long career. And yet it should not make any real difference. Great performers who have developed their own unique sounds can pick up any trumpet and sound like themselves. With an inferior instrument, the familiar sound will still be there even if the trumpeter has to try a bit harder to get it. With high-quality instruments, it shouldn't make any difference at all.

At the store, I did not take Eddie's advice. I concentrated on trumpets manufactured by Bach, Martin, and Yamaha, all brands popular with jazz artists. Dave Douglas plays a Bach, Miles Davis played a Martin, and Eddie himself has a Yamaha. Although I did put several horns to the test, and although I did play four different examples of the exact same model, I bought a trumpet on the same day I walked into the store. I couldn't wait. My choice was a middle-weight Bach Stradivarius with a middle-size bore, model number 180S37. Related to neither Johann Sebastian Bach nor the eighteenth-century Italian who made the famous violins, Bach Stradivarius trumpets were developed by a man named Vinzenz Schrottenbach, born in 1890 in Austria. In 1914, Schrottenbach immigrated to the United States, where he became Vincent Bach. When he began manufacturing high-quality trumpets, he chose to name his best professional horn after the legendary violin maker. My choice of a Bach Stradivarius was not an idiosyncratic choice. The Strad 37 is by far the best-selling trumpet in the world. The first-chair trumpeter in the New York Philharmonic plays one, as does the first-chair trumpeter in the Metropolitan Opera orchestra. So do countless other classical and jazz players.

And no wonder. It's a beautiful instrument with a silver finish so bright it glows. I love the design of the O-ring on top of the third valve slide, the slightly asymmetrical U on the first valve slide, and the gently stylized C on the lead pipe that perfectly accommodates my right pinkie. I also love the fact that, unlike most trumpets and cornets, a Bach Strad has no water key or spit valve on the third valve slide. When moisture builds up inside, you pull out the slide and let the water run out. You feel like a French horn player, whose instrument has no water keys at all. A Strad sounds beautiful too. One of the many trumpeters I know who also plays one says that it has a "sweet spot." I know just what he means. When you're playing mezzo forte and you have enough chops to take it into the upper register, the horn sings like a violin. Maybe that's why it's called a Stradivarius. I spent most of the first several days just staring at my new Bach when I wasn't playing it.

CREATING AN AMERICAN TRUMPET

The Strad 37 has a vibrant history. The story of its creator, Vincent Bach, parallels that of C. G. Conn, the maker of the Conn Wonder and a range of band instruments embraced by several generations of student and professional musicians. Both men started out making mouthpieces after a bit of bad luck with their own favorite models. Both then moved on to making top-of-the-line instruments and became successful after years of tirelessly promoting their wares in schools and communities. As a boy growing up in a little town a few miles from Vienna, Vinzenz Schrottenbach was surrounded by music. Both his parents were accomplished singers who also played musical instruments. His two sisters played piano. Vinzenz began playing the violin at age five. He became interested in the trumpet a few years later, but his musical education came to an abrupt end when his father died. In desperate need of a breadwinner for her family, Vinzenz's mother remarried when the boy was eleven. There was immediate friction between the son and his stepfather. Rather than sending Vinzenz to the conservatory as the boy had hoped, his stepfather insisted that he pursue a more practical career. Vinzenz chose mechanical engineering and graduated with a degree in 1910.

Schrottenbach had been surreptitiously playing the trumpet throughout his years at engineering school, and after graduation he immediately began taking lessons from the first-chair trumpeter at the Vienna Volksoper. He had carried out his obligation to his stepfather, and he now went back to what he loved. To fulfill his required year of military service, he joined the navy band and quickly became a featured soloist. Soon he was touring Europe and England. This phase of his career ended abruptly with the outbreak of World War I. Because he retained a commission in the Austro-Hungarian military, he was locked up as a prisoner of war when he was performing in England. Talking his way out of jail and adopting a Norwegian identity, he sailed for New York on the *Lusitania*.

The penniless Schrottenbach was soon looking for work in the New World. After a few auditions, he landed a place in the Boston Symphony. In fact, he was already sufficiently accomplished to be hired as first chair. For several years he played with various ensembles and as a soloist with the new name Vincent Bach. A turning point came when a fellow trumpeter asked to borrow his mouthpiece. To Bach's horror, the fellow reamed out the inside of the mouthpiece, thinking it would make the piece easier to play. It didn't. After searching in vain for a proper replacement, Bach wondered what would happen if he made his own mouthpiece. Finally putting his engineering background to use, he went to work in the back room of a Selmer Music store in New York, and using a lathe designed for mouthpieces, he made one as good as the one he had lost. In 1918, at age twenty-eight, Bach invested $300 in a foot-operated lathe and began manufacturing mouthpieces. By 1924, he was manufacturing trumpets.

For many of those early years, Bach was on the road performing and looking for buyers. Although he also manufactured cornets and trombones, much of his success came from America's new passion for trumpets, increasingly the favored instrument of the Jazz Age. Bach was highly entrepreneurial as a manufacturer and salesman, even writing books on trumpet technique and the art of making horns. As a designer of instruments he was much more cautious. Virtually all of the mouthpieces he manufactured were based on preexisting designs, and his trumpets were closely modeled on horns manufactured at the Besson factory in France in the late nineteenth and early twentieth centuries.

Zig Kanstul, who runs the factory in Anaheim, California, where Besson trumpets are now made, is one of the grand old men of the trumpet industry. He told me that turn-of-the-century Bessons were once considered the most desirable of all trumpets. Besson and his heirs hired the trumpet virtuoso and scholar Louis Saint-Jacome to test each horn personally. After the arduous process of manufacturing trumpets of the highest quality, Besson sold only the absolute best instruments to his most serious customers. According to Kanstul, it's almost impossible to find a good Besson trumpet from that period because they've all been used up. The few trumpets in good condition have remained that way because they were essentially rejects.

Like Besson, Vincent Bach closely supervised the manufacture of his trumpets and began experimenting with variations in bore, weight, and bell size. He worked closely with the most eminent symphony players to modify his designs. After making instruments in New York City for several years, he moved to a larger shop in Mount Vernon in 1953. He resisted the temptation to begin mass production, concentrating instead on filling special orders while constantly rethinking the design and the metallurgical components of his trumpets. In 1961, he sold his business to the Selmer Corporation, and by 1965 the entire Bach operation had been relocated to Elkhart, Indiana. Like Conn and several other instrument manufacturers, Selmer was located near the meeting of two rivers in Elkhart. The Native Americans who lived there in the eighteenth century said that the island where the two rivers met resembled the heart of an elk—hence the name. Although Bach continued to play a role in the production of trumpets engraved with his name, the Elkhart factory began a program of mass production that continues to this day.

BENDING BRASS

So how does Bach make the best-selling trumpets? How did they become the industry standard? And why does a Bach trumpet made in Mount Vernon or New York sell on eBay for more than a brand-new Elkhart model, even if it is more than fifty years old? I booked a flight to the Midwest. My plan was to make Chicago my base of operations. From there I would visit the Bach factory in Elkhart, a three-hour drive from Chicago in northern Indiana. The next day I would go north to Kenosha, only an hour from Chicago in southern Wisconsin, where Martin Committee trumpets are made. The Martin Committee has a long and honored past with several generations of jazz musicians. Miles Davis played a Martin Committee because Dizzy Gillespie played one, and Gillespie bought one because his idol Roy Eldridge was playing one. Kenny Dorham played a Martin Committee, as did Chet Baker. The eminent Wallace Roney plays one today. It's called a Committee because the Martin Company, which had been manufacturing musical instruments since the nineteenth century, decided in the 1930s to invite several of the best trumpet manufacturers, including Vincent Bach, Elden Benge, and Renold Schilke, to work together to create a new design. Although the trumpet that resulted was a success, it was initially marketed at a relatively low price and was thus especially desirable to jazz artists with limited cash on hand. The classic models are instantly recognizable by spit valves placed on the side of the slides rather than on the bottom.

I arrive bright and early at the Bach factory in Elkhart. From the outside it looks like any industrial building, but it covers a huge swath of land. Although Bach controls the larger share of the market for trumpets, it is not the only brand manufactured by the giant conglomerate Conn-Selmer. King, Benge, and Ludwig as well as Bach, Conn, and Selmer are all part of the same family. The conglomerate is itself part of Steinway Musical Instruments, Inc. Several boutique manufacturers such as Schilke, Calicchio, Callet, Stomvi, Cannonball, Getzen, and Challenger make a few trumpets each year. Besides Conn-Selmer, the only other large maker of professional-quality trumpets is Yamaha. Having moved its base of operations from Japan to Grand Rapids, Michigan, Yamaha contributes to the concentration of musical instrument factories in America's heartland.

Tedd Waggoner, a jovial and personable man of about fifty, welcomes me at the Bach factory's reception area. He gives me a pair of goggles and takes me on the grand tour of the factory. Although I'll be shown each step in the process of manufacturing the Bach Stradivarius, no secrets are disclosed. I am told very early in the tour that outsiders cannot know the source of the brass from which Bach trumpets are made. There can be only so many foundries where brass is manufactured, but there is, I suppose, a certain romance in keeping the precise spot a mystery.

At one of the first stations Tedd and I visit, a man takes a flat piece of this mysterious raw brass and places it on top of a tapered metal cylinder called a mandrel. The worker begins beating the metal with a baseball bat. Within minutes he has turned the metal plate into the long, conical, unbent bell of a trumpet. The mandrel is well worn from so much pounding. It also has a distinctly antique look. In fact, many of the mandrels still in use at the factory were made by Vincent Bach himself in the 1940s. The technique of shaping brass into a bell using a mandrel and a strong piece of wood goes back a long way, perhaps as far as back as Egypt in the fifteenth century B.C.E. It was essential to the art of the trumpet maker in the late Middle Ages and during the Renaissance.

At the next station, Tedd introduces me to a technician who takes the long bell and spins it on a lathe that allows him to the shape it more elegantly. Using a metal spike, he works from the narrow end of the bell up to the flared end. As he works on the spinning bell, the seam where the two sides of the original piece of metal were soldered together begins to disappear. At the wide end of the bell, the technician creates a perfectly circular rim. I ask him how long it took until he felt that the operation was second nature. He says, "Oh, about three years." An older fellow at the next station yells out, "He still hasn't got the hang of it." At the next station the bells are forced into a press and bits of metal are shaved off. The seam is now almost totally invisible.

Some of the most accomplished technicians at the Bach factory have the difficult task of placing a thin copper wire along the outer edge of the bell. The rim is then bent over the wire and soldered into place so that the wire is completely concealed in the circular rim. Tedd picks up a bell that has not yet been fitted with a wire and strikes the rim with a metal shaft. I hear a thud. He then strikes a bell that has been fitted with the wire and I hear a chime. This is one of the processes that make the Bach trumpets unique. The difficult process of fitting each bell with a metal wire can be costly if botched. If the wire is not properly fitted, the bell becomes unusable. Some manufacturers have decided to save money and time by skipping the process. Tedd makes sure I know this before I visit another factory.

The trumpet bells go through several stages of annealing, a process of heating and slow cooling that makes the metal strong and less brittle. The temperature varies for each stage of the process. Annealing is essential to working with brass, which can crack and deteriorate if not properly treated. Even brass doorknobs go through an annealing process. At the Bach factory, the precise nature of the annealing cycle is another trade secret. I'm not even allowed into the area where the annealing takes place. But I do have the pleasure of seeing several bells filled with ice in a refrigeration unit. When the metal reaches the proper temperature, the narrow end of the bell, still full of ice, is bent 180 degrees into a smooth curve. Like the tar or pitch that the earliest trumpet makers used—and that many manufacturers still use today—the ice maintains the integrity of the brass tube and prevents crimping. Once bent, the bells are hung up so that the ice can drip out as the metal returns to room temperature. The bells now look like part of a modern trumpet. But this is only a small part of the long process of making a horn. If nothing else, a great deal of polishing and finishing still needs to be done.

Trumpet pistons are made from Monel metal, a highly refined substance that resists rust and deterioration. If properly maintained, Monel valves can last several lifetimes. At the factory, technicians drill through the metal and deburr each porthole by hand. With a mixture of pumice and lard oil, the valve casing is reamed out so that the valves can be precisely fitted. If the fit is too tight, the valves will move sluggishly. If too loose, the lack of compression will make the instrument more difficult to play. The desired clearance within the valve casing is 5/10,000ths of an inch. The trumpet's long lead pipe— which begins at the mouthpiece, extends about fourteen inches, and then curves back 180 degrees to connect to the valve casing—goes through its own elaborate process before it is soldered into place along with all the other tubes and slides.

One entire room is devoted to buffing the instrument after it has been assembled. Several workmen stand at lathes firmly pressing trumpets into canvas strips attached to rapidly revolving wheels. The canvas strips are covered with a compound of ferric oxide suspended in animal fat. It is similar to jeweler's rouge and is especially useful for smoothing out the places where tubes have been soldered together. The same substance is used on the felt wheels that polish the brass until it has a mirrorlike finish. The rouge, however, creates an orange-red cloud throughout the room, and the men doing the buffing have striking red complexions. All are wearing the face masks of surgeons. Even though each of the workers in this unit will leave all his clothes in the factory and take a long shower before heading home in his street clothes, he will bring a good deal of the dust with him wherever he goes. Even if he stays away from work for several days, the inside of his shirt collars will turn a dull red. Because the buffing process is also hard physical labor, the men in the buffing room are among the highest-paid workers in the factory. They are also among the least skilled. Virtually every one of the other 120 employees who make Bach trumpets comes to the factory with substantial training or experience, but a strong young man with no experience of any kind can easily land a job as a buffer.

My complete tour of the Bach factory lasts several hours. Toward the end I watch as the insignia of the Bach label and a few particulars for the specific horn are engraved onto the bell (see figure 23). The entire process ends in a room where several highly accomplished trumpeters put each horn through its paces. The musicians hit the highest and lowest notes, blasting away at earsplitting decibels and then dropping back to a barely audible pianissimo. Like everyone else in the factory—except of course the buffers—these are highly skilled workers.

After lunch, Tedd takes me through the factory's business offices. I see numerous photographs of Vincent Bach in various stages of his career as well as several carefully posed portraits of eminent musicians who have played Bach instruments. From a wide cabinet Tedd extracts dog-eared blueprints that Vincent Bach himself drew up. As a mechanical engineer who also knew what a serious performer requires, Bach scrupulously noted the precise width of the tubing at numerous spots along the trumpet's body. In fact, those blueprints were about to be put to use to create exact duplicates of the revered C trumpets that Bach delivered to members of the Chicago Symphony in 1955.

Tedd takes me into his own office and with an impish smile turns to an old file cabinet near his desk. The dull green cabinet looks like it dates to the 1940s, but it may be older. Tedd tells me that it had been left in a deserted corner of the Elkhart factory and was almost thrown out several years ago. Because he long ago decided that he would be the company's "keeper of the flame," Waggoner decided that the cabinet ought to be preserved. It turned out to be a treasure-house. Tedd opens the top left drawer and pulls out a three-by-five card. At the top of the card is the number 0616, the serial number that would have been stamped onto the valve casing of the 616th horn to emerge from the factory. The information is written on the 616th card in the drawer. (Just to provide a sense of how far back that card goes, the Bach trumpet I bought in 2004 is stamped with the number 602,947.) In the middle of the card, in Bach's own handwriting, I see "Bix Beiderbecke, Cornet 1928." In that year, Beiderbecke was known to only a handful of jazz insiders. Bach could not have written it there because he knew he was selling to a great jazz artist. Rather, he made a card for every horn he sold. He was, in fact, running a small operation and making almost every sale on an individual basis. Each card in the file has a name and is numbered consecutively, right up to 28,000, the last serial number for horns made in Mount Vernon before the operation was fully relocated to Indiana in 1965. Tedd pulls out a few other cards, including one from the 1930s with the name of Adolphus Cheatham. Better known as Doc, Cheatham would have played the horn when he was lead trumpeter in the Cab Calloway big band.

JAZZING THE ASSEMBLY LINE

When a musician plays a Bach trumpet, the notes are precise. Pressing down the valves firmly, the musician locks in the notes. The sound is clear and direct. This is one of the reasons why musicians specializing in European classical music overwhelmingly choose the Bach Stradivarius. By contrast, a jazz trumpeter who likes to smear notes and produce bluesy half-valve effects is not as likely to choose a Bach. For a looser, more flexible approach to playing, many jazz artists prefer the Martin Committee. Just as their trumpet is more flexible, the people at the Martin factory in Kenosha are more laid-back. The fellow who shows me around is knowledgeable but somewhat affectless. He is no keeper of the flame. In fact, most of the people I spoke to at Martin seemed a little sad. Maybe it's because they knew they were about to be swallowed up. A few months after my visit, Conn-Selmer acquired LeBlanc, the French corporation that had its international headquarters in Kenosha and that once made Martin, Holton, and LeBlanc trumpets. Conn-Selmer then discontinued the manufacture of the Martin Committee trumpet.

When I was in Kenosha in 2004, however, the factory was still turning out new Committees, mostly on special order. Although there are many different models of the Bach Stradivarius, the company honors tradition by giving every trumpet the same distinctive look. Not so Martin. For one thing, Martin Committees were being produced with bright red and blue paint jobs. A blue Bach is impossible to imagine. During my tour of the LeBlanc factory, I was told on several occasions that I ought to speak with Larry Ramirez, one of the technical wizards who had maintained the high quality of the Martin Committee for several decades.

So I drive a few miles from Kenosha to see Larry in Elkhorn, Wisconsin. The apple never falls far from the tree when trumpet manufacturers strike out on their own. The Getzen Corporation has its factory a few blocks from Larry's workshop inside a facility devoted primarily to making saxophones and large brass instruments. In his workshop, Larry pulls down some cases from a shelf and shows me the prototype for a slide trumpet he had made for Maynard Ferguson. Larry is an accomplished jazz trumpeter as well as a technician. Working the slide as if he were playing a small trombone, Larry produces the smooth glissandi that Ferguson had requested. I also get a good look at the four-valve trumpet the Martin company had made for Don Ellis in the 1960s. An early member of the jazz avant-garde, Ellis wanted to be able to play quarter tones, taking jazz beyond the old functional tonality of Western art music. That fourth valve was designed to take the pitch down a quarter step, allowing the trumpeter to play a note midway between any two notes on the chromatic scale. Needless to say, the idea of a fourth valve for quarter tones never caught on.

Sitting prominently on Larry Ramirez's workbench is a beautiful case containing two identical Martin Committee trumpets that had just been made to the precise specifications of Wallace Roney, an excellent jazz musician who was profoundly influenced by Miles Davis. Just before he died, when Davis was reunited with Gil Evans to play the extraordinary music from the *Sketches of Spain* LP they had recorded in 1959 and 1960, it was Roney who stood next to the ailing Davis and performed the parts that Miles had originally played. Davis gave Roney one of his own Committees as a gesture of gratitude. Roney has remained faithful to the brand.

Ramirez himself has a story about Miles. In the 1980s, not long before his death in 1991, Davis went through several Martin Committees each year. He would call the factory in Kenosha to place his orders, but he was impatient with technicians who failed to understand his requirements. Possibly they could not understand his famously raspy voice. Or his vernacular. Regardless, when an exasperated Davis twice hung up on technicians, one of them said to Larry, "You play with jazz musicians. Next time Miles calls, you talk to him." When Davis next called, Ramirez was summoned to the phone. When he gave his name, Davis asked if he was related to Ram Ramirez, the bebop pianist who had written the beautiful ballad "Lover Man." Larry Ramirez grew up in Denver and is no relation. But he hesitated a moment before acknowledging the lack of a connection. By telling Davis that he was not related to someone Davis probably knew, Larry took a chance, but it was for the best. Larry is certain that he won the respect of Davis at that moment.

Miles had called the factory because he had decided he wanted a red, white, and blue trumpet. Ramirez knew how complicated it would be to put more than one color onto a trumpet. Thinking for a moment, he suggested that Davis ask for a black trumpet. The idea appealed to Davis, and Ramirez went to work complying with all of Davis's other specifications before figuring out how to color a trumpet black. The first coat of black lacquer did not cover it completely. There were still a few spots where the brass peaked out from underneath. The second coat did not cover it completely either. Ultimately it took four coats of lacquer, making the horn exceptionally heavy. Fortunately, throughout most of his career, Davis had preferred heavy horns with a large bore that produced the dark sound that was his trademark. Only toward the end of his life, when he was getting weak, did he prefer lighter horns. The technicians at LeBlanc were so pleased with the black trumpet that they suggested an in-person presentation to Davis.

By coincidence, Davis was about to give a concert in Denver, Larry's hometown. The day of the concert, Larry arrived in Davis's dressing room with the brand-new instrument. Davis examined the black trumpet and made approving sounds. Then he sat down and put the horn to his mouth. He began playing, but with the bell practically buried in Larry's stomach. Larry did not move. In situations of this nature, one does not move unless Miles himself directs one to move. Larry was relieved when Davis said that he was pleased with the sound. He said that he was playing quietly (into Larry's stomach) because his wife was asleep in the next room. Within a few minutes, the actress Cicely Tyson, Davis's fourth wife, emerged from the bedroom with an elaborately embroidered robe over her nightgown.

"What a beautiful trumpet, Miles," she said. "Why don't you offer your friend something to drink?" She opened the small refrigerator in the dressing room to reveal bottles of Diet Coke, mineral water, and Heineken beer.

"I'll have a Heineken," Larry said.

"I'll have one too," rasped Miles.

In a maternal voice, Cecily said, "Just one, Miles."

With a green bottle of beer sitting in front of each man, Miles Davis and Larry Ramirez discussed politics, boxing, and the art of making a trumpet while Tyson bustled about the dressing room. Miles had drunk most of his beer, but Larry had taken only a few sips. At a moment when his wife was looking the other way, Miles switched the bottles. When his wife turned around, Miles said, "I think Larry needs another beer." A second green bottle was placed in front of Larry while Davis went to work on the beer that Larry had been nursing. When Davis finished that one, he switched bottles again, and said, "Honey, get Larry another beer." Before he went home that evening, Larry had taken a sip from four different bottles that Miles eventually finished.

FETISHIZING THE HARDWARE

By the time I returned from my trip to Elkhart, Kenosha, and Elkhorn, I was a hopeless equipment geek. I wanted more trumpets.

Or at least the experience of playing more trumpets. I began by surfing the websites of the various trumpet manufacturers and hanging around the trumpet room at Dillon's music store in Woodbridge, New Jersey. Dillon's is the place to go if you want to try out a used horn before buying it. You can get great deals on eBay, but you will not have the luxury of playing an instrument before you commit to it. At Dillon's, there must be several hundred trumpets hanging from the walls. Anyone who walks in can sample the goods at random, even the ones along the top rows, thanks to a stepladder placed there for the customers' convenience. At Dillon's, I played brands of trumpet I never knew existed.

Before long, I could tell from a distance what make and model a trumpeter was playing, even in an old movie. I began to wonder if I had been too hasty in my sudden purchase of a Bach Stradivarius. Maybe I'd be happier with a Yamaha trumpet. Eddie once played a Bach, but now he is totally devoted to his Yamaha. And when I went to see a technician after I dropped a valve slide and needed a dent removed, he told me that Yamaha consistently turns out the horns with the best workmanship. I was soon cruising eBay and Dillon's for a good used Yamaha.

But then I read that Renold Schilke was the man the Japanese invited over to help develop Yamaha trumpets. Schilke was also the major player in the design of the original Martin Committee. The horns he made in his own factory in Chicago in the late 1950s and early 1960s are now the Cadillacs of the industry. When a friend let me play his 1962 Schilke, it blew so easily I was astonished. It sounded great too. On eBay, well-preserved Schilkes from the 1950s and '60s sell for almost as much as Mount Vernon Bachs. I began looking for a good used Schilke. At about this same time, I attended a brass conference in Purchase, New York, where most of the trumpet manufacturers lay out all their models on tables in individual rooms. Once you register for the conference, you can wander from room to room trying out brand-new horns. I was especially impressed by the new Cannonball trumpets. They sounded good, they were easy to blow, and each had a precious gem placed strategically on the tubing. I forget exactly why it had to be a precious gem and why it had to be placed at the precise point where the lead pipe connects to the valve casing, but I was sorely tempted to whip out my credit card and take one home.

And then there was the Conn Connstellation, no longer in production, but still the preferred trumpet of several musicians I respect, including the great jazz trumpeter and educator Bill Dixon. A direct line can be drawn from Buddy Bolden's Conn Wonder cornet to the Conn Connstellation and most recently to the Conn Vintage One. I wanted one of those too. And yes, I still wanted a Martin Committee.

When I told Eddie that I was thinking about buying a second trumpet and maybe a third, he gave me a skeptical look and said, "Are you a collector?" Actually, I am. I've been an obsessive collector of jazz recordings and books since I was sixteen. Much to the chagrin of my long-suffering wife, three of the five rooms of our apartment are almost completely filled with books, records, CDs, and tapes. But the answer to Eddie's question was supposed to be no. He was asking if I was devoted to learning to play a single instrument as well as possible, or if I would be flitting from horn to horn, more concerned with ownership than musicianship. Chastened, I stayed with my Bach.

THE NEXT WAVE IN TRUMPET TECHNOLOGY

It was David Monette, however, who got me thinking once again about buying another horn. Surely the most radical figure in the trumpet universe, and in some ways the most successful, David Monette was playing trumpet in a rock band in the 1970s when he wondered if it might be possible to make his work easier by redesigning his trumpet. On the one hand, the Stradivarius violin was made in the eighteenth century and is still regarded as the best, mostly because of the unique qualities of the wood and how it has aged. Antonio Stradivarius also had a formula for varnishing that has never been completely duplicated. On the other hand, Besson designed a trumpet in the 1880s that has been the model for Conn, Bach, and most manufacturers since, but there is no reason why design evolution must stop there. According to Dave Monette, hero worship of grand old men like Besson and Bach has stood in the way of imaginative solutions to problems that still exist.

Monette is a controversial figure if only because he has regularly told trumpeters that their equipment is no good. No one likes to hear that. But if you stop to wonder if the design of trumpets should move beyond nineteenth-century paradigms, he may have a point. His first project was to redesign the lead pipe, the length of tubing that begins where the mouthpiece is inserted. On most trumpets, the crook where the lead pipe curves backward is almost squared off, with two sudden bends at the top and the bottom. Monette made a lead pipe with more gentle curves and more elaborate fabrication techniques. Changing the way the air flows through the first bend in a trumpet's tubes to reduce turbulence, Monette made horns easier to blow. He successfully marketed his lead pipes to many professional trumpeters, who were pleased by the difference. A few of them even asked him if he planned to make his own trumpets.

By the mid-1980s he was doing exactly that. Then as now, the world of professional trumpeters was small. Word spread quickly that Monette was making trumpets. He had the distinction of selling his first products to three of the world's most distinguished trumpet players: Charles Schlueter, the first chair trumpet in the Boston Symphony Orchestra; Adolph "Bud" Herseth, who had played principal trumpet in the Chicago Symphony since 1948; and Charles Gorham, the esteemed trumpet teacher at Indiana University's eminent and enormous School of Music. All three of these men had been playing Bach Strads with Monette lead pipes.

Another of Monette's first clients was Wynton Marsalis (see figure 24), who had also been playing a Bach during his years as a young prodigy winning Grammy Awards for jazz *and* classical recordings. Marsalis was so taken with the new horn that he presented Monette with a new lathe for making mouthpieces. He has played a Monette trumpet ever since, and every time he appears with one of Monette's distinctively designed trumpets, even when it's in a magazine advertisement, he is promoting Dave's horns. For a while, Marsalis was playing a horn with a mouthpiece that was not detachable—the lead pipe and the mouthpiece were both part of the same piece of tubing. Many in the jazz community think of Wynton as a conservative musician, more interested in preserving the past than in following the usual goal of taking jazz into the future. And yet in his choice of trumpets, Wynton is highly experimental, constantly trying out Monette's latest models.

When he first began manufacturing his own horns in Chicago, Monette was outsourcing a good deal of the work and concentrating primarily on designing bells, lead pipes, and mouthpieces. When he set up shop in Portland, Oregon, in 1992, he continued to experiment, constantly looking for new ways to make his trumpets easier to play and more beautiful to hear. By continuing to outsource a few parts of his horns, including the valves and valve casings, he was able to build about six horns per week with a staff of four employees. By the end of 2006, however, his factory was manufacturing every part of the horn except the valve springs. And although he had built up a staff of nine employees, the factory was turning out only six horns *per month*. Building each part of the trumpet (or cornet or flügelhorn) inside the factory and maintaining a high standard of workmanship has made his horns more labor-intensive than ever, each instrument requiring 150 person-hours of labor. A good deal of that labor goes into making the horns tighter. If the clearance between the valve piston and the casing is 5/10,000ths of an inch on a Bach Strad, it's closer to 3/10,000ths of an inch on a Monette. This tightness allows the player to expend a little less air, and in the world of trumpet players, that little bit can make a huge difference.

Making everything from scratch with the best materials has also made Monette horns very expensive—so expensive that all but professional and/or wealthy artists can afford them. But they do have their champions among jazz artists. Terence Blanchard, Ryan Kisor, Scotty Barnhart, and Ron Miles all play Monettes. It was a major coup for Dave Monette when Maynard Ferguson became a convert, and for a period before his death in 2006, everyone in the trumpet section of his big band was playing a Monette. A few of the trumpeters I interviewed grumbled about the sound of Monette's trumpets, but few criticized the ease with which they can be played. With Monette constantly experimenting with new approaches to sound, and with a small but steady stream of Monette trumpets working their way into the population of professional trumpeters, his horns may someday be the industry standard. Or at least the first item on a player's wish list.

When I made my first visit to his factory in Portland in 2004, Monette was trying a new mouthpiece for the Swedish symphonic trumpeter Urban Agnas. Dave took me to the far end of his one-room factory and gave a signal to an employee who stood at the other end with a trumpet next to a table covered with mouthpieces. Each time the trumpeter changed mouthpieces, Dave and I would walk along the far wall. Dave could locate precisely the place where the tone changed. Part of his success as a designer comes from his uncanny ability to hear tiny changes in sound. When he custom-makes a trumpet for distinguished musicians such as Marsalis and Schlueter, Monette takes pains to find the proper thickness of metal, the right degree of taper, and many other small adjustments to produce the ideal sound for each player. Experimenting with the Agnas mouthpieces, Monette would find the exact place where the sound center moved as each mouthpiece was sampled. In some cases, a tiny change in mouthpiece construction moved the center several feet at the far end of the factory. By the end of the process, I was beginning to hear the difference too. Or at least that's what I told myself.

Monette was especially proud of the new computerized lathe he had recently purchased for his factory. It allowed him to enter the precise coordinates for a new mouthpiece into a computer and then hold the finished product in his hand within a few minutes. The results of the tests he was performing in the factory that day were about to be fed into the computer to produce the prototype for a new line of mouthpieces.

With his bushy beard, his complete disregard for tradition, and his animated manner, Monette at first seems like an unreconstructed hippie. When he begins talking about his work, Thomas Edison pops into mind, but not the Edison of the Hollywood films with Mickey Rooney and Spencer Tracy. He is more like Edison the charismatic showman who made movies and figured out how to record music. Monette is also an avocational pilot. The distinctive curve in the tuning slides on all his horns resembles nothing so much as the wing of a jet airplane. Besson was creating the canonical trumpet design a few years before the Wright Brothers took to the skies and decades before aeronautical engineers learned how to design a wing that allows a large tube of metal with a heavy engine to take flight. More than a century passed before Monette put contemporary aeronautics to work and rethought trumpet design.

Although he had played the trumpet professionally for a brief period, Monette had never been a serious musician. But he did understand how the instrument's design could be changed. When he first opened a shop in Chicago in the 1980s, he was, like any struggling

businessman, in a stressful situation. He was looking for a way to reduce that stress, but he was also on a lifelong search for a way to connect with spirituality. Organized religion as it's usually practiced in
America just wasn't doing it for him. When he read the Hindu sutras
and discovered kundalini yoga, he knew he had found the answer.
Soon he was teaching yoga even as he continued to experiment with
trumpet design at his factory. For the first three years after his arrival
in Portland, he ran the Kundalini Institute of Portland.

Like C. G. Conn and Vincent Bach before him, Monette is regularly on the road demonstrating trumpet technique at the same time
that he is promoting his equipment. His knowledge of yoga has made
an indelible impact on what he teaches trumpet players in particular
and musicians in general. After I'd met his coworkers and joined
them for an informal lunch in the common area next to the factory
room, Monette showed me how to breathe. It was a revelation. First,
he tells me to stand up and take a deep breath, monitoring how
much of my body fills with air. Without adjusting my posture, I pull
in the air and feel it enter my stomach and chest. Then he tells me to
square up my feet and place them shoulder-width apart. He tells me
to bend my knees slightly, push my pelvis back several inches, and
hold my head so that my throat and windpipe are both on a vertical
axis. "Now take another deep breath," he says. I can immediately tell
the difference—the air fills up my stomach and my chest, and then
keeps going. I can feel it at the very top of my chest. It even seems to
be working its way into my shoulders.

"Wow," I say.

"That's what most people say," he tells me.

Breathing is, of course, an important element in the practice of
yoga, and the Monette environment is suffused with yoga. Dave has
given Hindu names to his horns and mouthpieces. His top-of-the-line
mouthpieces are called Prana, the Sanskrit word for life principle or

"vital air." Another horn is called Ajna, meaning command as in the spiritual guidance offered by a guru. When he developed a trumpet for Maynard Ferguson, Monette called it a Raja, Hindu for prince.

In Portland, I was also hoping to get to know Dave Monette the salesman, the one who managed to sell the world's greatest trumpet players on his revolutionary approach to building a horn. Even if his trumpets are unquestionably the best, it is not inevitable that musicians as eminent and as different as Wynton Marsalis and Charles Schlueter would be playing them. So I ask Dave to sell me a mouthpiece. I know that they are expensive, but I'm certain that it will be worth it. For one thing, I'll get to see Dave the mouthpiece expert in action. For another, I'll have the opportunity to try several different models, feeling and hearing the differences among them. Remember that there are at least a million different combinations among the tiny adjustments that can made to any custom-built mouthpiece. Dave has surely been through a large portion of those variations as a manufacturer of mouthpieces.

In fact, Monette does most of his business in mouthpieces. Each of the six horns he makes in a month is a special order. At the time of this writing, there is a fourteen-month wait from the time a customer places an order until the new trumpet is delivered. And they're not cheap. Anyone can purchase a brand-new discounted Bach Stradivarius for $1,800 or so. The cheapest Monette trumpet costs about $9,000. If money is no object, and if you devoutly want your horn to have a sound as big as all outdoors and as thick as molasses, you can pick out a heavy, twenty-four-karat-gold-plated Raja for more than $25,000. And since all horns are made to order for individual players, who almost always come to Portland to experiment with sample instruments, the only prices are retail.

Monette mouthpieces, however, can be purchased from dealers, and the chances of getting a deal are a bit better. Still, a store that sells a Bach mouthpiece for $20 will usually sell Monette mouthpieces for $200. The price is at least partially the result of gold plating. For me it's worth it. The gold feels soft and cool on the mouth. I also find gold mouthpieces to be more responsive and comfortable. Although it does not affect the price, Monette tells me that mouthpieces for standard B-flat trumpets are too long, more appropriate for trumpets pitched in lower keys. He talks about "pitch centers," maintaining that standard mouthpieces make the horn sound flat in the upper register and sharp in the lower register. He explains that the standard mouthpiece that goes with a B-flat trumpet is more appropriate to an A trumpet. To make his point, he pulls the tuning slide all the way out on a B-flat trumpet so that it is effectively an A trumpet. He then sticks my Bach 7C mouthpiece into the horn and invites me to play a middle C and a high C. They do sound more in tune than the same notes I play with the slide pushed back in.

Monette brings a large collection of gold-plated mouthpieces into the factory room where the acoustics are best. To get the full sense of what each mouthpiece can do, I need to play each one on a variety of trumpets. One after another, I hold prototypes for each of the trumpets Monette manufacturers. The care with which he hands me each model is almost ritualistic. When I pick up a horn on my own by grabbing it around the valve casing, he thanks me for not picking up the horn by the bell. Dean Comley, one of the Monette employees and a terrific trumpet player in his own right, rummages around for a defective bell that never became part of a trumpet, and he shows me what happens when he gently pushes the rim with his finger: it easily gives way and bends at least an inch. Dean then shows me a trumpet that once belonged to Wynton Marsalis. There is a noticeable ring of slightly protruding brass a few inches from the rim of the bell. Wynton had pushed a mute into the bell a little too firmly one day.

Why the brass is so delicate and how it gets that way is a trade secret. The Bach people would not let me watch the annealing process; Monette will not even discuss it. The extremely delicate brass may partially explain the high prices of Monette horns. When you pay five figures for a trumpet, you're going to take extremely good care of it, and the people at the Monette factory are less likely to see it come back with dents and dings. In fact, Monette will not honor the warranty on his trumpets unless you buy a custom-built case along with the instrument. The case is hard as a rock on the outside and lavishly padded inside.

One of the last trumpets I try is a heavy Raja with a brushed gold coating. As bits of the surface catch the light, the effect is tintinnabulating, like thousands of tiny bells briefly flashing. Before I am allowed to hold the Raja, Dave asks me to take off my wedding ring. A good gold finish will last a long time if properly maintained. But because the gold plating represents only 1/10,000th of an inch of a horn's surface, a little bit of contact with metal can cause a great deal of damage.

Throughout the process, Dave invites me to observe the way each mouthpiece has its own special characteristics. Some produce wider, darker sounds, while others are what he calls "slappy," giving the notes more of a pop when they are tongued sharply. He also shows me how I can change my embouchure slightly to get the most out of each piece. When it's all over, he suggests a slightly larger cup than I had been playing with my Bach 7C. He says he'll make me a B4S. The S is for Lew Soloff, who began his career (like Monette) playing in a rock band (Blood, Sweat & Tears) before he became one of the most admired lead trumpet players in jazz. Soloff's constant search for the most serviceable mouthpieces led him, like so many others, to Monette. Dave promises to make my mouthpiece on his brand-new lathe and put a little bend in the stem so that my trumpet will stick straight out. (I still have a bit of an overjet even after those two and half years of orthodontia.) As always, the factory is backed up on mouthpiece orders, but he promises to ship it to me within a month.

By the time I have picked out my mouthpiece, it's late in the afternoon, and I'm ready to head back to my hotel. Dave gives me a hug and wishes me well. I am literally halfway out the door when he comes running over and says, "Have you seen Art Farmer's flumpet?" My God, the same Art Farmer who changed my life. For this, I'm more than happy to stick around.

To understand Monette's connections with Farmer, you need to know that Farmer began playing flügelhorn as often as trumpet in midcareer. Compared to the trumpet, a flügelhorn has a larger bore and is more conical. Just as the cornet evolved from the post horn, the flügelhorn evolved from the keyed bugle. For most of the twentieth century, flügelhorns were more associated with German marching bands than with jazz, but in the 1950s, several jazz artists were attracted to its round, dusky sound and began playing it as a solo instrument. Monette, who was never shy about approaching well-established artists, went into his workshop and created a horn that was midway between the trumpet and the flügelhorn. Thus was the flumpet born. Farmer loved Monette's flumpet and played it regularly until his death. Monette was pleasantly surprised to learn that Farmer's will stipulated that the horn be returned to him after Farmer's death. (See figure 25.)

Dave goes to a cabinet and pulls out an elegant case. In it is a horn like nothing I've ever seen before. Like many of the Monette horns, it has at least double the amount of metal as a conventional trumpet. Instead of small tubelike braces between the bell and the lead pipe, there are plates at least an inch wide. Where the tubes curve there are additional plates, taking up almost all of the empty space between. Most remarkably, Art Farmer's flumpet is decorated. At least ten tiny images appear on the several flat surfaces that the instrument's design provides. Dave tells me that the icons were carefully engraved by his friend Tami Dean, who has her own studio in Portland where she makes strikingly original jewelry. He points to one of the icons and asks me who it is.

"Who? It looks like a foreshortened railroad locomotive," I say.

"No. It's a camera," he says. "You may have had one of these when you were younger."

I'm stumped.

"Didn't you have a Brownie camera?" he asks. As a matter of fact, I did. Then I get it. Brownie. The nickname for Clifford Brown, the trumpet genius who sat next to Art Farmer in the Lionel Hampton big band in the early 1950s. The icon is a puzzle, but it's also a tribute to one of the people who inspired Farmer when he was young.

Then Dave points to another symbol, a tiny representation of a trumpet with lightning bolts coming out of it. "What's that?"

Again I'm stumped. Lightning Hopkins was a blues singer. Was there a trumpeter named Lightning?

"Give up? It's Louis."

Hmmm. I never would have figured that one out, but it's fair to say that Armstrong was the Zeus of the trumpet, tossing bolts of fire out of his horn.

Another one of the icons is a horn with its bell turned up. Before I can say "Dizzy Gillespie," Dave says, "That one's too easy."

Then he makes me an offer: "If you can identify three of the remaining icons, I'll give you your mouthpiece for free." Suddenly $200 is on the line. I begin to look very carefully at the little designs on the flumpet's braces. I see a book opened with a large *L* on one page. It takes a minute, but I get it. It's Booker Little, who played with Eric Dolphy, John Coltrane, and Max Roach before dying at the tragically young age of twenty-three in 1963. Art Farmer admired his playing, and his flumpet bears a tribute to him.

That's one.

Encouraged, I look at what appears to be a dress that a little girl might wear except that it is wider than normal. I eventually figure that one out too. It's Theodore "Fats" Navarro, who might have been the best of them all. Because he had a high-pitched voice, and because he was overweight—at least until the last months of his life, when he was wasting away—his nickname was "Fat Girl." One more icon to go. I see the representation of a string bass. Although my memory is not as sharp as it used to be, I remember that Art's twin brother, Addison Farmer, was a jazz bass player.

A few weeks later, I get a package containing a beautiful gold-plated mouthpiece with a slight bend on its shank. It has been carefully packaged in an elegant mouthpiece box. There is no bill.

I love my Monette mouthpiece. I also love my Bach trumpet. But I have decided that there is nothing wrong with having two trumpets that I play regularly. I will not be, in Eddie's terms, a mere collector. My Monette LTJ trumpet, very much like the one that Wynton Marsalis was playing in 2006, will arrive at my door shortly after this book goes to press. I may soon decide whether I was born for a Bach or for a Monette. Or both. Or maybe for a Bach, a Monette, and a Martin Committee . . .

chapter 5

Caution: The Trumpet May Be
Hazardous to Your Health

Professional players asked Dave Monette to build a trumpet because they liked his lead pipes. Aerodynamic design and tightly fitted parts made it easier for the musicians to coax music out of their recalcitrant horns. Even musicians who don't like the sound of Monette's trumpets will tell you that they are easier to play. Of course, every musician has his or her own sense of what sounds good and what is easy to play. *Chacun à son goût.* But there is a consensus that Monette has succeeded in making the air flow more smoothly through the tubes. Even an amateur like me can tell the difference. Allowing the player to expend less energy has made Monette's horns highly desirable. And highly expensive.

Even the eminent Armstrong was constantly looking for a quick fix. Richard Wang, the respected jazz educator in Chicago, says that Louis Armstrong regularly visited the workshop of Charlie Allen whenever he was in town. Allen was famous for his mouthpieces as well as his knack for repairing damaged or aging horns. When he walked into Allen's shop, the first words out of Armstrong's mouth were always "Can you make it any easier?" Armstrong smoked marijuana every day of his life in order to relax and make playing the trumpet less stressful. Other musicians have taken more extreme pharmacological paths toward stress relief. We'll get to them soon enough.

HERNIAS, BLEEDING LIPS, AND SLIPPED DISKS

Whether it was the marijuana or some adjustment to his instrument, Armstrong made it *seem* easy. But he paid a high price. Examine a close-up photograph of Wynton Marsalis or some other distinguished trumpeter and look closely at the lips. There may be a few marks and indentations, but nothing like the bulging, twisted, callused lips of Satchmo. In the 1920s, Armstrong was not afraid to go on playing even when his lips were bleeding. Mezz Mezzrow famously observed Armstrong "holding his horn and panting, his mangled lip oozing blood that he licked away."[1] And watch any video or listen to any recording of Armstrong before 1959. That was the year when he suffered his first heart attack and began to ease up a bit. Before 1959, however, Armstrong played with the same superhuman intensity, vibrating his hand on the valves of his horn for his trademark vibrato. That wasn't good for him either. Even when he began to sing more and play less in the final decade of his life, Armstrong kept the fires burning. His sidemen always spoke of him as an iron man.

In 1968, when he became gravely ill, Armstrong did not play in public for two years. Hospitalized with heart, kidney, and lung problems, his doctors told him to stop playing altogether. They knew that the effort it takes to hit a few high notes could kill a man with a weak set of lungs and an even weaker heart. Knowing that Armstrong's long, glorious career was nearing its end, impresario George Wein, who founded the Newport Jazz Festival in 1954, arranged a celebration at Newport in 1970. Armstrong was saluted by trumpeters from three generations, all of them profoundly in his debt. In the film of the concert, a much weakened and visibly aged Armstrong is clearly touched by the tribute. Although he sings a chorus of "Mack the Knife," he is without his trumpet. Perhaps buoyed by the cheers he received at Newport, Armstrong felt good enough to begin practicing again, at first in his bathroom so that no one could hear. A few weeks later he was out of the bathroom and performing in public again. He made several television appearances, the last of which was on *The Tonight Show* with Johnny Carson. Those who remember the appearance say that he played as well as he ever had during his final years. He even made a few successful stabs into the upper register. Armstrong returned to the hospital in June 1971 after still another heart attack. Shortly after he was released, he was resting in his house in Corona, Queens, and starting to feel better. He decided to return to his touring schedule. The night after he called his sidemen to schedule a rehearsal, he died quietly in bed.[2]

Roy Eldridge, another giant of the jazz trumpet, also died inconspicuously after a distinguished career. Like Armstrong, he reached a stage when playing the trumpet could have been deadly. Dizzy Gillespie, who based his early style on Eldridge's, once said that Roy would rather injure himself than be outplayed. This is exactly what his physicians feared. When Eldridge's heart attack came at age sixty-nine, doctors gave him the same warnings they had given Armstrong: stop playing or die. Although he would play along softly with records at home, Eldridge never played in public again. He lived another eight years, often singing and playing drums and piano at various venues. When his wife of fifty-three years died in 1989, everyone who knew him agrees that he gave up on life. He stopped eating and passed away in a hospital bed three weeks later.[3]

The final years of the lives of old masters like Armstrong and Eldridge are not important parts of their legends. Dying peacefully in bed does not for good legends make. If you're after good legends, consider Buddy Bolden blowing his brains out. Or consider the head of Roland, the hero of the eleventh-century French epic, exploding when he plays the battle call on his oliphant. And then there is the eighteenth-century natural trumpet virtuoso Gottfried Reiche, who died a few hours after playing a hellishly difficult trumpet solo written especially for him by J. S. Bach.

Not all of the legends end with trumpet death, but all serious trumpet players have a tale or two about injuries suffered by their peers, sometimes even by themselves. Bleeding lips are hardly the worst of it. In the 1960s, a trumpeter named John Glenn Little was playing an especially loud solo when he suddenly experienced an intense pain in the back of his head. He later discovered that he had two slipped disks in his neck. After a week in the hospital, his doctors warned him not to play for at least a year. Even seasoned lead trumpeters who play the crucial role in a jazz orchestra have had their troubles. One of the most skillful lead trumpeters to pass through the Stan Kenton Orchestra was Al Porcino. One night at a concert, while Kenton was holding out his arms to end a piece, he caught the eye of an attractive woman in the audience. Temporarily distracted, he made the band sustain a final chord a few seconds longer than usual while Porcino held the top note. It wasn't even an exceptionally high note. But because he had to keep blowing for those few additional seconds, Porcino passed out and fell over backward.[4]

There is no question that the trumpet is the most difficult of all instruments. Two hundred muscles are mobilized when a trumpeter plays a single note. Muscles in the face, lips, tongue, throat, arms, fingers, spinal column, diaphragm, and even the bowels are recruited. All of this is complicated by a small mouthpiece that requires a tiny opening between the lips to get that soprano sound. As the trumpeter plays higher, he must press the mouthpiece more firmly against the lips to make the opening even smaller. One researcher calculated that a trumpeter must exert three pounds per square inch of pressure on the mouth to hit a D above high C, a note that most accomplished trumpeters can reach without difficulty. When the trumpeter hits that note, however, it's not just the lips that take the punishment. Enormous stress is also placed on several vital organs, especially the lungs, which must process all that air, and the heart, which must pump extra blood into the lungs so that they can do their job. Blood then rushes away from the rest of the body, including the brain. Feeling light-headed is an inevitable and unavoidable part of trumpet playing.

Since trombonists, tuba players, and anyone who plays a large brass instrument must also divert a great deal of air into the horn, they might seem to be in an even worse predicament than the trumpeters. But brass instruments pitched lower have much larger mouthpieces, so the pressure is spread around the lips more efficiently. Good tuba players and trombonists need strong breath support, but they do not have to play with the same intensity as the trumpeters. A tuba player can keep it going for an entire performance while the trumpeter needs frequent breaks to rest his lips, not to mention the rest of his body.

Oboists suffer similar ailments. They too need to apply immense pressure to produce a clear sound, and there are jokes about oboists going a bit crazy because brain cells die every time they have to play high or loud. Trumpeters lose brain cells too, but there is a significant difference between what they endure and what oboe players are faced with. Oboists are seldom asked to make their delicate instruments soar loudly above the orchestra. And if the oboist fluffs a note, only a fraction of the audience will notice. But the trumpeter is like the Olympic ice-skater. Anyone who watches the sport on television for a few minutes quickly becomes an expert. The skater who falls on his or her ass is obviously not as skilled as the one who does not. And judges rate the performances accordingly. At the symphony—even at a jazz club—it is painfully obvious to everyone when a trumpeter falls on his ass. Even a cool cucumber like Miles Davis was so eaten up with anxiety in the early years of his career that he regularly vomited before a performance.

IT DOESN'T COME EASY

Because of the extreme difficulty of the instrument, and because of the profound humiliation that is always a strong possibility in performance, trumpeters have acquired various talismans and personal habits that border on the superstitious. I once sat next to a trumpeter who seemed to be lining up his mouthpiece every time he put it into his horn. I watched him do it on several occasions, always noting that the capital C on his Courtois mouthpiece was at the exact bottom when it was inserted. Trumpet mouthpieces are precisely circular and symmetrical. Unless the mouthpiece is damaged in some way, it shouldn't make any difference how the rim is rotated. And my section mate's mouthpiece was not in any way damaged. When I asked him about it, he assured me that a professional trumpeter once urged him to find the place where the mouthpiece was most comfortable. For several months, he made a note of how it felt to play with the mouthpiece in each position. He eventually became convinced that he played best when the C was in the exact right place.

Now, I admit that I've tried it, and I can't tell any difference, no matter how my mouthpiece is situated. But this does not mean that it could not make a real difference for someone else. My highly uninformed guess is that trumpeters, desperate to find anything that will give them an edge, will fall back on something that has more to do with psychology and confidence than music. In other words, if they *believe* a trick works, that's enough for them. Lew Soloff regularly brings several mouthpieces to a gig. He has been known to change mouthpieces in the middle of a solo, sometimes more than once. Players who have sat next to him and watched him go back and forth between mouthpieces have said they cannot hear any difference in his sound. But it obviously makes a difference to Soloff.

Many trumpeters wear the same lucky tie, jacket, or cuff links to performances. One player kept a tiny stuffed bear dangling from the end of his third valve slide. When asked what it was, he responded, "Cracked note catcher." And trumpeters are obsessed with their teeth, which must be in excellent condition to support all that pressure from the mouthpiece. Harry Glantz, principal trumpeter in the NBC Symphony under Arturo Toscanini, was so diligent about brushing his teeth that he began to wear away the enamel. His dentist had to tell him to ease up.[5] Other trumpeters have taken the more severe step of filing down their teeth. The jazz trumpet master Jon Faddis, who has an astounding ability to play high and loud, has a gap between his two front teeth. And the left tooth is severely chipped because of a childhood accident. Faddis has said that he can channel more air into his horn because his teeth do not provide much of an obstruction. He may be right about this. Randy Sandke, another first-rate soloist and trumpet virtuoso, told me that he has actually gone to the dentist to have parts of his front teeth shaved off.

Even without the anxiety, expertise on the trumpet requires constant practice. To have any facility and command over the instrument's range, a trumpeter must commit to at least an hour a day, and many professionals put in much more than that. Wynton Marsalis told an interviewer that he practices five or six hours a day. On days when they can stay home, trumpeters leave the horn out of its case, playing it for stretches of twenty or so minutes throughout the day. Brain specialists agree that twenty minutes is about as long as anyone can productively concentrate on a single task. It's also about as long as a good trumpeter can continue playing without beginning to feel fatigued. The best players know when to rest, even if for only a few minutes. And if, for whatever reason, trumpeters put their instruments away for even a few days, they need to work extra hard to get back up to speed. "Come-back players" like me need several years of regular practice to get back to where they left off. At age sixty, after more than four years of daily practice, I think I play about as well as I did when I was eighteen.

By contrast, a decent saxophone player can afford to take off long periods of time without losing prowess. Jazz saxophonist Art Pepper tells an extraordinary tale in *Straight Life*, the autobiography he wrote with his third wife, Laurie LaPan Pepper.[6] Struggling with a lifelong heroin habit, Pepper often went for months without playing, devoting all his energy to scoring drugs and "goofing" in his heroin euphoria. At one point, after six months of inactivity, his second wife, Diane, lined up a recording date but did not tell him until the last minute. To Pepper's horror, Diane and the highly respected producer Lester Koenig had arranged for him to make a record for Koenig's Contemporary label. Pepper was even more appalled by the accompanists Koenig had lined up—Red Garland, Paul Chambers, and Philly Joe Jones, exactly the same rhythm section with which Miles Davis had been working regularly for more than a year. Cursing Diane and frantically trying to get his alto saxophone working after months of neglect, Pepper showed up at the studio to make the record. Intimidated at first by the extraordinary array of musicians, Pepper eventually began to play a series of stunningly brilliant improvisations. Portions of this story may be apocryphal—published discographies suggest that Pepper made a few recordings during the months when he said he was inactive—but the proof of his exceptional performance that day in 1957 is on the CD *Art Pepper Meets the Rhythm Section*. Listen to how Pepper expertly navigates his way through tortuously complex lines on his up-tempo solos. No trumpet player, no matter how accomplished, could play that well after a long period of inactivity. Even Hollywood filmmakers know this.

TRUMPET ANXIETY (CINEMATIC)

In the 1959 film *The Five Pennies*, Danny Kaye plays Red Nichols, a minor jazz cornetist who had a hit in 1927 with "Ida, Sweet as Apple Cider." Nichols himself recorded the cornet solos that Kaye pantomimes in the film. In fact, Kaye does much more than pantomime. The screenwriters for *The Five Pennies* reworked the Red Nichols story so that Kaye can sing and clown around in the same demure style he brought to his popular television program in the 1960s. But Kaye also gets to do some acting with a capital A when the story turns melodramatic and his daughter is stricken with polio. Blaming himself for traveling with his band instead of staying home to look after her, Kaye's Nichols chooses to give up music completely. The real Red Nichols did in fact stop performing and worked in the shipyards from 1942 until 1944. In the film, Nichols comes home to find his teenage daughter and her friends listening to a record by Harry James. Highly offended by one boy's suggestion that the jazz parade has passed him by, Nichols picks up a cornet that his wife (Barbara Bel Geddes) has conveniently brought out of the closet. Having once sung with his band, the wife knows that Nichols would be happier if he returned to performing. With the woman standing close by, Nichols struggles with a chorus of "Indiana" before he fails to pin a high note and gives up. One of his daughter's friends breaks the embarrassed silence by saying, "I have homework to do." All the teenagers then leave the house of the humiliated cornetist.

The Five Pennies is not the only film in which a trumpeter fails to hit a high note while a woman stands by. In 1950, Kirk Douglas starred in *Young Man with a Horn*, a film based on the novel inspired by Bix Beiderbecke. Near the end of the film, Rick Martin, the trumpeter hero played by Douglas, begins drinking heavily after his beloved trumpet teacher dies and after his wife takes up with a woman who is as close to being a lesbian as the cinema industry of 1950 would allow. Doris Day plays Jo Jordan, a singer in his band who understands the enigmatic trumpeter and waits patiently for him to turn to her. Rick is playing behind Jo at a recording session when he fails in midsolo to hit a high note. After flailing about in the upper register in hopes of finding the right note, Rick flees the studio and begins a quick slide into alcoholism and vagrancy. The hero's low point is marked by an especially symbolic moment when he collapses in the street and the wheels of a passing car flatten his trumpet.

Spike Lee surely watched *Young Man with a Horn* at some point. Consciously or unconsciously, Lee re-created the crisis of the trumpeter hero in *Mo' Better Blues* (1990). Bleek Gilliam (Denzel Washington) is a jazz trumpeter whose success is undermined by the incompetence of his manager and childhood friend Giant (played by Spike Lee himself). One night, when Bleek comes to Giant's aid as two thugs are beating him for not paying his gambling debts, the thugs gleefully turn on Bleek and smash his mouth with his own trumpet. Bleek spends an indeterminate amount of time in seclusion, waiting for his lips to heal and presumably practicing. When he finally emerges to pick up where he left off, he joins his old band in a club. Like Barbara Bel Geddes in *The Five Pennies* and Doris Day in *Young Man with a Horn*, Clarke Bentancourt (Cynda Williams) is the singer with the hero's band as well as his former lover. In a scene that made regularly wood-shedding musicians rub their eyes, Bleek shows that he is still a long way from recovering. As the beautiful Clarke looks on with compassion, he flubs his way through a few bars of a solo and then walks out of the club into the rain. In the compelling scene that follows, the disgraced Bleek hands his trumpet to Giant as he walks off into the night. Giant holds the horn high in the air while rain streams down and the camera drifts upward. "I won't sell it, Bleek. I won't sell it," he cries out.

In each of the these three films, the trumpeter's masculinity as well as his sexuality are at stake. In the films' logic, the trumpeter who can't hit the high note is effectively impotent. The presence of a sexually desirable woman is essential to the equation. We trumpeters have enough problems playing those high notes without the movies giving us performance anxiety.

Far away from the overheated territory of Hollywood movies, in the horse latitudes where failed trumpeters are thrown overboard, floats Ralph Cramden, the henpecked bus driver played by Jackie Gleason in the 1950s sitcom *The Honeymooners*. Ralph would occasionally pull out a battered cornet and make a pass at the upper register. When he would pinch out the beginnings of a high note, he would say to his wife, "I got a piece of it, Alice." Alice was seldom impressed.

Even Harry James, the matinee-idol trumpeter who starred with Benny Goodman's band before forming his own orchestra, was rendered impotent at least once in the movies. In *Best Foot Forward*, a 1943 film based on a Broadway show, James and his band are playing for a prom at a military school. On the one hand, the filmmakers allowed James plenty of room to dazzle the audience with his solos, including his trademark "Flight of the Bumble Bee," which he plays impossibly fast. He also gets to hit his share of high notes without so much as knitting his brow. (As always in the movies, James and his band prerecorded the music and then pantomimed it for the camera. But no matter.) On the other hand, James does not fare well when he is matched with Nancy, an unattached female at the dance played by Nancy Walker. Short, Jewish, and chubby, Nancy wisecracks her way through much of the film, providing relief from the bland lead characters. When she rubs her aching feet and a girlfriend asks if her shoes are too small, she replies, "No, they're the right size, but my feet don't believe it."

Nevertheless, Nancy gets a dance with Harry James. She coaxes him onto the dance floor by taking away his trumpet. While Nancy moves about the floor holding his horn, James continues to reach out sheepishly for the trumpet. Nancy always pulls it away at the last moment. When she finally throws the horn over James's head into the wings, the audience does not hear a crash, but James's face and posture become that of a little lost boy. The number concludes with the trumpetless trumpeter performing an awkward dance with the awkward, aggressive woman. Even a performer with the prowess of Harry James—he married the pinup goddess Betty Grable in the same year that *Best Foot Forward* was released—can be emasculated once his trumpet is taken away.

TRUMPET ANXIETY (SYMPHONIC)

In real life, or at least in the day-to-day world of the professional trumpeter, missing a note or losing a trumpet is seldom as drastic as a sexual meltdown. But the humiliation of public failure is still just a fraction of a millimeter away. That's the distance between the wrong lip position and the right position for whatever note the player must produce on demand. Because the symphonic trumpeter is always the person in the organization whose mistakes are most obvious, the majority of conductors appreciate their players and do not expect them to play like automatons. But on at least one occasion, a conductor was not so sympathetic. The story of Seiji Ozawa's persecution of Charles Schlueter has been thoroughly documented by Carl Vigeland in his book *In Concert*,[7] which narrates the interactions among musicians, administrators, and orchestra supporters leading up to performances of Gustav Mahler's Second Symphony when Ozawa was conducting the Boston Symphony Orchestra in the 1980s. Although many other musicians and orchestra employees are introduced, the hero of the book is Schlueter. Vigeland surely regarded the trumpeter as a sympathetic fellow whose fortunes made his story more compelling. Although Ozawa looms large throughout the book, he is not a likable figure.

Charles Schlueter had already established himself as a world-class musician when he auditioned for the BSO's principal trumpet position in 1982. At the audition he played brilliantly and won out against stiff competition. By the end of his first and probationary year with the orchestra, Ozawa consented to give him tenure, the right to remain in the orchestra indefinitely. At the end of Schlueter's second year, however, Ozawa said that Schlueter's playing was unacceptable and asked him to leave. Schlueter was devastated. He did not, however, take the insult lying down. After deciding that he wanted to remain in the BSO despite Ozawa's opposition, he went to the musicians' union to fight for his job. Ultimately, the carefully constructed rules of arbitration worked to Schlueter's advantage. The arbitrator ruled that Ozawa had not followed the proper procedures when he tried to fire his principal trumpeter. Schlueter kept his job, but by no means was he vindicated. Nothing in the arbitrator's decision said that Ozawa was wrong about the quality of Schlueter's playing.

Because his victory was procedural rather than artistic, Schlueter had to go on playing with a conductor who did not want him. Partially because of an exhausting schedule as an international celebrity and partially because of his temperament, Ozawa kept his distance from the members of the BSO. His staff soon realized it was their job to handle personal interactions. More to the point, Ozawa was reluctant to spell out exactly what he wanted from each musician. He expected his musicians simply to understand his concept of the pieces they were playing. And because Ozawa was younger than many of the orchestra's senior musicians, he needed to find a way to assert his authority. Ozawa may therefore have decided to pick on a recent addition to the orchestra. Because several eminent members in the BSO organization also had problems with Schlueter's sound, he was the victim.

Ozawa essentially said that Schlueter played too loud and with too much vibrato. He also mentioned that Schlueter had problems with intonation. In his attempts to be fair to Ozawa, Vigeland says that the conductor did not take the obvious step of telling Schlueter to reduce his volume because he believed that musicians should simply *know* what he wanted. The issue of vibrato is more complex. Many trumpet teachers today discourage the use of vibrato, especially for beginning students. Unless executed properly, the fast up-and-down movement of a note's pitch can be annoying. It can also substitute for good intonation, although it is difficult to imagine that a musician as dedicated as Charles Schlueter would have intonation problems. The best trumpeters in jazz, classical, and Latin music develop their own unique sound, and vibrato is often an essential component. Schlueter had personalized a vibrato that connoisseurs have characterized as highly musical if vaguely mournful. Vigeland does not say whether or not Ozawa liked that particular sound. More likely, Schlueter was simply playing in a way that was too individualized for a conductor who wanted the entire orchestra to reflect *his* personality.

During the period in which Schlueter's case was arbitrated and for years afterward, the trumpeter had to play difficult solos and heroic lead trumpet parts knowing that he had no support from his conductor. He was also painfully aware that others in the BSO organization shared Ozawa's dislike of his style. To make matters worse, an important newspaper critic always singled out Schlueter for special criticism when he was less then perfect and ignored his playing when he was at his best. Schlueter was in a dreadful predicament. Every mistake added to people's low opinion of his playing, thus greatly increasing his anxiety at each performance. And playing with that anxiety made him more likely to make mistakes. Which increased his anxiety.

David Monette appears in Vigeland's book as something of an angel. Monette was especially devoted to Schlueter, one of his first internationally famous customers. Working closely with Schlueter, he created a trumpet that responded perfectly to his strengths and weaknesses. Ultimately, Schlueter's Monette horn required a bit more effort than the standard issue, thus taking some of the edge off of Schlueter's uniquely powerful sound. Regardless of whether or not he was playing too loud and not blending well with the orchestra, Monette made it possible for Schlueter to play with a less overwhelming sound. By the time Dave began giving Schlueter yoga lessons, the trumpeter had begun to think of Monette as a son. Thanks to the support of Monette and a few other loved ones, Schlueter was able to manage his contested role in the BSO. Gradually he overcame enough anxiety to play at a consistently high level, so high that no one could argue that he did not belong in the orchestra. The book ends with Ozawa putting aside his war with Schlueter and briefly patting him on the back after a short tête-à-tête during a rehearsal. For Ozawa, it was an exceptionally dramatic gesture.

DEATH AND THE TRUMPET

For Charles Schlueter, the trumpet was a unique source of distinction and accomplishment. Although he might have been wounded by his treatment, he probably never would have suggested that Ozawa was trying to "emasculate" him. Buddy Bolden, Louis Armstrong, and several generations of black musicians also sought to distinguish themselves by making great music on an exceptionally difficult instrument. But for them, the trumpet presented a unique opportunity for powerful affirmations of manhood. If they had expressed their masculinity in almost any other fashion, they would have faced brutal reprisals from racist whites. In the first half of the twentieth century, black trumpet masculinity was appropriated by white artists, especially white jazz artists. Like the white athlete and the white rock 'n' roller of subsequent generations, white musicians discovered that they could boost their masculine presentation by imitating black men, even by having black men close by. In the 1940s, several white swing bands hired a single black trumpeter to play "hot" jazz solos. Cootie Williams left the Ellington band to join Benny Goodman, inspiring Raymond Scott to write a dirge, "When Cootie Left the Duke." Tommy Dorsey put Charlie Shavers in his trumpet section, and Artie Shaw hired Oran "Hot Lips" Page. Roy Eldridge worked with Gene Krupa and later with Shaw as well. But as American popular culture began to cast large firearms, fast automobiles, and bulging muscles as more legitimate signs of masculinity, the trumpet seemed a fragile vessel indeed.

The fragility of the trumpet and the trumpeter have coexisted with myths of the trumpeter's masculinity. Hence the cinematic myth of the accomplished trumpet player who suddenly fails to "get it up" when a female love object is nearby. Hence also the myth of the trumpeter who distinguishes himself with his prowess on the instrument and then dies young. Vance Bourjaily has noticed how many times this second myth has been attached to the lives of jazz artists. In an essay about jazz and fiction, Bourjaily has called this myth "The Story." "The Story goes like this: a musician of genius, frustrated by the discrepancy between what he can achieve and the crummy life musicians lead (because of racial discrimination, or the demand that the music be made commercial, or because he has a potential he can't reach), goes mad, or destroys himself with alcohol and drugs. The Story might be a romance, but it is a valid one."[8] The Story could begin with Buddy Bolden, who may have turned to alcohol when his fragile success and the pressures of the jazz life became too much for him. More likely, Bolden had a chemical imbalance in his brain and would probably have suffered some kind of breakdown even if he were a shoe salesman.

For Bourjaily, The Story first appears in print as *Young Man with a Horn*, Dorothy Baker's 1938 novel that was the source for the 1950 film with Kirk Douglas. Baker took her title from a 1936 essay by Otis Ferguson, one of the first people to write about Bix Beiderbecke, the white trumpeter from Davenport, Iowa. Beiderbecke was practically unknown during his brief career except to a few aficionados. Only after his death in 1931 did jazz writers such as Ferguson begin listening carefully to his recorded solos and assessing his genius, and not until much later were the details of his biography widely known. The biographical details certainly were not available to Dorothy Baker.

Regardless, when Baker inaugurated The Story with *Young Man with a Horn*, she was working with what little was known about Bix but even more so with what she and other jazz lovers believed to be true about the jazz life—that in order to make a living, the jazz artist must make severe compromises, even if it kills him. In Baker's novel, Rick Martin (the Bix character) is orphaned at an early age and raised by a neglectful older sister. Left to his own devices, Rick takes up with a young black man who introduces him to jazz. He devotes himself to learning piano and then trumpet. Soon he is playing with enough skill to attract the attention of Phil Morrison, a character based on Paul Whiteman, the highly successful musical entrepreneur who called himself the King of Jazz. Whiteman did in fact hire the best white jazz artists, including Beiderbecke. He even brought Billie Holiday into the studio for a recording with his band. Whiteman regularly featured Beiderbecke's horn, and some of the trumpeter's best solos are on Whiteman's records.

For Dorothy Baker, however, Phil Morrison forces Rick Martin to play the same drivel night after night, driving him to despair and eventually to drink. As the novel's narrator puts it, "There is music that is turned out sweet in hotel ballrooms and there is music that comes right out of the genuine urge and doesn't come for money."[9] The real Bix Beiderbecke died of pneumonia complicated by the effects of heavy drinking. During his short life he was never much of a success even though his recordings consistently reveal a musical genius who could and did change the meaning of the trumpet for a large group of musicians and listeners. Whether or not he would have developed a drinking problem if he *had* become a success is another question. Think of the 1960s pop stars Janis Joplin, Jimi Hendrix, Brian Jones, and Jim Morrison. All died from drugs at the pinnacle of their success. In fact, all four of these artists were twenty-seven when they died, just one year younger than Beiderbecke at the time of his death. Success did not prevent them from destroying themselves.

A recent biography of Beiderbecke, however, offers new evidence that the trumpeter may have had serious problems that were unrelated to his musical career. In 1921, when Beiderbecke was eighteen, he was arrested for committing a "lewd and lascivious" act with a five-year-old girl.[10] According to witnesses, he had taken the child into a garage and asked her to lift her skirt. There is the possibility that he had made sexual advances to other girls as well. Although no charges were filed, Beiderbecke's relations with his parents were permanently changed. He was always a loner and a rebel, but this level of antisocial behavior reveals a deeply troubled young man. Shortly after the incident, he was sent away to Lake Forest Academy near Chicago, a school that submitted troublesome children from wealthy families to military discipline. Although his exile from Davenport gave Bix an opportunity to begin forging his career in the crucible of Chicago nightlife, he may never have been able to put what happened at home behind him.

The legend of Bix Beiderbecke as a sensitive artist brought down by a society of philistines is especially compelling. He was never a folk hero like Louis Armstrong because his playing was not sensational. He was uninterested in high notes and in overpowering other trumpeters at cutting contests. He never strayed from the middle register of his instrument, and his solos were understated and poetic. They were as elegantly structured as they were winsome. With very few exceptions, audiences at clubs surely kept right on talking and drinking while he soloed. Even his parents ignored his music. Or perhaps they had simply written him out of their lives after his arrest in 1921. Beiderbecke began making records in 1925, dutifully sending copies to his parents, devout burghers of German descent living comfortably in Davenport. One day when he was home for a visit, he found all his records in a closet, still in their original wrappings. After devoting his life to his craft, it must have broken his heart to discover that his own parents weren't paying attention.

Buddy Bolden and Bix Beiderbecke both had severe drinking problems and both died in 1931. In some ways, their legends have fed off each other. Bunny Berigan, although he died a bit later, was another double-B trumpeter who drank to excess. In Berigan's case, alcoholism probably killed him.[11] The biographies of all three of these musicians can be made to fit The Story without too much imagination. With Bolden, The Story is embodied most elegantly in Michael Ondaatje's *Coming Through Slaughter,* in which Buddy loses his mind because he cannot play the notes he hears in his head. Somehow the cornet is inadequate to his aspirations, however great his mastery, and the gap is his undoing. Dorothy Baker served up a similar if more prosaic story for Beiderbecke.

Like Harry James, Bunny Berigan got his start with Benny Goodman and then formed his own band. Perhaps even more than James, he had the looks of a movie star. His big hit came in 1937 with "I Can't Get Started," a great tune by Vernon Duke with witty lyrics by Ira Gershwin invoking tea with Greta Garbo and consultations with FDR.

Still I'm broken-hearted
'cause I can't get started with you

On the recording, Berigan sings lyrics of worldliness and longing that are of a piece with the trumpet solo that follows. Louis Armstrong once said that Berigan was his favorite among the many white trumpeters who emerged in his wake. From all accounts, however, Berigan was a ferocious alcoholic, and his death was the direct result of his drinking. As with Janis Joplin, Jim Morrison, and the other wildly successful rockers, Berigan may have perished from success rather than neglect.

The Story might also apply to James "Bubber" Miley, who was twenty-nine when he died of tuberculosis. Like Beiderbecke, his disease was exacerbated by his alcoholism. And like so many of the trumpet geniuses who died young, his impact on the music was formidable. A young Duke Ellington, just starting out as a composer and bandleader, recognized that Miley could growl and talk through his trumpet even more extravagantly than King Oliver and the great New Orleans cornetists of the 1920s. If Ellington was to compete with the other dance bands in Jazz Age New York, he knew that his band had to play something more affecting than the sweet dance music his peers were turning out.

With Miley, Duke found the perfect foil. Ellington grew up in a middle-class family in Washington, took piano lessons as a child, and was admitted to art school with a scholarship. He was many steps away from the gutbucket traditions in which jazz was born. Little is known about Miley except that he was born in South Carolina in 1903 and was six when his family settled in New York City. His family was probably much less affluent than Ellington's. Regardless, Miley grew up in New York temperamentally disposed toward a more raw style of music. Early in his career, he looked up to Johnny Dunn, a good blues player who was also known as a bon vivant. Dunn some-times used a mute to produce a wah-wah sound, but it was nothing like the extravagantly vernacular effects that King Oliver regularly created. When Miley heard Oliver in 1921, he quickly turned to bath-room plungers and other gadgets to sound like Oliver. With Elling-ton, he would growl and curse with his horn all night, using the difficult technique of singing with a guttural rumble in his throat while simultaneously sounding dark notes on his horn and waving mutes in front of the bell. While Ellington was working out ideas that were derived primarily from classical music and Tin Pan Alley, Miley was, like many African American performers, lavishly importing the blues and blurring the distinction between vocal and instrumental music. With Ellington, he was also blurring the distinction between white and black music. Jazz historians wonder if Ellington could have succeeded—or have gained success so quickly—without Miley's early impact on his style.

After Miley's departure, Ellington always had a growling trum-peter, even if the men he hired initially had no idea how it was done. Cootie Williams came in as Miley's replacement and had to listen carefully to Joe Nanton—the band's trombonist, who had learned how to growl from Miley—to figure out how to play the parts Miley had left behind. When Cootie Williams left in 1940, Ray Nance took over the chair and the growl responsibilities.

Although Miley was responsible for the Ellington orchestra's sig-nature sound in the mid-1920s, he was an unreliable employee who showed up drunk or not at all. Ellington fired him in 1929. Miley may have been ready to move on anyway, and his poor attendance record probably reflected ambition rather than irresponsibility. But he ran out of time before he could succeed as a solo artist. He died in 1931, the same year in the midst of the Great Depression when Bolden and Beiderbecke also passed away. There is no published biography of Miley, so it's impossible to know if he was searching for some impossible note or looking for a level of professional satisfaction that was unavailable to him. It's more likely that a bad case of tuberculosis simply took his life.

The diagnosis of tuberculosis exacerbated by drug abuse is also what brought down Fats Navarro at the age of twenty-six in 1950. Navarro's drug of choice, however, was not alcohol but heroin. Shortly before his death, he was poised to become the most important trumpeter of his generation. With his effortlessly fluid playing and fertile imagination as an improviser, he might have surpassed Miles Davis and perhaps even Dizzy Gillespie. He is mythologized in Charles Mingus's autobiography, *Beneath the Underdog*, perhaps the most intriguing book ever written by a major jazz artist. Mingus, the composer and bassist whose career spanned most of jazz history and all of its stylistic peregrinations, worked with Navarro when they were both members of the Lionel Hampton orchestra in the late 1940s. Both Mingus and Navarro were part of an elite circle of bebop pioneers that also included Charlie Parker, Gillespie, Bud Powell, and Thelonious Monk. In the last pages of his autobiography, Mingus recreates two long conversations with Navarro that range widely over numerous topics, especially religion and racial politics.

According to Mingus, the ravages of disease had taken Navarro's weight from three hundred pounds down to a scant one hundred ten. When Mingus asks him why he won't go to a doctor to stop his internal bleeding, Navarro responds, "Mingus, I'm bleeding 'cause I want to bleed. I got T.B. intentionally and I'm hoping there ain't no heaven or hell like you say there is. Think how drug I'd be to get there and find the white man owns that too and it's rent-controlled in heaven and hell's like the slums. I'd tell them, 'Kill me, white faggot cocksucking angels, like you did down on earth,' 'cause you sure ain't gonna get no work or rent from my soul.' "[12] The jazz life was brutal for musicians of Navarro's generation, especially black ones. Although the black beboppers thought of themselves as professionals and not as crowd-pleasing entertainers, racist Americans treated them like sharecroppers. When Navarro's peer Charlie Parker died of pneumonia and a variety of self-inflicted complications at the age of thirty-four, the first doctor on the scene listed his age as fifty-three.

In Mingus's book, Navarro does not share Mingus's religious convictions. A gospel beat and the shout of the black folk preacher always played a role in Mingus's music, and expressions of Christian faith appear regularly in *Beneath the Underdog*. Mingus was on the way to a long and distinguished career when he died from amyotrophic lateral sclerosis at the age of fifty-six in 1979. Dizzy Gillespie, whose career was even longer and more celebrated, was a proponent of the Baha'i faith. Several black jazz artists who escaped an early grave embraced Islam. Perhaps their faith kept them away from the temptations that brought down musicians like Navarro. They may also have thought long and hard about what happens to musicians like Navarro, who expressed disdain for religion.

Then there was Freddie Webster, who left only a handful of recordings but was also poised to be a major figure in jazz history. He made his mark with the first generation of beboppers, playing at the legendary jam sessions at Minton's in Harlem in the early 1940s. Gillespie, with whom he played regularly, said he had the best sound of any trumpeter he knew. Touring the Middle West a few years later, Webster took the young Miles Davis under his wing. In his autobiography, Davis called Webster "my real main man in those first days." On one of his first recordings, Davis actually re-created one of Webster's solos note for note. Webster was extremely generous with the young Davis, but he could also be difficult and self-destructive. When Count Basie invited Webster to join his orchestra in 1947, he asked Webster what kind of salary he deserved. Webster replied, "After you've paid the rest of those guys, you and I split 50–50!" He didn't get the job. Shortly after his disastrous encounter with Basie, Webster died at age thirty from a heroin overdose. Rumor has it that a mortal enemy of saxophonist Sonny Stitt, who was working with Webster at the time, had prepared a fatal dose for Stitt but that Webster got to the drugs first.

Although Miles Davis lived to sixty-five, it's a miracle that he lasted as long as he did. After twice kicking a serious heroin habit, Davis spent a good portion of his final years addicted to cocaine, painkillers, or alcohol. Consider this list of subheadings that appear under Davis's own name in the index to his autobiography: "arthritis, auto accident, cocaine used by, diabetes, drinking, drug-induced delusions, gallstone operation, hallucinations, heart palpitations, heroin habit, hip operations, larynx nodes, liver infection, police beating, shooting of, sickle-cell anemia, stroke, throat operation, ulcer."[13] His cause of death was listed as a stroke.

There is no question that African American trumpeters such as Bolden, Miley, Navarro, and Webster suffered because of what they had to endure throughout their lives. And few of these musicians were recognized in a way that was at all appropriate to their stature as artists. Even if racism and public neglect were what killed them, there is another group of brilliant trumpet players who died young but not because of self-destructive tendencies. On the one hand, they can be seen as refutations of The Story. On another, they might have survived in a world that afforded better treatment to jazz artists. Clifford Brown surely stands as the best example. He died in an automobile accident in 1956, when he was twenty-six.

Along with his pianist, Richie Powell, and Powell's wife, Nancy, Brownie was en route from Philadelphia to Chicago for a club date with the band he co-led with the great bop drummer Max Roach. Ordinarily, Brown and Roach traveled together. But Brown wanted to stop in Elkhart, Indiana, a few hours east of Chicago, to check out some new trumpets. While Roach went on ahead, Brown invited Powell and his wife to join him in his car. The detour to Chicago prolonged a trip that was already arduous. Jazz musicians had to take whatever jobs they could get, even if it meant crossing long distances in a short time. While Brown and Richie Powell slept, the young wife took the wheel. Nancy apparently lost control of the car on a rainy Pennsylvania Turnpike, back in the day when Route 70 was legendary for its twists and curves and its bizarre array of road signs. A few years after the accident that took the life of Clifford Brown, the jazz singer Dave Lambert, one third of the vocal trio Lambert, Hendricks, and Ross, was killed by a passing car on the Pennsylvania Turnpike when he stopped to change a tire.

When the car with Brownie, Richie, and Nancy went off the road, it tumbled over several times. All three passengers died instantly. Brown left behind a six-month-old son and a wife to whom he had been married exactly two years to the day.[14] The loss was especially tragic because Clifford Brown was not a doomed soul. Never a junkie, he had been a paragon of clean living. When he first went off to college, he majored in mathematics. Although he spent hour upon hour perfecting his trumpet style each day, he also found time to become an expert chess player. His nickname was "Sweet Clifford." You'll understand why if you see the only surviving video of him, a kinescope of an old Soupy Sales television program in which he smiles graciously at Sales's clowning. You can also hear the sweetness in his voice when he speaks into the microphone at the end of a live performance that is available on a Columbia CD, *The Beginning and the End*. After thanking the appreciative audience, he says shyly but ingenuously, "You make me feel . . . so wonderful." The album Brown made of ballads with string accompaniment in 1955 still gets regular airplay, even on stations that seldom feature jazz. My trumpet teacher Eddie Allen says that he once spent three weeks devoting most of his daily practice sessions to re-creating the first three notes of Brown's solo on "Laura" on the album with strings. To this day, many trumpeters still name Brownie as their favorite.

Booker Little's story may be more tragic if only because he was

even younger when he died. In 1961, at age twenty-three, he suc-
cumbed to uremia, a species of kidney failure that channels toxins
into the blood. Max Roach, who co-led the group with Brown at the
end of his life, was devastated by the loss of Clifford. He says that
when he heard the news he took two bottles of cognac to his hotel
room and remained there for several days. Roach soon re-formed his
quintet with Kenny Dorham on trumpet, but by 1958 he had hired
the twenty-year-old Little. The difference between the quintet with
Dorham and the one with Little is striking. While the Dorham
band has the same peppery, gregarious sound as the old Clifford
Brown/Max Roach Quintet, the band with Little is more pensive, occasionally even solemn in its tonalities. Barely out of his teens, Little
was providing the band with his extremely personal arrangements as
well as his contemplative trumpet solos. He would go on to write
arrangements for the large ensemble on John Coltrane's *Africa/Brass*
LP, and he would record memorably with Eric Dolphy just a few
months before his death. Uremia is hereditary. According to the jazz
scholar and ethnomusicologist Paul Berliner, who has begun a biography of Little, the trumpeter knew what he was up against several
years before his death, and he probably knew that he was dying at
least a few months before the end. And yet many of those closest to
him were unaware that he had a life-threatening disease. Booker devoted himself to writing and playing and left little time for self-pity.[15]

Another heartbreaking accident took the life of Lee Morgan when
he was thirty-one. Much of his life was self-destructive. A child
prodigy, he had begun playing professionally at age seventeen. He
played with Dizzy Gillespie's big band and with Art Blakey and the
Jazz Messengers. But in 1961, when his heroin habit began to affect
his behavior and his playing, Blakey had to fire him. Although he
continued to work fairly regularly throughout the 1960s, Morgan
never really kicked the habit until about 1971, when he was struck in
the mouth with a large metal pipe wielded by an unpaid drug dealer

or a jealous husband, depending on which rumors are true. Lee's teeth were so loose that he had to wear braces and wires to keep them from falling out. In heroic fashion, he continued playing in spite of incredible pain.[16]

Even when he was most addicted to drugs, Morgan was able to make some good money in 1963 when his *Sidewinder* LP was the biggest hit ever for Blue Note records. He was extremely well liked and respected by his fellow musicians. Even before his *Sidewinder* success, he was always generous with friends who needed a little financial help.

By the early 1970s, Morgan was turning his life around. He had kicked the heroin habit and was in the process of giving up the methadone that many addicts take to avoid the agonies of withdrawal. He even quit smoking. Part of his self-renewal came from the woman he was seeing at the time, Judith Johnson.[17] She was clearly the inspirational soul he needed. Unfortunately, he had to contend with a woman named Helen More, with whom he had been living long enough for her to be listed as his wife in press reports.[18] One night he was performing at a club called Slug's in New York's East Village. While the band was on a break, More came to the club and began arguing with Morgan. Then she pulled out a gun. Earlier the couple had bought the pistol for protection, but they had agreed that Morgan would always hold the bullets. More somehow got her hands on the bullets. She shot Morgan, and he died shortly afterward.

I should also mention a group of brilliant jazz trumpeters who lived longer than Bolden et al., but who still didn't make it to age fifty. The clean-living, much-beloved Blue Mitchell died of cancer at age forty-nine. Woody Shaw, who may be the most important jazz trumpeter after Miles Davis, fell in front of a New York subway train in 1989. One of his arms was amputated, and he passed away a few weeks later at age forty-five. Kenny Dorham died in 1972 at age forty-eight after years of suffering from high blood pressure and kidney disease.

Chet Baker somehow survived until he was fifty-eight in spite of a voracious appetite for illegal drugs. During the last decades of his life, Baker insisted on being paid in cash so that he could score drugs as soon as possible. According to his biographer, James Gavin, Baker regularly injected himself in his jugular vein. He died mysteriously in Amsterdam in 1988, when he either fell or was pushed from a hotel window.[19]

SURVIVORS

But there is another story of the brilliant players who were not brought down by murder, racism, disease, or the jazz life. Dizzy Gillespie (figure 26) is an excellent place to begin. Never interested in drugs or excessive drinking, he tried to convince Charlie Parker, whom he called "the other half of my heartbeat," to give up drugs. Parker didn't listen. Gillespie, however, lived long enough to be feted at the White House in 1978. In what may have been one of Jimmy Carter's finest moments as president, he invited a large group of jazz artists to perform there. He even included the pianist Cecil Taylor, who has played a relentlessly difficult music throughout his career. Charles Mingus, who was dying from ALS and confined to a wheel-chair at the time, was photographed weeping as he was embraced by the president. In his public remarks, unlike any president before him, Carter attributed his nation's neglect of its greatest native art form to racism. Later he joined Gillespie on the bandstand and sang a note-perfect version of "Salt Peanuts" with Dizzy's band. After the performance, Gillespie asked, "Mr. President, when are you going on the road with us?" Carter laughingly replied, "After this, I may have to." Gillespie died of pancreatic cancer in 1993 at seventy-five.

Of course, the careers of Louis Armstrong and Roy Eldridge also spanned several glorious decades. So did (and have) those of Clark Terry, Harry Sweets Edison, Henry Red Allen, Buck Clayton, Rex Stewart, Thad Jones, Donald Byrd, Freddie Hubbard, Art Farmer, Joe Wilder, Charlie Shavers, Eddie Henderson, Cootie Williams, Howard McGhee, Snooky Young, Clora Bryant, Ray Nance, Bobby Shew, Ruby Braff, Bill Dixon, Kenny Wheeler, Maynard Ferguson, Charles Tolliver, Cecil Bridgewater, Johnny Coles, Valaida Snow, Bobby Hackett, Marcus Belgrave, Lew Soloff, Marvin Stamm, Jimmy Owens, Claudio Roditi, Enrico Rava, Max Kaminsky, Bill Coleman, Jonah Jones, Jack Sheldon, Arturo Sandoval, Billy Butterfield, Wild Bill Davidson, and Digby Fairweather, to name a few. These players all stand as inspirations to anyone who has ever tried to master the demon trumpet.

There are a handful of trumpeters who may be even more inspirational. Tom Harrell is an extremely talented musician and improviser who has suffered from schizophrenia throughout his adult life. With heavy medication he has been able to maintain his high level of performance. But the side effects of the drugs have made him a ghostly presence on the bandstand. When not playing, he takes on a stiffly frozen posture, staring out into empty space, his arms pasted against his sides.

Doc Cheatham began a solo career late in life and was playing beautifully at age ninety. He was even able to get a few spikes into the upper register at an age when virtually no other trumpeter is able to maintain such mastery over the instrument. One explanation for his longevity is that he spent the greater part of his life as a section player rather than a soloist. In the early 1920s, Cheatham played with blues singers and vaudeville bands. He played lead trumpet with Cab Calloway's big band in the 1930s and then went on to decades of obscurity performing with Latin bands, Dixieland ensembles, and whatever other work he could find. Standing next to Lester Young, Roy Eldridge, Ben Webster, Coleman Hawkins, Vic Dickenson, and Gerry Mulligan, he was the only horn man who did not solo when Billie Holiday sang "Fine and Mellow" in the great 1957 television program *The Sound of Jazz*. Cheatham began a solo career in the 1970s and continued to make it seem very easy during a long series of club dates and recordings. On his last album, he showed that he could keep up with the young lion Nicholas Payton. He died of a stroke just a few days shy of his ninety-second birthday.

How do they do it? How does a musician master an instrument as demanding as the trumpet? Doc Cheatham said he could maintain his control at an advanced age because he never drank. Others talk about proper breathing and contraptions that allow them to put less pressure on the mouthpiece when they're practicing. Some swear by the art of playing as quietly as possible during practice sessions. Clark Terry, who has been making memorable recordings for at least sixty years, attributes it all to lip buzzing. According to Don Sickler, an important trumpeter, arranger, and jazz entrepreneur with whom I have been fortunate to take a few lessons, Terry could "play" the difficult études of Herbert Clarke simply by buzzing his lips. Late in life, after a long spell when his doctors told him he was too sick to play, Terry was able to jump right back into a regular performance schedule because he had been practicing daily only by buzzing.

Outside of jazz, some famous soloists have been legendary for obsessive practice regimes that give them astounding abilities. The Mexican virtuoso Rafael Méndez (1906–81) started out as a ten-year-old soloist in his father's band. He allegedly became the favorite trumpeter of the Mexican guerrilla leader Pancho Villa. According to legend, Villa was so taken with the young Méndez's ability that he drafted the child into his army band, effectively holding him prisoner. At the time, Méndez's father could not afford to buy him a new trumpet, so the boy made do with an old horn held together with nothing but wax. He was scared to death one day when the notorious bandit made him play under a hot sun. Young Méndez was certain that Villa would kill him when the wax melted and his trumpet fell apart. Villa, however, took the boy out and bought him a new horn. He sent him back home to his family a few months later. Méndez eventually went to Hollywood, where he appeared in a few MGM films of the late 1940s and 1950s, including one with an especially appropriate title, *For Whom the Bulls Toil* (1953). He subsequently toured the world as a soloist and performed regularly on television variety shows. He flaunted his amazingly clear articulation of rapid-fire notes throughout the upper ranges of his instrument, often pointing his shining trumpet skyward as he soloed. When he was not on the road, he spent virtually all of his waking hours practicing. His wife told interviewers that she would bring him a sandwich during his nonstop days of practice, and that he would continue to practice as he chewed.

Another trumpeter with a physician's nickname may live as long as Doc Cheatham and still play at the same high level. Doc Severinsen is now in his seventies and still commands the upper register with authority. Don Sickler tells of being an impressionable young musician and seizing an opportunity to meet Severinsen at the airport when he was arriving for a performance. Severinsen led the big band that played every weeknight behind Johnny Carson on *The Tonight Show* from 1967 until Carson's retirement in 1992. Before then, he had established himself as a reliable studio musician and a high-note specialist. Sickler says that when he met Severinsen at the airport, he eagerly reached down to pick up his suitcase but went flying over the top. The bag was so heavy he could barely move it. Severinsen regularly worked out with dumbbells to increase his strength and breath control. As Sickler discovered, he took his dumbbells with him on the road. Although Severinsen is short and slender, Sickler has said that the trumpeter's body would double in size when he took a deep breath.

Of all the high-note specialists, Maynard Ferguson (1928–2006) is

17. Conn Wonder B-flat cornet, dated 1888 (bottom), with Bach Stradivarius trumpet, circa 2004. (*Author's collection. Photograph by the author*)

18. Ingrid Jensen. (*Photograph by Peter Nimsky*)

19. Louis Armstrong in the 1930s. (*Jerry Ohlinger's Movie Material Store*)

20. Louis Armstrong (standing) with King Oliver, circa 1923. (*Courtesy William Ransom Hogan Jazz Archive, Tulane University*)

21. Lil Hardin with Louis Armstrong and his Hot Five. (*Courtesy William Ransom Hogan Jazz Archive, Tulane University*)

22. Sammy Davis Jr. with Louis Armstrong in *A Man Called Adam* (1966). (*Trace-Mark Productions and Embassy Pictures. Jerry Ohlinger's Movie Material Store*)

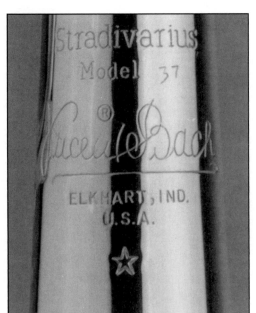

23. The bell of a new Bach Stradivarius trumpet. (*Courtesy Conn-Selmer, Inc.*)

24. David Monette with Wynton Marsalis and Tami Dean.
(*Courtesy David G. Monette Corporation*)

25. Art Farmer late in life with one of David Monette's flumpets. (*Courtesy of Ydo Sol*)

26. Dizzy Gillespie, the bell of his horn pointed ever skyward.
(*Jerry Ohlinger's Movie Material Store*)

27. The young Miles Davis.
(*Jerry Ohlinger's Movie Material Store*)

28. The older Miles Davis.
(*Jerry Ohlinger's Movie Material Store*)

29. Zampanò (Anthony Quinn) and Gelsomina (Giulietta Masina) in *La Strada*. (*Ponti–De Laurentiis Cinematografica. Jerry Ohlinger's Movie Material Store*)

30. The Trumpet Geek.
(*Drawing by Chris Kemp*)

the most heroic. He may be best known for his recording of "Gonna Fly Now," the theme from the 1976 film *Rocky*. Although Ferguson had no use for the song when he first recorded it, "Gonna Fly Now" seems to be as much about Ferguson's stratospheric playing as it is about the achievements of Rocky Balboa. Ferguson goes well beyond the many trumpeters who manage to hit a high note or two at the climax of a solo. He would camp out in the upper register, improvising elegantly structured solos in the upper reaches without running out of steam. And he could do it while still playing in tune. The classical virtuoso Adolph "Bud" Herseth, who was the principal trumpet player with the Chicago Symphony for more than fifty years, was asked to name the man he considered to be the greatest living trumpet player. When Herseth said Maynard Ferguson, the interviewer rephrased the question. He was *not* asking about Herseth's pick for the best *jazz* trumpeter; he wanted his choice for the best trumpeter period. Herseth still picked Ferguson, praising his complete control over the upper register.

When Ferguson was asked about his technique, he usually said it all was about breathing. Many trumpeters think of their upper body as a glass that must be filled with water. When they take a breath, they visualize the torso filling with air from the bottom up just like the glass when water is poured in. First the stomach swells, then the chest. Ferguson, however, visualized filling pockets of his body well below the torso, seeking out previously unexplored areas as reservoirs of air. Like the trumpeter who dials in the "right" position on his perfectly symmetrical mouthpiece, Ferguson's visualization had more to do with what works psychologically than physiologically. But it most definitely worked for him.

Ferguson also said the structure of his mouth was unique. Trumpet pitch may be related to the placement of the tongue in the mouth—the higher the tongue, the higher the pitch. Because the roof of Ferguson's mouth was unusually high, it gave him more room to raise his tongue. And like Jon Faddis, Ferguson was born with a gap between his teeth. When an orthodontist fixed his teeth, however, Ferguson could still play the high notes. I find it even more astounding that when Dave Monette handed Ferguson one of his horns and mouthpieces a few years before his death, the trumpeter went right out on stage and started playing. Unlike the vast majority of trumpeters, Ferguson did not worry about whether a new piece of equipment was right for him.[20] Like Louis Armstrong, Ferguson was born with the perfect body for playing the trumpet—big chested and stocky. I like that idea because it gives me an excuse for not being able to play more than a few notes in the upper register without fainting. I simply don't have the body for it. It's not my fault.

Indeed, the trumpet world includes many freaks of nature. Others may practice longer and more diligently, but they will never be able to play as high or with the same big sound that the "natural" players have. One day I was sampling the merchandise at Dillon's, the store that specializes in used trumpets, when a Spanish-speaking family walked in. The father was picking out a trumpet for a son who looked to be about fourteen. A younger son, no more than nine, was also trying out the horns. At one point, the younger boy began playing incredibly high notes, well above high C. I looked over at him and said, "How do you do that?" He looked at me blankly. His father then said, "He doesn't speak English." So I asked the father how the boy could climb so high into the upper register. "I taught him," he said. When I asked him what the secret was, he just smiled. My guess is that the secret is the physical equipment the boy was born with. He was barrel chested, large headed, and stout.

So was Cat Anderson, who played in the Duke Ellington orchestra for several decades and was the band's screech specialist. Ellington often ended a number with Anderson's piercing assaults on the top register. When the tune was over, Duke would tell the audience that the last screeching note was "a high C above Hyannis Port." In addition to a broad physique, Anderson had an exceptionally wide jaw. The notion that Anderson simply had the body for the high notes did not stop experienced trumpet players who attended Ellington concerts from coming backstage after a show hoping to learn how Anderson did it. When asked to show his mouthpiece, Anderson would reach into his pocket and hold out a conventional mouthpiece, not unlike the Bach 7C with which most schoolchildren begin. That he was able to scale the heights without special equipment seemed impossible to the experts. It probably was impossible.

The issue of mouthpieces is central to the art of the trumpet player. With a million different possibilities, trumpeters must find the right combinations of depth, width, length, gradation, and the rest. Even today trumpet players will purchase a preferred model and then make their own modifications, usually reaming out the bore to make it wider and to give their horns a darker, bigger sound. Eddie Allen told me about his youthful experimentations with mouthpieces. He started out with an exceptionally wide bore to get that fat sound so many jazz musicians have mastered. He called his mouthpiece "a cannon." Later, however, when he was asked to play lead trumpet, he bought "a peashooter," a mouthpiece with a very shallow cup and a narrow bore. Most mouthpiece manufacturers produce a model like this for lead trumpeters who need to play comfortably in the ether above high C. Clark Terry, who sat next to Cat Anderson in the Ellington trumpet section for most of the 1950s, helped solve the mystery of how Cat could hit the high notes with an ordinary mouthpiece. He has said that the mouthpiece Anderson actually used was a piece of metal with a dent and a pinprick.

LEARNING FROM THE MASTERS

But these are only anecdotes. They don't help an amateur or a comeback player like me to become a better trumpeter. For a more thorough explanation of what it takes, I paid a visit to Indiana University's School of Music. There I looked up William Adam, for several decades the esteemed and beloved teacher of trumpeters. His students occupy principal chairs in numerous orchestras and big bands throughout the world. We spoke extensively about issues that I never thought would be important to a trumpeter. For example, is the speed of sound relevant to what we do? Since it takes longer for a tuba player to send his breath through yards of brass tubing, does he have to start his lips vibrating before the trumpeter, whose breath must traverse a much shorter distance? (The answer appears to be no. It's all about a vibrating column of air and not about the distance the air must travel.) Professor Adam also spoke about his visit to the university's anatomy department, where he looked closely at preserved human lungs and contemplated the best way to make the organs do their work. He conferred with psychologists about gestalt psychology and how each note—no matter how short and insignificant—can play a crucial role within a holistic phenomenon in which the player, the music, and the instrument become one. Adam even visited colleagues in the physics department to discuss how trumpeters can make the laws of physics their allies and not their enemies. At the end of a long and far-ranging discussion, I asked Adam what he had learned from decades of research on every aspect of the trumpeter's work. His answer was, "You must put yourself inside the music."

Adam's response reminded me of the joke about the king and the royal economists. In order to understand his country's economy, the king asked his economists to tutor him on the laws of finance. Every time they appeared before him with their lessons, he was dissatisfied. Either he had no time for a long discussion or he was not bright enough to grasp all of their explanations. As he continued to ask for more concise accounts, the economists came in with shorter and shorter presentations. Finally, the king demanded that they boil all of economic theory down to a single sentence. After several days of heated debate, the economists agreed on the sentence: "There is no such thing as a free lunch." After four years of hard labor with the mouthpiece and the metal tubes of my trumpet, and after two years of playing with various ensembles, I think I know what Adam means. I also think I understand why there are no free lunches.

There is, however, the issue of execution. It's very different from musical metaphysics and the theories of economics. For execution, I decided to take a few lessons with Laurie Frink, one of the premier trumpet teachers in New York City. Frink is widely known as the teacher professional trumpeters consult when they are having difficulty. When Freddie Hubbard, one of the greatest of them all, severely injured himself in a trumpet battle with Jon Faddis, he lost almost all of his ability to play in the upper register. After a glorious career as a brilliant improviser and technician, he spent several years playing at the level of a near novice. Whenever I heard trumpeters talk about Hubbard's difficulties, sooner or later almost all of them would say something like, "If he were to go see Laurie, she could fix it."

Although she tours occasionally with the first-rate jazz orchestra led by Maria Schneider, Frink spends most of her time with students in her apartment on the Upper West Side of Manhattan. She had studied with Carmine Caruso, the teacher of many promising young trumpeters in the 1970s and 1980s. Caruso wrote a book titled *Trumpet Calisthenics*, a good description of the kind of exercises he assigned his students. At least in the early stages of a trumpeter's progress, Caruso was unconcerned with how beautiful the trumpeter sounds. He was much more concerned with exercises that build flexibility, endurance, and range. For years Frink would sit in on Caruso's lessons with other trumpeters, learning exactly how his method could work with different players with different needs. She has effectively picked up where Caruso left off.

Somehow the acoustics in Frink's building allow for nonstop

noise throughout the day without complaints from neighbors. I came to my first lesson with two carefully prepared "Characteristic Studies" from the back pages of the Arban book, but I never played them. Instead, Laurie began by asking me to play a chromatic scale from middle C up two octaves to high C. That was all she needed to hear. She went right to work teaching me how to buzz my lips without the horn. (I knew about Clark Terry's devotion to lip buzzing, but never having really tried it, I was intrigued.) Laurie told me to begin each of my practice sessions trying to hit a few pitches with just my buzzing lips. Then I was to play the same pitches with just the mouthpiece. Only after the lip and mouthpiece exercises could I play the entire trumpet. But in these early stages, it wasn't just about pitches; it was about bending pitches. The idea was to hit a note, lip it down a half step, and then slowly lip it back to the original pitch, which always sounds clearer and more in tune. Needless to say, no one listening to these exercises will find them pretty. The idea behind these and the many other exercises in the Caruso/Frink tradition is to gain control over the most fundamental aspects of making the lips work within the mouthpiece. After that, the trumpeter can begin finding notes inside the mouthpiece. Ultimately, after realizing how close the notes are within the mouthpiece, the player becomes more confident moving among the upper, middle, and lower registers.

Following Caruso, Frink also asks students to make quick jumps from the lower to the upper register. She tells students not to be discouraged when they can't hit a high note or make a big jump between registers. "Your body has to learn how to do it," she told me. "You can't intellectualize your way to better playing. What were you thinking when you learned how to ride a bicycle, when your parent was no longer holding you up, or when you no longer needed the training wheels? It was not in your mind. It was in your body."

After a few lessons, I thought I understood the Frink method. But when I asked her to summarize what she considered to be the secret of good trumpet playing, she said, "Put the little end into your mouth, not the big end." Her point was that there is no one secret because every individual has a different set of issues when he or she encounters the trumpet. She thinks that one of her strengths as a teacher is the ability to watch closely and determine what a player is doing right or wrong. With me, she went right to work on buzzing lips and bending pitches because my breathing seemed to be all right and because I seemed to have a positive attitude about playing. Because attitude is so important, Frink often has to play shrink with her students, searching for ways to make them think differently about the horn. Sometimes she actually witnesses a breakthrough that is entirely accidental. One student could not play more than a few notes in the middle register, no matter how many times she told him how to move his lips to slur from one note to another. Then, one day, she accidentally used the word "trill" when she meant to say "slur." That did it. The student left her studio with two and a half octaves of notes at his disposal. Somehow the word "trill" set off a chain of connections that changed his approach to playing.

Laurie says that regular practice does not build muscles and endurance so much as it builds refinement. Early on, players cannot make the horn sound right as they try different exercises. "No one wants to sound ugly," she say, "even when they're alone." People back off from playing ugly sounds, but they cannot master a note until they have first made those awkward, halting attempts at playing it. The body makes movements each time it plays a note, but those movements must be refined. Laurie offered another metaphor: the act of bringing down a sledgehammer to break a big rock is very similar to what jewelers do when they use a special tool to cut a diamond. The difference is that one movement is more refined than the other.

Thanks to Laurie, Eddie Allen, and Don Sickler, I no longer play with a sledgehammer. And I realize that I moved on from that stage simply by letting my body make the movements and not by trying to think it through the way I do as when, well, as when I'm writing this book. Little by little my body is learning, and little by little I'm reaching out for that little jeweler's tool. I still have a long way to go, and it will not be easy. It's also sobering to think of Bix Beiderbecke, Clifford Brown, Fats Navarro, and all the other geniuses who paid so high a price to get to that special little hammer and to play with brilliance and finesse.

chapter 6

Miles Runs the Voodoo Down

t the beginning of the twenty-first century, the image of Miles Davis has taken on a life of its own. Dark glasses covering his eyes, Davis's face appears in a TV commercial for Mercedes-Benz that had wide distribution in the summer of 2001. An announcer asks, "If you were loading the ark today, what would you bring?" We see animals walk up the plank two by two along with a line of people carrying works of art such as Van Gogh's *Sunflowers*, Michelangelo's *David*, and the piano scores of Bach and Mozart. They also carry items with less cultural cachet such as an Apple computer and a refrigerator full of Häagen-Dazs ice cream. As the camera cuts from one item to another, we see a pair of hands carrying a stack of LPs with Miles Davis's *Birth of the Cool* prominently displayed on top. The commercial ends as two silver E-Class Mercedeses drive up the plank and the rain begins.

Even before Ken Burns, jazz was well on its way to being considered high art. This was especially true with older jazz, including the *Birth of the Cool* sessions, recorded at midcentury. At Lincoln Center, a ticket to a jazz show now costs as much as a ticket to the opera.

Perhaps the stack of LPs in the Mercedes commercial is meant to be associated with the ice cream and the computer, but I doubt it. The camera deliberately focuses tightly on the LPs, *not* on the person carrying them, just as the camera had gone in tight to show the names of Bach and Mozart on the books of scores. Jazz, especially when it's packaged with the ultracool image of Miles Davis, can symbolize affluence and elegance in the same way as Michelangelo's *David*, Van Gogh's *Sunflowers*, and the music of Mozart. And the old photograph of Miles Davis makes him the only black person whose work is being carried onto the ark. In a commercial for a product aimed squarely at upper-middle-class Americans, the "jazzness," the coolness, and the masculine mystique of Miles Davis have made him a valuable icon for a company trying to sell status symbols.

There was, however, no financial incentive when *Birth of the Cool* was honored in an animated television series. In an episode of *The Simpsons* broadcast in 2003, Homer learns that *Birth of the Cool* is the favorite record of Lisa, the baritone-saxophone-playing, jazz-loving second-grader who is by far the smartest person in the Simpson household if not in the entire town of Springfield. We even hear a few seconds of Miles Davis's music as Homer takes the unusual step of trying to make peace with his daughter.

While *The Simpsons* has made Davis the favorite of an extremely bright and ethical eight-year-old, and Mercedes-Benz has made him the peer of Mozart and Michelangelo, the cable channel VH1 has placed him in the august company of the Beatles, Bob Dylan, and the Beach Boys. In the early 1990s, the pop culture specialists at VH1 made up their list of the "100 Greatest Artists of Rock 'n' Roll." In that list, Miles Davis is ranked number 39, between Elvis Costello (38) and Michael Jackson (40). Then, in another of VH1's blandly provocative lists, Miles Davis is represented by not one but two items among the "100 Greatest Albums of Rock 'n' Roll": *Bitches Brew* comes in at 64, and *Kind of Blue* is 66.

No other figure from popular culture is in the Mercedes-Benz ad, and unless you think that Steely Dan, Stevie Wonder, and Joni Mitchell play jazz, no other jazz artist appears on either of VH1's rock 'n' roll lists. Just as Davis becomes the peer of great dead white males in the Mercedes-Benz ad, he is in the same league with Janis Joplin, Kurt Cobain, and Crosby, Stills & Nash, all of whom he *outranks* in the VH1 list of the greatest artists. As the twenty-first century picks up steam, it's easier than ever to hear Davis's music. Columbia Records has released a stack of lavishly produced boxes of his recordings on compact disc as well as on high-priced, vinyl LPs for purists, all of it with new, previously unreleased material. As Will Friedwald might put it, when you buy these boxes you're buying furniture, not music. Along with multiple biographies and reminiscences, there are three books of critical essays about Davis, two books devoted entirely to the *Kind of Blue* LP, and two romans à clef: the main characters in Herbert Simmons's *Man Walking on Eggshells* (1962) and Walter Ellis's *Prince of Darkness* (1998) do not bear Davis's name, but they are closely modeled on him.

If few other artists have become so ingrained in the popular imagination, it may be because Davis worked very hard at supervising how people saw him. Even late in his life, when his zeal to exert exclusive control over his image had waned slightly, he complained bitterly about a photo that appeared on the back of the first printing of his autobiography. He said he was smiling too broadly. Davis was as devoted to controlling how people perceived him as he was to how people heard him.

AFTER NEW ORLEANS

The jazz life was not always so easy to manage. The first trumpeters who played jazz or something like it were primarily interested in making a living. And they were hoping to attract the black audiences that were most likely to appreciate their music. But without knowing that they were creating anything revolutionary, Buddy Bolden and his peers were reformulating the vernacular music of black America into a highly malleable art form. Playing the blues and improvising solos, they created jazz. And by bringing the trumpet up front to replace the violin, they were able to reach an audience outside the black community. When Bolden's band gave concerts in Johnson Park, he would lift his cornet and "call his children home." The children who came running were not only black. White players soon figured out what Bolden was doing, and white audiences began listening seriously to black music, perhaps for the first time. As the poet/critic/playwright Amiri Baraka has written, in the early years of the twentieth century, jazz inspired some whites finally to regard black Americans as human beings.[1]

During slavery, music was an essential part of life on the plantation. Slave owners believed that a singing slave was a happy slave, and in a sense they were right. While slaves in the field sang spirituals and chants, the slaves in the house played polite dance music, usually with string instruments. Buddy Bolden, Louis Armstrong, Freddie Keppard, and King Oliver were liberated men not afraid to inject the old styles of polite music with highly impolite eruptions of the blues and ragtime. They would make their horns growl like wild animals or purr like lovers in bed. If these men had tried to express their masculinity and their sexuality in just about any other fashion, they would have been lynched. Don't forget that a teenage Emmett Till was killed by white racists in Mississippi after he whistled at a white women. And that was in 1955.

We can learn a lot by comparing the recordings of the white Bix Beiderbecke to those of his contemporary Louis Armstrong. As a young man growing up in Davenport, Iowa, Beiderbecke definitely had his problems, and he was openly rebelling against his Victorian, repressed family. But he did not have to stand up to people who said that he was not a man. Much was at stake for Bix, but not his man-hood. There was no compelling reason for him to play at top volume or to sing the dirty blues. This may explain why he seldom bothered hitting the high notes and why there was no swagger in his playing.

In New Orleans, when jazz was being born, black men swaggered with their trumpets in parks, dance halls, and parades. By the 1920s, while Armstrong was remaking the Fletcher Henderson band and while Bubber Miley was defining the sound of the Ellington orches-tra, trumpets began driving the big bands throughout the Swing Era. In the 1940s, beboppers like Dizzy Gillespie, Fats Navarro, and Fred-die Webster took the trumpet to the next level, battling in late-night jam sessions as robustly competitive as in New Orleans when jazz was being born. But if the Crescent City horn men were looking for work and hoping to outplay their peers, the boppers knew that they were creating art.

By developing a more challenging music, however, the boppers left the public behind. Jazz critics embraced bebop as the future of jazz, a natural outgrowth of all that was good in the music of the 1920s and 1930s. Even though they regarded Armstrong as something of an embarrassment, modernist trumpeters like Gillespie also knew that they were simply refining a style that came directly from Armstrong. But the popular audience had little use for bop, not least because the musicians prided themselves on *not* being entertainers, refusing to engage in the ingratiating theatrics of people like Armstrong. The most common complaint about bop was that you couldn't dance to it. Gillespie's response was always, "*You* can't dance to it." The bop-pers would dress like bankers, wear deadpan expressions, and then play an experimental music with strange harmonies and idiosyncratic rhythms. Armstrong joined Cab Calloway in referring to bop as "Chi-nese music" or even crazy music. Always attentive to the ironies of their situation, boppers and their hipster fans began using "crazy" as a term of praise. "Crazy, man!"

Those who were deeply invested in New Orleans jazz and big-band swing regarded bebop as a dead end. If bop was jazz and the audience for jazz was therefore drying up, then maybe it was time to stop calling it jazz. In 1949, when it was more of a trade journal than a guide to what's new in the music, *Down Beat* magazine ran a contest to find a name for a music that could include swing and some of its aftermath but not bebop. The winning entry was "crewcut music," contrasting the youthful, hip hairstyle of an artist like Stan Kenton to the mop-haired virtuosi of classical or "longhair" music. Needless to say, crewcut music did not catch on.

For many young black musicians, however, bebop was thrilling. In the first sentences of his autobiography, Miles Davis describes the first time he heard Dizzy Gillespie and Charlie Parker in person. It was 1944, and Bird and Diz were playing in St. Louis as members of Billy Eckstine's big band. Davis said that hearing that band was "the greatest feeling I ever had in my life—with my clothes on."[2] He may have been responding to the sensual appeal of Eckstine, one of the most beautiful men ever to sing jazz. He also may have been responding to the hypermasculine chops of Gillespie.

Improvising jazzmen learn a series of musical and physical gestures that connote masculinity. Body language can be as important as hitting the high notes. Gillespie used to make pelvic thrusts while conducting his own big band in the late 1940s. But he could also hit a high note and then glissando dramatically into a much higher one. Once the jazz musician learns these gestures of masculinity, he can embrace them unproblematically or have fun with them. To use a term from the African American vernacular, jazz artists can signify on the trumpet's masculine side. Later in his career, Gillespie could play high, fast, and loud solos whenever he wished. But when young trumpet turks challenged him in solo duels, he responded to their assaults on the upper register with short, quiet, often humorous phrases, thus setting himself apart from the pretensions of the challenger and winning a laugh in the process. Affecting a look of well-earned insouciance, Gillespie would toy with the challenger as well as his own role as the patriarch of the jazz trumpet. Miles Davis (figure 27) surely developed the most flamboyant revision of the trumpet as masculine signifier by seeming to reject the heights of jazz virtuosity, preferring instead to strive for a broad range of emotional expression. When he first heard Eckstine's band, Miles Davis had just graduated from high school in East St. Louis, Illinois, where his father was a successful dentist and a landowner who owned a 160-acre farm where he raised horses. The family lived in a predominantly white neighborhood, but they were still part of black culture, even if it bore little resemblance to the black New Orleans that produced Louis Armstrong and Buddy Bolden. For one thing, Davis was not raised in the Sanctified Church. Although young Miles took most of his early education in public schools, he attended a Catholic school for a few years. Later in life, in a passage in his autobiography, he said that the religion that most interested him was Islam. Otherwise, he seems to have picked up his talent for the blues and African American rhythms outside the church.

Recognizing that his son also had real talent with "legitimate" music, the older Davis paid Joseph Gustat, the principal trumpeter with the St. Louis Symphony, to give lessons to the boy. Miles was already playing with local jazz bands when he heard Eckstine, but his father sent him to New York to continue his classical training at Juilliard. There he took lessons with William Vacchiano, the first-chair trumpeter with the New York Philharmonic. When Davis auditioned for the Juilliard faculty, he played one of the more difficult études that Herbert L. Clarke composed in the early years of the century.

According to jazz myth, Davis blew off Juilliard as soon as he arrived in Manhattan and spent all of his time with the boppers on Fifty-second Street or in Harlem. He was indeed hanging with jazz artists almost from the moment he arrived, but he attended classes at

Juilliard for an entire year, earning a B average in his first semester. He did not do so well in the spring semester, but he took courses during the summer in hopes of catching up. Even after leaving Juilliard and plunging into the hothouse conservatory of the boppers, Davis remained attentive to classical music. He has said that he carried Stravinsky scores in his pockets while he was playing with Charlie Parker.

If the young Miles seemed to reject a large share of jazz virtuosity, he made his peace early with conservatory training. He may be the first great classically trained trumpet player to successfully apply his lessons to the art of jazz. In fact, he was among the first trumpeters to accept a new pedagogy. As the ethnomusicologist and jazz scholar Paul Berliner has pointed out, the first generations of jazz trumpeters took few formal lessons, maybe in grade school. Most just listened and were informally trained by other musicians. Certainly they never went to the conservatory. Even a white player from the earliest generations like Bix Beiderbecke never studied music after secondary school. Some of the early black players scorned the conservatory teachers, insisting that they tried to make their students "sound white." After the ascendancy of Miles Davis, however, many black artists looked with less suspicion on the conservatory. Lee Morgan, Clifford Brown, and Booker Little all paid careful attention to what their classically trained teachers were telling them.[3] Dizzy Gillespie and a few older jazz artists knew their music theory, but their trumpet playing developed before they began experimenting with altered chords. When a younger player like Freddie Hubbard runs through the changes in his solos, you can hear a command of music theory as he negotiates the passing tones, suspended chords, and diminished ninths.

Jazz history continued, of course, even if the newer jazz never found much of an audience in the 1940s. After World War II, the GIs came home, women left their factory jobs, and people spent more time raising children than dancing to the big bands. The suburbs were born. Charismatic vocalists like Frank Sinatra and Peggy Lee, who had begun their careers with the big bands, built up enough star power to eclipse the instrumentalists, even the show-off trumpet players.

For me, the dramatic rise of singers over players is epitomized in the story of Louis Prima and Keely Smith. Raised in New Orleans and clearly inspired by Louis Armstrong, Prima played trumpet in Dixieland groups before forming his own big band during the Swing Era. By the end of the 1940s, most of the big bands were breaking up. Kay Kyser, he of the wildly successful radio program *The Kollege of Musical Knowledge* and the leader of one of the most popular bands of the day, retired in 1949. In that same year, Count Basie began leading a small group. Also in 1949, Louis Prima began recording with Keely Smith, a demure singer with Cherokee Indians among her ancestors. By the time the two were married and performing together regularly, Prima was no longer leading his own big band. Instead, he was dancing and blowing hot trumpet solos as if his only goal was to impress his beautiful brunette wife. Smith, however, steadfastly deadpanned her way through the performances, occasionally pausing to roll her eyes at the hyperingratiating Prima. Louis and Keely eventually took their act to Las Vegas, where it must have inspired Sonny and Cher, another duo with an overachieving Italian American and a beautiful, affectless singer whose mother was Cherokee. Sonny and Cher were Louis and Keely without the trumpet.

COOLING OFF THE BOP

The young Miles Davis was too busy with the music to notice that the trumpet was in danger of losing its cultural cachet. He had already recorded with Parker and Gillespie in 1945. But listen to how delicately he solos in the company of the great boppers. In a session with

Parker a few years later in 1947, Davis follows Bird's two astounding choruses on "Embraceable You" with one muted chorus of thoughtful, softly expressive improvisation that almost suggests Beiderbecke. Certainly the Miles of the 1940s had none of the quicksilver technique you can hear in Diz and Bird's solos at this time. Miles realized he could never play with Dizzy's speed and fire, perhaps not even with his harmonic imagination. Nevertheless, in the middle of the century Davis transformed the trumpet and American culture just as dramatically as Buddy Bolden and Louis Armstrong had at the beginning of the century.

In fact, Miles Davis changed the music more than once. In 1987, when he attended a White House event honoring Ray Charles, he showed up in a flamboyant red-and-white outfit with leather pants and silver chains, and he quickly decided that the few African Americans in the room—to honor Ray Charles, no less—were tokens. When an older, well-dressed woman asked him what he had done in order to be invited, there was a certain truth in his response: "Well, I've changed music four or five times. What have you done of any importance other than be white?"

Davis's need for change was compulsive, but for most of his career he had the talent and the imagination to deliver the goods. In 1949, less than five years after he began recording with the boppers, he invented cool jazz. Five years after that, he had a hit with "Walkin' " and became a key figure in the rise of hard bop or soul jazz. Five years later, in 1959, with the *Kind of Blue* LP, he created modal jazz. Five years after that, he dramatically deepened the expressive possibilities of the trumpet solo with his stunning album *My Funny Valentine*. And five years after that, with *Bitches Brew* becoming a huge hit, he invented jazz-rock. At each of these junctures there were others who deserve credit for their contributions, but Davis always seemed to be at the center of the transformation.

In spite of his life as a musical chameleon, Davis's legacy will always be cool jazz. He used his trumpet—as well as his image—to create a music that was as understated as it was expressive. He first realized what he could accomplish as he looked for alternatives to the high-wire acts of the beboppers. It wasn't just a question of turning away from bop virtuosity. Davis had cut his musical teeth during the Swing Era, and he had a strong affinity for the ensemble playing of the big bands. He could see that bebop, primarily a soloist's art, was running out of steam in the late 1940s. Without returning to the familiar conventions of the big bands—the shout choruses and the call-and-response dialogue between the sections—Davis remade jazz as a composer's art.

Young Miles was fond of the Claude Thornhill Big Band, especially when it played the arrangements of Gil Evans. Born in Toronto and raised in California, Evans was already arranging Charlie Parker tunes for Thornhill's big band in the mid-1940s. Adding French horns, flutes, and a tuba to the standard instrumental array, and instructing the sax and brass players to play with less vibrato, Evans created sounds that were closer to tone poems than to dance music, as much Claude Debussy as Count Basie.

In 1948, Evans was living in an apartment in midtown Manhattan that was wide-open to jazz artists, day and night. Davis was one of many who dropped in to talk about the music, play Evans's piano, or sleep on his bed. Like Davis, many of the kindred spirits who hung out at Evans's place were looking for ways to move beyond bebop or at least to make it more accessible. So much was happening in the elaborate solos of Parker and Gillespie that only the aficionados could get it. Or at least some of it. Inaccessibility was, of course, what the boppers had in mind, but Davis and Evans realized that they could slow the pace and orchestrate the harmonic ideas but still create something as elegant as bop. This new music would be more listenable, especially for the white audiences who bought the drinks and kept the jazz clubs in business. In 1948, Davis led a group of nine musicians for several nights at a New York club called the Royal Roost. They recorded a few months later. The music was subsequently collected on a Capitol LP called *Birth of the Cool*. As a twelve-inch LP and then as a CD, the music has been selling steadily for more than fifty years now, even showing up in that episode of *The Simpsons*.

Gil Evans was fourteen years older than Davis and definitely the spiritual leader of the *Birth of the Cool* nonet. Along with Gerry Mulligan and John Lewis, Evans also did most of the arranging. But the twenty-three-year-old Davis was the one who booked the band, having exploited his contacts with club owners who remembered him from his high-profile days with Charlie Parker. Thanks to Davis, a rehearsal band ended up with a public forum to present a music that foregrounded musical textures rather than the soloists. With his understated, nuanced trumpet style, and with his classical training, Davis was the practical choice for leader.

Like bebop, the cool jazz of the Miles Davis Nonet was not an instant hit. But by establishing a new, less complex direction for jazz, it gradually brought back some of the audience the boppers had driven away. And the laid-back sound of Miles's trumpet and Lee Konitz's alto sax over the warm rumble of an ensemble with a tuba and a French horn was widely imitated, especially among white musicians in California. Cool jazz and West Coast jazz soon became interchangeable terms. But no one, on either the West Coast or the East Coast, was playing quite like Miles Davis. He was making his trumpet moan, laugh, and cry. King Oliver, Bubber Miley, and other premodern trumpeters had extended the African American tradition of making an instrument sound like a human voice. But if the trumpets of Oliver and the rest suggested a joking, cursing, vulgar voice, Davis's trumpet conjured up a sensitive, plaintive, occasionally playful voice. Just as important, Davis was among first major jazz improvisers— saxophonist Lester Young was another—for whom less was more. He made silence work for him, creating spaces between his solo phrases and tightening the tension. Davis put audiences at the edges of their chairs, where they sat wondering what was coming next.

Davis went on to make some of his most memorable records with Gil Evans. With *Miles Ahead, Sketches of Spain,* and *Porgy and Bess,* all recorded between 1957 and 1961, Evans established a rich orchestral showcase for Davis's spare, evocative solos. During these same years, however, Davis was working regularly with a quintet or a sextet that included bop-inspired saxophone players whose flashy solos also set off his more economical statements. In the 1950s, he played with Sonny Stitt, Jackie McLean, and Dave Schildkraut, all devout disciples of Charlie Parker, but most prominently with John Coltrane, who was already taking Parker's innovations to the next level of intensity. This is not to say that Davis never displayed virtuosity. He was fully capable of shooting spikes into the upper register and running the changes at breakneck speed. He could play loud too. But the typical Miles Davis solo primarily communicated vulnerability, emotion, and thoughtfulness. The occasional flurries of fast runs and high notes actually served to make the rest of his solo more compelling.

Davis's affluent background surely had much to do with his style. Raised with more privilege than the vast majority of African Americans of his generation, Davis did not feel the need to present an ingratiating stage persona. His autobiography includes a photo of Armstrong, under which appears the phrase "I loved Satchmo, but I couldn't stand all that grinning he did." Older black jazz musicians such as Teddy Wilson had comported themselves in a dignified fashion, declining to smile effusively at the audience. But Davis went much farther, scowling on stage, turning away from the audience, not bothering to announce the titles of songs, and leaving the stage entirely when someone else was soloing. At Juilliard, if he learned nothing else, he learned what a serious artist should expect from his audience.

Nevertheless, he was still a black man in white America. In an event that made headlines in 1959, Davis was the featured performer at Birdland, a major jazz venue on Broadway and Fifty-second Street named after Charlie Parker. In between sets he escorted a white woman out of the club and saw her off in a taxi. He then stood outside the club to smoke a cigarette. A white policeman, who may or may not have seen Miles with the white woman, told him to move along. Miles stayed put, saying, "I work here." What happened next is open to debate, but everyone agrees that Davis and the cop were in some kind of a scuffle when a New York detective, who might have been drunk, drove by and saw a white cop with a black man on the street. The detective walked up behind Davis and struck him repeatedly on the head with his nightstick. Miles needed five stitches in his scalp. He was arrested and taken into custody, but the charges were dropped a few weeks later. For some time Davis had been training as a boxer, and he later said about his encounter with the cop, "If I had hit him, he wouldn't be here today."

MILES AND THE MOVIES, PART I

While Davis was making jazz history with Gil Evans, John Coltrane, and the elite of the jazz world, something else was happening in American music. Young people were less likely to feel that jazz artists spoke for them. From its beginnings, jazz had been denounced by America's moral guardians as the devil's music. In the 1930s and 1940s, young whites who jitterbugged to big-band swing, with its powerful African American rhythms and harmonies, were thumbing their noses at the late Victorian values of their parents. By the 1950s, there were still young people who took jazz seriously and sought out the latest thing. Dave Brubeck's *Jazz Goes to College* (1954) was marketed directly at smart young people. But for an increasing segment of teenagers in the 1950s, jazz and swing represented the obsolete, used-up music of their parents. Rock 'n' roll arrived in American culture in about 1955, when Little Richard recorded "Tutti Frutti," and Chuck Berry released "Maybellene." In 1956, Elvis Presley had his first number one hit with "Heartbreak Hotel," and Gene Vincent recorded "Be-Bop-a-Lula," a song that had nothing whatever to do with Diz and Bird. Even in the twenty-first century, pop musicians and their legions of fans are still deeply invested in the music of Presley, Berry, and Little Richard. It's as if Glenn Miller and Kay Kyser were still major figures for teenagers in the 1990s. The first rockers were right— it's here to stay.

In 1955, MGM released a film called *Blackboard Jungle*, starring Glenn Ford as a GI back from Korea who takes a job teaching high school in an impoverished New York neighborhood where he turns around the lives of rebellious, even violent teenage students. The filmmakers may have thought they were being ironic when they put a recording of "Rock Around the Clock" by the obscure rockabilly group Bill Haley and the Comets over the opening credits. The film was conceived as another postwar film about social problems. Rather than racial prejudice (*Pinky*), anti-Semitism (*Gentleman's Agreement*), or mental illness (*Snake Pit*), *Blackboard Jungle* took on juvenile delinquency. Basically the film carried the message: "Isn't it sad how these young people have lost their way? Thank goodness we have strong father figures like Glenn Ford to get them back on track." But the actors who played the students, most notably Vic Morrow with his Brandoesque contempt for bourgeois propriety, appealed to an audience that Hollywood did not even know existed. *Blackboard Jungle* turned out to be a recruiting poster for a youth movement that embraced black leather jackets, duck's ass haircuts, and contempt for authority. Even teenagers who never dreamed of gang violence thought it was cool to refer to the man at the chalkboard as "Teach." And of course they listened to rock 'n' roll. Thanks to *Blackboard Jungle*, "Rock Around the Clock" became a surprise hit. Hollywood was soon cranking out films like *Rock, Pretty Baby* and *Don't Knock the*

Rock (both 1956) that were intentionally rather than unintentionally aimed at the youth market.

In 1955 and 1956, Miles Davis was busy making the crucial move from Prestige records to Columbia. George Avakian, the fabled record producer who invented the Columbia Record Club and who recorded Louis Armstrong, Thelonious Monk, and Duke Ellington, was marshaling the machinery at Columbia to make Davis a star. Or at least a well-paid recording artist. In 1957, Davis toured Europe and came home to record *Miles Ahead*, the first of his great LPs with a large orchestra led by Gil Evans.

Also in 1957, Elvis Presley was appearing in his third film, *Jailhouse Rock*. The film begins with the hero Vince Everett (Presley) protecting the honor of a woman in a bar who is being abused by her tough guy husband. Vince impulsively teaches the husband a lesson, but he overdoes it and winds up in prison. Behind bars, he borrows a guitar and makes a recording that finds its way to the hands of a pretty young record producer named Peggy (Judy Tyler), who picks up on his star quality. As soon as he is out of jail, Peggy takes Vince to his first recording session and then brings him home to meet her college professor father. The couple arrives on a night when the professor has invited over some of his stuffy friends to listen to his record collection. They are discussing an LP by "Stubby Ritemeyer," a fictional musician probably based on the West Coast trumpeter/composer Shorty Rogers.

"I think Stubby's gone overboard with those altered chords," says one of the pompous guests. "I agree," says another. "I think Brubeck and Desmond have gone just as far with dissonance as I care to go." "Oh, nonsense," says a man. "Have you heard Lennie Tristano's latest recording? He reached outer space." A young woman adds, "Someday they'll make the cycle and go back to pure old Dixieland." A well-dressed, older woman says, "I say atonality is just a passing phase in jazz music." Turning to Presley, she asks, "What do you think, Mr. Everett?" He answers, "Lady, I don't know what the hell you're talking about," and storms out of the house.

Followed and scolded by Peggy, Vince protests that he was being forced into a corner by a stupid question from "some old broad." After Peggy tries to assure him that the woman was only trying to bring him into the conversation, Everett says he wasn't sure "that she was even talkin' English." He then kisses her forcefully. She protests, "How dare you think such cheap tactics would work with me?" Everett kisses her again and adds, "I ain't tactics, honey. That's just the beast in me."

In 1957, jazz belonged to the professoriate and "old broads" at cocktail parties. Elvis himself delivered the message. Like Shorty Rogers, Presley made black music acceptable to a larger whiter audience. But if Presley had been listening to Otis Blackwell and Big Mama Thornton, Shorty Rogers had been listening to Miles Davis. As cool as he was, and in spite of the best efforts of even Columbia Records, Davis would never see the same level of profit as Elvis and the most successful generations of white rockers. Ten years later, with his embrace of jazz-rock, Davis would try to do something about that.

Davis may not have seen *Jailhouse Rock*, but he may have agreed with the fellow who thought that Stubby had gone too far with those altered chords. Shortly after the Presley film was released, Davis recorded *Kind of Blue*. If nothing else, the album contained no altered chords. The musicians simply improvised around a set of scales. Modal jazz was born. With Cannonball Adderley, Bill Evans, Paul Chambers, and Jimmy Cobb, Davis worked his way through a brandnew set of tunes, each beginning with a catchy introduction and continuing with solo choruses. Adderley on alto sax and Coltrane on tenor had moments of lyricism, but they were also likely to tear through the chords whenever it suited them. Davis was the minimalist, playing some of his most engaging and accessible solos. *Kind of Blue*, which begins with that anthem of cool, "So What," has become the best-selling album in jazz history.

After *Kind of Blue*, Davis was not content to continue improvising over an unstructured modal platform. As always, he was ready to move on. *Birth of the Cool* had emphasized ensemble textures. The "Walkin'" recordings in the midfifties moved out of the cool and punched up the rhythmic pulse. At the end of the decade, *Kind of Blue* invited the soloists to dispense with the familiar chord changes of the pop tune. By the mid-1960s, Davis's innovations were about emotional expression. He found the perfect rhythm section in Herbie Hancock, Ron Carter, and Tony Williams, each of whom had the uncanny ability to follow Davis wherever he went without getting in his way.

For me, Davis does his absolute best playing with Hancock, Carter, Williams, and tenor saxophonist George Coleman on two LPs made at a 1964 concert at Philharmonic Hall in New York. Davis eventually replaced Coleman with Wayne Shorter, and that quintet also made great music, but I'll stick with the 1964 band. Originally released as *My Funny Valentine* and *Four and More*, the music from Philharmonic Hall eventually became the two-CD set *The Complete Concert: 1964*. I would love this music even if it had not been staged to raise money for voter registration efforts in Louisiana and Mississippi. In fact, as Ingrid Monson speculates, Miles may have used the idea of a benefit concert to provoke his sidemen into some inspired playing. The members of the quintet arrived at Philarmonic Hall not knowing that they were about to play for free. The band had not performed for several weeks, so they could have used the money. Davis may have hoped his men would play with more fire if they were angry about not getting paid. He was also testing their loyalty—if they really wanted to play with someone as great as Davis, they had to do what he said. That might have made them angry too, but his strategy worked. Everyone played brilliantly. Especially on the slow tunes, Miles is at his most dramatic, alternating passages of supreme lyricism with earthy intrusions of gutbucket blues. Monson is surely right when she argues that Davis's music acquired gravitas through its association with people risking their lives to register voters and to undo decades of institutionalized racism.[4] He had already put his body on the line when he stood up to cops in front of Birdland. Part of his genius was his ability to make his experiences as a black American—his sufferings as well as his aspirations—speak through his trumpet.

THE BRANDO CONNECTION

In his essential biography of Davis, John Szwed says that Frances Taylor, Davis's second wife, was convinced that Miles consciously imitated the voice that Marlon Brando used as Stanley Kowalski in *A Streetcar Named Desire*. Keep in mind that *Streetcar* was released in 1951, several years before Davis's voice acquired the rasp and gravel it would have for the rest of his life. Davis even expressed admiration for the jazz-inflected score that Alex North wrote for *Streetcar*. After seeing the film, Davis said to his brother, "Fuck jazz! Alex North is the man."[5]

For his part, Brando had a brief encounter in 1965 with Frances Taylor Davis. She was in Hollywood just after she left Davis because of his escalating drug abuse. She ended up at a party where Brando sat and listened sympathetically to her stories. Frances eventually went home with Brando, but she was appalled when he sat her down in front of a pornographic movie in his bedroom.[6]

If Davis was imitating Brando's voice, Brando returned the compliment by emulating Davis's notorious practice of leaving the stage while other musicians soloed during his club appearances. Rod Steiger bitterly complained about Brando's behavior during the crucial scene between the two men in the back of a car in the 1954 film

On the Waterfront ("I coulda been a contenda! I coulda been some-body!"). After the shots with both men in the frame had been filmed, Steiger says he sat patiently and reacted in character while the cam-era took close-ups of Brando. But when the camera was turned toward Steiger for his close-ups, Brando went home. Steiger's com-plaint, "He left the set, he left the set," parallels the familiar complaint about Davis, "He left the stage, he left the stage," when he walked into the wings during the solos of his sidemen.

Still another Davis/Brando connection involves their understand-ing of recording technology. Brando was often accused of mumbling. In fact, he was relying on the technological amplification of his voice in order to avoid the stale old declamatory styles of stage speech. Davis was also keenly sensitive to the possibilities of the microphone. He would take the stem out of a Harmon mute and place it right up against a microphone. On its own, a stemless Harmon greatly reduces a trumpet's volume. But with a decent microphone and a little help from the men in the recording booth, Davis could play as softly as he wanted and still be heard. Later, he worked with producer Teo Macero to attach a wah-wah pedal to his horn so that he could pro-duce an entirely new sound by manipulating a pedal with his foot. Only fifty years after Buddy Bolden redefined the trumpet by blowing louder than anyone else, Miles redefined it all over by playing softer than anyone else.

THE GUITAR VS. THE TRUMPET

Twenty years after the revolutionary *Birth of the Cool* sessions, and ten years after *Kind of Blue* and his first LPs with Gil Evans, Davis took the audacious step of embracing electronic music, reaching out to a young audience more attuned to Jimi Hendrix than to Charlie Parker. In one sense, Davis was finally hearing the message that Elvis was delivering in the 1950s, that jazz belonged to an older generation and that electrified rock was the music of youthful passion and sexuality. The central instrument in the new music was not the trumpet. It was the electric guitar. And no one had exploited the potential of that instrument as extensively as Hendrix. Davis actually wanted to record with Hendrix, even going so far as to invite Gil Evans to orchestrate their collaboration. But the self-destructive guitarist died before he could join Davis and Evans in the studio. It might have been an extraordinary session.

According to the rock bassist Jack Bruce, Davis was trying to do with his trumpet what Hendrix had been doing with his guitar.[7] For one thing, the sound of a trumpet with a stemless Harmon has a certain metallic resonance that recalls an electric guitar. And the wah-wah pedal allowed Davis to achieve effects comparable to what guitarists can do with a tremolo arm, or "whammy bar," that can quickly raise and lower the pitch. Even though he had taken some of the macho swagger out of the jazz trumpet, Davis must have known that the young musicians everywhere were now defining their masculinity by strapping on an electric guitar rather than by putting their lips to a brass instrument. Hendrix in particular was making the connection between the guitar and male sexuality as explicit as possible. Steve Waksman has said that Hendrix transformed his guitar into a "technophallus" when he repeatedly spread his legs and let the instrument extend directly from his crotch.[8] Some suspected that Dizzy Gillespie had bent the bell of his horn upward to suggest an erection, but this was something else altogether.

Although Davis was almost universally reviled by jazz purists for abandoning the true faith of acoustic music, some of the music on albums such as *Bitches Brew* (1969), *Live Evil* (1970), and *Get Up with It* (1970–74) is as complex and challenging as anything he ever recorded. Many of the critics saw Davis's jump from his acoustic quintet of the mid-1960s to the large fusion ensembles of the 1970s as an opportunistic move toward a larger market. Davis was in fact looking for a new audience and a bigger paycheck. But his need to rede-fine himself also was a part of a gradual and coherent progression to-ward more abstract, texturally based music. The beginnings of that progression can be heard in the *Birth of the Cool* collaborations with Gil Evans and in their later work, where it continues to evolve. Listen to the prophetic 1963 recording "The Time of the Barracudas" in-cluded in the box set *Miles Davis and Gil Evans: The Complete Co-lumbia Studio Recordings*. Six years before *Bitches Brew* and without electrification, Davis and Evans were laying down nonmelodic frag-ments of sound from French horns, flutes, bassoon, and harp along-side statements from conventional jazz instruments. As with the best of the electric recordings, the result sounds nothing like a jazz tune with a series of solos but much more like a progression of musical environments.

In his book *Miles Beyond*, Paul Tingen goes so far as to argue that Davis's career culminates with his electric recordings.[9] Most of the many Davis biographies concentrate on the twenty-two years between his first recordings as a leader in 1947 and *Bitches Brew*, dismissing much of the music he produced in the twenty-two years after *Bitches Brew*. Tingen, however, regards everything prior to 1969 as the pre-lude to a great period when Davis began playing alongside electric guitarists and musicians from Africa, India, and Latin America. He was engaging in intense musical dialogues without regard to borders, geographic or otherwise. For Tingen and a handful of other writers for whom the old acoustic jazz was no longer the ideal, Davis was striving for "the electronic sublime."

I admire much of what Davis played in his later years. Let me re-peat: I admire this music. But my admiration exists alongside the wish that I could listen to it with greater pleasure. I agree with the British jazz writer Richard Cook that almost all of it is "joyless." In the recordings of the 1950s, I hear playfulness. Davis is making his notes dance and taking great delight in it. Even later, when he is digging deep for emotional expression in the *My Funny Valentine* performances, there are flashes of joy. I hear little of that in the electric recordings, and I'm probably not alone. The rock critics adored the novelty of *Bitches Brew* and made it a major crossover success for Davis. But few of his electric recordings reached a large audience after that. And as a trumpet player, Davis was in decline due to a long history with drugs and alcohol as well as diabetes, sickle-cell anemia, bleeding ulcers, a stroke, a serious automobile accident, and a heart attack (see figure 28). He also underwent a series of hip operations that left him in constant pain and dependent on painkillers. Between 1975 and 1980, he nearly gave up music, spending most of his days alone in his apartment drinking heavily and dosing himself with cocaine and painkillers. During this period he also became impotent, literally as well as musically.

Davis's late ensembles may not have played the thoroughbred jazz of his early 1960s bands, but they were highly theatrical. Dressed in what another British writer, Richard Williams, has called a "dodgy collection of duster coats, boleros and harem pants in a variety of diaphanous boudoir fabrics,"[10] Davis would stalk a stage filled with towering stacks of speakers and instruments that could have been designed for a science fiction film. He would wander over to a sideman and engage in intimate, improvised dialogue before moving on to the next encounter. Sometimes he would even lean on his sidemen, as if he needed their physical as well as musical support. Davis's flair for the theatrical goes back at least to the 1950s, when he began dressing in ostentatiously good taste and posing with expensive sports cars and beautiful women. In retrospect, albums such as *Kind of Blue* can be conceived as acoustic dramas in their own right. Soloists step forward like actors delivering soliloquies while the rest of the ensemble provides an atmosphere of portentous anticipation. When Davis steps forth, the drama intensifies. Whether he liked it or not, he was the heir of Louis Armstrong.

DARKNESS AUDIBLE

Thanks in part to the ideas of Debbie Ishlom, a resourceful publicist at Columbia Records, Davis began developing a unique visual identity in the 1950s. Part of that identity included the image of himself in silhouette on the cover of his LPs in his trademark posture with the trumpet. It also included his impeccably tailored suits and elegant sports cars. Davis's image work also included an effort to establish his bona fides as a proud black artist. He acted as if his every gesture had a deep purpose. Walking impassively into a club, he would call his broker to check on his portfolio, and then without so much as a nod to the audience or his sidemen, he would put the trumpet to his mouth and begin playing. If anyone spoke to him during this process, Davis displayed various levels of resentment over the intrusion, as if his concentration were being broken.

Ralph Ellison may have been reacting to this pose when he wrote to his friend Albert Murray in 1958. Ellison had just seen a performance by "poor, evil, lost little Miles Davis, who on this occasion just couldn't get it together."[11] Ellison had heard Davis at the Plaza Hotel, an event that was recorded by Columbia Records and released as *Jazz at the Plaza*. Like many who have listened to that record, I firmly believe that Davis did in fact have it together. Ellison always wrote brilliantly about music, but his tastes were formed in the 1930s, and he was never able to get a handle on bop and its aftermath. What I find important here is Ellison's use of the word *evil* to describe Davis. Did Ellison know how often Miles backed up the menacing face he presented to audiences with vicious verbal assaults? Quincy Troupe, the coauthor of Davis's autobiography and a longtime fan, recalls a night in the 1950s when a well-dressed white man and his wife approached

Davis after a set as he was standing at the bar with a beer and a cigarette. The young man held out his hand and began to introduce himself. Davis cut him off with the words, "Fuck you, you jive punkass motherfucka! Get the fuck outta my face and take yo silly little bitch with you!"[12]

Although many of his old friends still speak of him with genuine affection, Davis could be as arrogant and insulting as he was vulnerable and defensive. He had the kind of personality that drove loved ones close to madness and that only the most eminent artists can get away with. When he told his band they had a gig at Philharmonic Hall in 1964 without telling them that they were not being paid, they were not the first to be subjected to Davis's elaborate testing rituals. When he hired the white pianist Bill Evans in 1958, he told him that he had to have sex with each of the men in his band before he could join. Evans thought it over and respectfully refused. Miles laughed and hired him anyway. His abrupt dismissal of sidemen was less jocular. He unceremoniously fired Vincent Wilburn Jr., the son of his beloved sister in Chicago, after Wilburn had played drums in the band from 1985 until 1987. Davis gave his nephew notice when the band was on tour and just about to arrive in Chicago. When asked why he fired his nephew at that time, knowing full well that Wilburn's friends would be at the concert, Miles said, "Music doesn't have friends like that." And yet in a later interview with Sy Johnson, Davis spoke with genuine sadness and hurt as he listed the former sidemen who never called or visited him.

Most disturbingly, Davis speaks openly in his autobiography about his attacks on women. None of the many women who were close to him seems to have escaped his assaults. Jo Gelbard, who lived with Davis during the last years of his life, was an athlete and much younger than the aging Davis. Although she insists that she was never really afraid when he turned violent, Gelbard said that Davis was capable of "unspeakable cruelty." In *Miles, the Autobiography*, he brags about sitting in his living room in the mid-1980s, joking with police-men about how to treat women, while his third wife, Cicely Tyson, was hiding downstairs after he "slapped the shit out of her" and she dialed 911. "I just slapped her once," he told the police. One re-sponded that they were obliged to investigate whenever emergency calls came through. Davis responded, "Well, if she's beating my ass you gonna come with your guns ready, too?" Then, according to Davis, "They just laughed and left."[13]

In the same book, however, Davis insists that Tyson's constant at-tentions saved his life after he nearly died from various ailments and extended drug abuse in the 1970s. Like many who read about Davis's attacks on women, the black feminist writer Pearl Cleage publicly agonized over how she could have fallen in love with the music of someone capable of such violence. "Can we continue to celebrate ge-nius in the face of the monster?"[14]

Robin D. G. Kelley may have provided the most satisfying expla-nation of how Davis could play what he did at the same time that he was viciously abusing the women he supposedly loved. According to Kelley, Davis's seductive music as well as his violent misogyny can be understood as part of a "pimp aesthetic": "listening for the pimp in Miles ought to make us aware of the pleasures of cool as well as the dark side of romance. We get nostalgic for the old romantic Miles, for that feeling of being in love, but who understands this better than the mack, that despicable character we find so compelling and attrac-tive?"[15] Art Farmer, himself profoundly influenced by Davis, put it more succinctly: "Miles plays the way he'd like to be."[16] All evidence suggests that, by contrast, Farmer really did play the way he was.

MILES AND THE MOVIES, PART II

Davis the mack daddy performed his magic on many levels, some of them subliminal. When I was in college, I visited the apartment of

Robert, a classmate living lavishly on his wealthy father's largesse. After a tour of his spacious apartment high above the city, I noticed an issue of *Playboy* on a table next to a pipe. I realized that Robert had built his life on the model of the hip, affluent bachelors who appeared in the magazine's series of self-promoting advertisements, "What kind of a man reads *Playboy*?" It seemed that every time I ran into Robert, he was with a different woman, all of them tall and beautiful. He once confided in me that he had programmed his record collection to coax his female companions into bed. I don't recall what music was at the bottom of the stack of LPs on his changer. It really didn't matter. The important thing was that the last LP was always a Miles Davis album. In Robert's *Playboy* fantasy world, Davis was there to lubricate the gears of seduction. Before Davis came along, it's hard to imagine a trumpet serving quite that same purpose.

As we might expect, Davis's trumpet is heard in various love scenes in Hollywood movies. In *The Runaway Bride* (1999), when Julia Roberts first picks up Richard Gere's cassette tape with the word "Miles" on the cover, the two have been eyeing each other suspiciously. But when she takes it home and listens to Davis's intensely romantic 1954 version of "It Never Entered My Mind," we know that Roberts's and Gere's characters are made for each other. Davis's music even serves a homoerotic purpose when Matt Damon, playing a gay man in *The Talented Mr. Ripley* (1999), asks if he can climb into a bathtub with the naked Jude Law as the two listen to Davis's 1955 recording of "Nature Boy."

Davis died in 1991, years before *The Runaway Bride* and *The Talented Mr. Ripley* were made. On the several occasions when he directly participated in putting music into movies, it was seldom a successful venture. *Jack Johnson* (1971), *Street Smart* (1987), *Siesta* (1987), and *The Hot Spot* (1990) were not hits, and few in the audience knew that they were listening to the trumpet of Miles Davis. His music had been put to much better use in the 1957 French film *As-*

censeur pour l'échafaud, directed by Louis Malle and released in the United States as *Elevator to the Gallows*. In fact, no other film has married jazz and cinema quite so elegantly.

After Malle invited Davis to improvise music for his film, the trumpeter went into a Paris studio with three French musicians (pianist René Urtreger, tenor saxist Barney Wilen, and bassist Pierre Michelot) as well as the American expatriate drummer Kenny Clarke. This group, with which Davis had been touring Europe for several months, was afforded the same privileges as almost every film composer in mainstream movies since the 1930s: they were given a complete copy of the film and allowed to put their own music where they thought it worked best. The musicians actually improvised as they watched the film. The CD of the music for *Elevator to the Gallows*, reissued in 1988 with several alternate takes, reveals how many times Davis and his sidemen went through the exercise until they knew they had it right. And in many ways they did. Thanks largely to the music, in 1957 the film won the prestigious Prix Louis Delluc, the French equivalent of the Academy Award.

Elevator to the Gallows, however, contains a stern lesson for anyone seeking the perfect marriage of jazz and cinema. In only one scene does the music really transform the images on the screen, specifically when the film's female protagonist, Florence (Jeanne Moreau), slowly walks through the Paris night while Davis and his quintet read her mind with their improvisations. Florence has conspired with her lover Julien (Maurice Ronet) to kill her husband, a wealthy industrialist. After Julien has carried out the carefully planned murder in the victim's own office, he prepares to drive away to meet Florence. But once he arrives at his car, he looks up at the office building where the dead body remains undiscovered and sees that the rope he used for surreptitious entry is visible from the street. Leaving the motor of his car running, he reenters the building and is immediately trapped in the elevator when the custodian shuts down the power as the workday comes to an end. The florist who works across the street and her petty thief boyfriend take the car for a joyride while Julien is desperately looking for a way out of the elevator. A few blocks down the street, Florence sees Julien's car driving off, but she sees only the young woman in the passenger seat. She suspects that the driver is Julien, but she cannot be certain.

The director has written a scene for Florence that perfectly accommodates the improvisations of a jazz group. In fact, Malle filmed the scene without dialogue, hoping that he would eventually find the appropriate music. Only after the film was essentially finished was he able to convince Davis to provide the music. In the crucial scene, the camera follows Florence for several minutes through the streets of Paris. As she wonders if her husband is dead, if Julien has betrayed her, and if she will ever see her lover again, Davis solos on his trumpet. Like so many African American jazz instrumentalists, Davis brings the sound of a human voice into his improvisations. At one point his trumpet even sounds as if it's singing in French. Davis was engaging in an elaborate dialogue with the character, trying to find musical means for expressing what she is feeling. Moreau utters only one word of dialogue in this scene when she sees a car that looks like Julien's. She calls out his name, only to see that the car is being driven by a man she does not know. At this point, Davis lays low, holding a long note as the man gets out of the car and the audience has a moment to sort out whether or not Florence has found her lover. Davis returns to his agitated but soulful improvisation when the heroine realizes that the driver is not Julien and continues her slow walk through the city. Either instinctively or by instruction, Davis knew that music must not get in the way when the audience expects a crucial plot point. Regardless, the combination of the music and the beautiful actress's night walk is stunning.

Another film makes fascinating use of Davis's trumpet, even if it deserves little respect otherwise. In *Pleasantville* (1998), two teenage siblings, David (Tobey Maguire) and Jennifer (Reese Witherspoon), are arguing over what to watch on television. The film asks for a great deal of suspension of disbelief when the brother and sister are magically transported into the black-and-white world of an old TV sitcom called *Pleasantville*, based most obviously on *Father Knows Best*, a staple of American television from 1954 until 1963. David is geekishly devoted to the old program, and he is more than happy to live in a much simpler world than the teen hell we see him experiencing in the film's early scenes. Jennifer, however, is a sexually active alpha girl, appalled to find herself "stuck in nerdville." But she changes her mind when she meets a young blond fellow with a winning smile.

In the logic of *Pleasantville*, the people in the TV sitcom world have only as much information as is presented in the episodes of the old program. So, because no one on the show ever reads a book, the volumes in the library have nothing but blank pages. Because no one ever leaves town, teachers present geography lessons about roads that never leave the city limits. And because no one in the show has sex, it's up to Jennifer, the teen from the future, to show them the way. Suddenly, the black-and-white world of Pleasantville begins to have some color. The film suggests that people turn colorful on the outside only after they have undergone some kind of transformation on the inside. Since teenagers are most open to novelty and can be easily transformed by sexual encounters, they are the first to make the change. Other characters become colorful when they become angry or when they see the world in a new light. The older citizens of the town do not change so quickly and unite against the colorful. A black-and-white man even puts a sign in his store reading NO COLORED. David is eventually arrested for his part in disrupting the "normal" life of the town. Although there are no African American actors in the film, the citizens of Pleasantville have a civil rights revolution. By the end, however, the film has completely sidestepped the racial issues it has raised. David finds ways to see that everyone in town takes on color. The case against him is dismissed, and people discover that they are all the same on the inside *and* on the outside. If only it were so easy.

For me, however, the most crucial scene in *Pleasantville* takes place when a group of teenagers in the soda shop ask David to tell them about the rest of the world. They also ask him about books that are suddenly full of words once Jennifer and David begin describing the plots. When David begins to talk about *Huckleberry Finn* and *Catcher in the Rye*, we suddenly hear Davis's solo on "So What," the first selection on *Kind of Blue*. The solo continues uninterrupted on the soundtrack for almost a full minute while the small-town teenagers line up to take books out of the public library. Earlier in the film, as the first teenagers become sexualized and hence colorful, the audience hears the sounds of pop musicians such as Gene Vincent, Elvis Presley, and Lloyd Price. We hear only brief moments of "Be-Bop-a-Lula," "Teddy Bear," and "Lawdy Miss Clawdy." But when the young people of Pleasantville begin to wonder about literature and the outside world, when they begin to *think*, we hear the music of Miles Davis. If rock and pop are the music of the body, jazz in general and Davis in particular are the music of the mind.

In most Hollywood films, the audience is not asked to listen carefully to the music. They are expected to feel it. In *Pleasantville*, Davis's subliminal trumpet delivers a precise message to the spectators, even the ones who have no idea that they are listening to Miles Davis or even to a trumpet. The music tells them that young people are embarking on a journey of wonder, one leading to sophistication and worldliness, even to danger. This is what the music has come to mean in the twenty-first century. We're a long way from the manly assertions that came out of the trumpets that the first African American jazz musicians played.

The legacy of Miles Davis is a sound that speaks to us on a unique level. In the late 1960s, long after he had changed the meaning of the trumpet, Miles tried to do with his horn what others had done with the electric guitar, the new default instrument for masculine self-presentation. He didn't exactly succeed, but then, for many years now, his *Kind of Blue* has sold more than any other jazz album. This most iconic work of Davis is not what he cooked up to compete with the phallic histrionics of Hendrix; it is the album he made when the trumpet was still king. Yes, Davis valiantly adapted to what was new, but *Kind of Blue* has his most beloved music. Almost everything he recorded (even the most marginal electronic experiments) now has its own boxed set. In the end, the sales figures, driven by true believers as well as by casual listeners seeking a cool moment, speak for themselves.

Conclusion:

Beyond the Brute

n the 1954 Italian film *La Strada*, Federico Fellini directed his wife, Giulietta Masina, in the role of Gelsomina. A dim-witted but compassionate waif who can break your heart with her smile, Gelsomina is sold by her impoverished mother to Zampanò. As played by Anthony Quinn, Zampanò is an unsmiling, brutal strongman who has apparently been expelled from a circus troupe. (See figure 29.) The film begins with Zampanò recruiting Gelsomina to replace her sister, who has presumably died or run away. Zampanò drives from town to town on that most hypermasculine form of transportation, a motorcycle. His motorcycle, however, is attached to the covered wagon where he keeps his belongings. At each town he earns a few lire by attracting a crowd and then creating the simple illusion that he has broken a chain by expanding his chest. At least at first, Gelsomina's job is to play a tattoo on a snare drum and then declare, "Here he is: Zampanò!" When she fails to announce the faux strongman with the proper execution, Zampanò shows neither sympathy with

Gelsomina's limitations nor appreciation of her charm. He whips her with the branch of a bush. Gelsomina nevertheless perseveres, even learning to play the old trumpet with rotary valves that Zampanò keeps in his wagon.

The film is not clear about exactly how Gelsomina learns to play the trumpet. We see Zampanò play only a few notes, all of them enunciated clearly enough to establish that he knows his way around the instrument. He then hands the horn to Gelsomina. Later in the film, when Zampanò has signed on with a traveling circus, Gelsomina encounters "il Matto," or the Fool, a talented acrobat and circus clown played by the American actor Richard Basehart. The Fool gives Gelsomina a brief lesson with his valved trombone as he attempts to bring her into his act. Zampanò forbids Gelsomina the extra work, however, in part because the Fool regularly taunts him, calling him "Trifle."[1] Eventually Zampanò runs after the Fool with a knife, resulting in both men being expelled from the circus. Zampanò receives the additional punishment of a night in jail.

When we actually hear Gelsomina play the trumpet, she and Zampanò have briefly stopped at a convent where she performs a mournful song with excellent technique. (At this point, we have seen her take only two brief lessons, but ah, the magic of the cinema.) Audiences had already heard an orchestral rendition of the song over the film's opening credits, but Gelsomina herself first hears it when the Fool plays it on a tiny violin. The song, later marketed simply as "La Strada," was written for the film by Nino Rota, the extraordinary composer whose music has transformed the movies of Fellini and many other filmmakers. "La Strada" is one of his most moving compositions, especially when we hear it as tenderhearted Gelsomina's tribute to one of the few people ever to take an interest in her.

Gelsomina might have stayed with the Fool and performed at his side, but the Fool seems to realize that she belongs with Zampanò and encourages her to stay with him. She has not, however, seen the last of the Fool. Later, driving through the countryside on his motor-cycle with Gelsomina in the wagon, Zampanò discovers the Fool on the side of the road tending to a flat tire. Still bearing a grudge from their last encounter, Zampanò goes after the Fool one more time. Zampanò does not intend to kill him, but the Fool expires shortly after Zampanò smashes his head against the car. With Gelsomina looking on in horror, Zampanò disposes of the body and the automobile. Gelsomina never recovers from the shock. Days later, she continues to mutter, "The Fool is hurt."

Because Gelsomina is constantly reminding him of his crime, and because she is too traumatized to be of much use to him as a performer, Zampanò abandons her one night as she sleeps. Significantly, he lays the trumpet alongside her as he takes his leave. In the last moments of the film, long after he has abandoned Gelsomina, Zampanò wanders through a strange town on foot. He appears to have lost his motorcycle and his wagon. When he sees a woman tending to her laundry and singing the tune that Gelsomina had played on the trumpet, he asks her about the song. The woman says she heard it from a girl who passed through town several years earlier and seemed to be crazy. She never spoke, the woman tells him, but she would play her song on the trumpet. One day she died of a fever. The film ends with the aged, dissolute Zampanò weeping on a deserted beach and regretting his wasted life.

FOR ME, IT is significant that Zampanò is a trumpet player. I'm also intrigued that the film was made just as Miles Davis was transforming the trumpet with his expressions of sensitivity and vulnerability. And keep in mind that Zampanò relinquishes his trumpet after Gelsomina has used it to speak her sorrows rather than to provide fanfares for a strong man's display of his body. The trumpet's associations with unreconstructed masculinity date back at least to Homer's Greece, and in spite of Miles and Federico, it retains this association today, especially in men endowed with a powerfully competitive spirit. Members of the International Trumpet Guild, probably the major professional organization for trumpeters, joke that the official greeting of the guild is "I'm better than you." Indeed, the man who swells his chest and belts out the high notes has much in common with Zampanò the brute.

The men who play lead trumpet in a large jazz group, a Latin big band, or a symphony orchestra must have a bit of the brute in them. These men know that they can be heard above all the other instruments, including drums and percussion. If they make a mistake, they realize that even the most musically naïve listener will notice. The daughter of Harry Glantz, who was principal trumpet in the NBC Symphony when it was conducted by Arturo Toscanini, told me that her father always believed that the man sitting next to him playing second was a better trumpeter—he simply could not take the pressure that goes with the first chair.[2] The principal trumpet and the leadman must be hardwired with the strength to forge on and withstand that pressure.

If you can take the heat, however, there are rewards. Especially in a jazz or Latin band, the lead trumpet is the man in control. He sets the tone, determines the rhythmic feel, and brings the rest of the band along with him. Not surprisingly, leadmen are notoriously arrogant and monomaniacal. Chris Washburne, a respected jazz scholar, teacher, and bandleader as well as an accomplished trombonist, told me some stories about his experiences with lead trumpeters. One threatened him with brass knuckles when Washburne lightly brushed against him while they were playing in a cramped orchestra pit. Chris was also at a recording session for a Latin band when two trumpeters arrived, both of them determined to play lead. As they argued over who would play which part, one took a large knife out of his pocket and placed it on his music stand. The other then placed a handgun on his. The trumpeter with the handgun played lead. Washburne's most disturbing stories are about aging leadmen who know that they are on the verge of being outplayed by younger musicians. He watched one of these men trying to rattle the concentration of his section mates with various strategies. One was criticizing their intonation just seconds before they were about to begin playing.

Of course, not everyone who plays trumpet, even the leadman, is a brute with a lethal weapon or a nasty bag of tricks for dealing with the competition. Brutishness is not the only form of masculinity, and masculinity is hardly monolothic. No one would say that Donald Rumsfeld, Barry Bonds, Jackie Chan, Denzel Washington, Ian McKellen, George Clooney, or Brian Urlacher is a nerd or a weakling, but each man expresses his masculinity in entirely different ways. Urlacher, a linebacker for the Chicago Bears, is probably the closest thing to a brute, a man who uses his bulk and his muscle instinctively and unreflectively. The brute seems to have been born with a body and an attitude that forcefully propel him through life. We can't imagine such a man stopping to contemplate whether or not he is being obnoxious, let alone apologizing for it.

Even the man who *looks* like a brute may not possess exactly this kind of masculinity. Think of the weight lifter who creates the illusion that his bulky muscles are a natural part of his physique and his character. Some bodybuilders walk and carry themselves in a fashion that seems to say, "Out of my way, bitch." But every now and then the weight lifter reveals the nerd beneath his skin. Watch him at the gym when he picks up his little notebook and scrupulously marks down how many sets and reps he has performed for each body part. Like the brute, the nerd has little in the way of social graces. But if the brute thinks too little, the nerd thinks too much, mastering the language of computers, immersing himself in statistics about batting averages, memorizing personnel listings on record covers, or researching the exact right exercise for each portion of each of his muscles. The nerd inside the bodybuilder is obsessed with *looking* like his masculinity is instinctive and natural. For a picture of the archetypal nerd, take a look at a photograph of the young Arnold Schwarzenegger before he began looking like a condom filled with walnuts.

Like the bodybuilder, a lead trumpeter might also be a nerd masquerading as a brute. While some may have been born with the wide chest and the deep jaw that make the high notes easier to come by, absolutely no one plays only with instinct and natural strength. Every successful trumpeter spends hours and hours each and every week developing the two hundred muscles it takes to play the trumpet properly, not to mention making sure that his or her horn is functioning correctly. Many trumpeters joke about how they or their section mates are obsessed with every aspect of their equipment and their practice regimens. They often use the term "trumpet geek," a good description of a person in the space where the brute and the nerd overlap. (See figure 30.)

Whether or not they play lead, devoted trumpeters will memorize solos by favorite artists and play them back with meticulous attention to detail. They will study tai chi, yoga, and complex breathing techniques. They will meditate and carefully monitor their diets. They will pamper their lips with their own preferred brand of lip balm. They will work through the fiendishly difficult exercises in the practice manuals by Carmine Caruso, Théo Charlier, and Marcel Bitsch, whose last name is pronounced "beech" although many refer to his manual as "the Bitch Book." Brian Lynch, who played trumpet with Art Blakey in the 1980s and who today performs with as much intensity and imagination as anyone in jazz, told me that it takes him more than an hour just to warm up. Then he'll work through a series of exercises created by Jimmy Stamp, all of them to be played just with the trumpet mouthpiece. Only after all of this will he begin playing what most of us regard as "music."

Brian Lynch, by the way, is well-read, articulate, and personable. He is neither a brute nor a nerd. And I have met plenty of other trumpeters who comport themselves with grace and good humor, even if you occasionally hear a bit of brute strength and geeky discipline when they perform. Long before Miles Davis made the trumpet express warmth and sincerity, the best trumpeters knew their way around a ballad. Even Buddy Bolden, who became famous largely by playing loud, could also play slow and soft, with what witnesses called "heartbreaking warmth."

The masculinity that Bolden, Louis Armstrong, and the first black trumpeters created was rooted in their devotion to the instrument and to the music. But it was also the result of an existential need to express themselves as men at a time when whites regularly addressed them as "boy." If some of those first black jazz pioneers had been born several generations later, they might have become running backs, power forwards, or boxers. Others might have channeled their aspirations toward professional careers in law, medicine, or commerce. Would Louis Armstrong have become a major league catcher or a trial lawyer if he'd had the opportunity? I doubt it. We are all extremely fortunate that he came along at a time when his prodigious musical ability, the limitations he faced as a black American, and his need to express himself as a man were in perfect alignment. The same is surely true of Roy Eldridge, Dizzy Gillespie, and many of the other African American geniuses who made jazz history.

The white men who were inspired by black trumpeters like Armstrong unquestionably possessed a special breed of masculinity. Any one of them could have chosen athletics, the professions, or some other career, but instead they played jazz. When all is said and done, the trumpeter is neither a brute nor a nerd. A man who has devoted himself to the trumpet—as an instrument of self-assertion as well as romance—has found an alternative model of masculinity. Ultimately, he has little in common with athletes or even with the professional men who persuade juries in courtrooms or clients in business meetings. The trumpeter is an artist who must be in touch with his emotions. He is seeking a way to express those emotions as truly as possible, even if, like Miles Davis, he is playing "the way he wants to be." If the trumpeter expresses masculinity in his playing, it is because he is expressing himself in an artful manner.

Then there are the white men who were inspired by the gentle side of a player like Armstrong. Or by the finesse of a black musician like Art Farmer. Or by the subtle imagination of a white trumpeter like Bix Beiderbecke. At this point, it becomes clear why women can be as successful as men when they play the trumpet. It's not just about that Y chromosome. If a woman like Clora Bryant or Ingrid Jensen rips through a phrase like Armstrong or Gillespie at his most intense, we might say that she is expressing the masculine side of herself. Or we could simply say that she is expressing her feminine side with unusual force.

AFTER I HAD taken lessons with Eddie Allen for about two years, he announced that I was ready to start playing with other people. He recommended a Latin band that played entirely for fun on Monday nights in East Harlem. The group met in a grade school band room that was otherwise unoccupied during the evening. The conductor was Ramón Rodríguez, an eminently musical and patient man who taught at the school during the day and resembled a Puerto Rican Orson Welles. The band included at least half a dozen singers and a small contingent of percussionists. Different people showed up on different Monday nights, but along with the collected singers and percussionists, there was almost always a guitarist, a pianist, a bass player, two trombonists, a baritone saxophonist, and three trumpeters. At the rehearsals, it usually seemed as if a party was on the verge of breaking out, especially among the percussionists.

The trumpet has always had its special role in Latino culture, whether in bullfights, mariachi bands, or in the career of an international celebrity like Rafael Méndez. The Latin big bands of Tito Puente, Chico O'Farrill, and Machito always featured flamboyant trumpet solos. Almost as much as the driving clave rhythm, a high-pitched trumpet soaring over the ensemble is the signature of the Latin jazz orchestra.

When I sat down to play with the Latin band for the first time, there were already two trumpeters at the rear of the room, where the trumpet section is always placed. One was clearly the leadman—barrel chested, nattily dressed, brimming with self-confidence. Testosterone, not blood, flowed in his veins. The other trumpeter seemed less confident, even though he was a tall, well-built man in his early thirties. Without hesitation, I picked up the third trumpet folder. The rhythms were tricky, and I laid low as much as I played on that first day. When I came back on the second Monday, the lead player was gone. I turned to the man who had played second and asked if he wanted to move up. He reached out for the second trumpet folder, grabbed the sheets, and said, "These are mine." He had been practicing the second trumpet parts for a long time, and he had no desire to play anything else. So I waited several more minutes for the leadman—or anyone else with a trumpet—to arrive. Finally, after a decent interval, I took a deep breath and assumed the first trumpet chair.

The leadman from that first night never returned, and no new leadman showed up. The first chair was mine. Other than me, the only person in the band who was not Puerto Rican or Latin was the pianist, a young woman who had joined the band because her boyfriend was one of the singers. She was good. Very few other members of the band were as talented, least of all me. We were not preparing for a concert, and few people showed up to listen to the band rehearse. It was simply an opportunity for some amateur musicians to get together and enjoy themselves. For this reason, very few of the arrangements we played were especially challenging. Some of the parts for first trumpet went into the upper registers, but I simply played them an octave lower. The fellow in the second chair dropped his part down an octave as well. We were good together, especially when the band played a bolero called "Yo Se Que Volveras" with a section written as a duet for two trumpets. I would hold a note while he played a gracefully moving passage in the middle register. Then he would hold a note while I came in with a passage slightly higher. One of the percussionists would hold up her arms and slowly sway back and forth whenever we played that duet. I loved it.

There was another piece written by Ramón himself called "Bar-rigita Llena," a mambo with lyrics celebrating the joys of eating one's fill of a good meal. The music featured a brief solo for the first trumpet. I could handle most of it, but I had trouble hitting the seven high Cs studded throughout the solo. If I played all or part of the solo an octave lower it sounded all wrong. The band must have played that piece every week for several months, and I usually fluffed the high notes, sometimes flamboyantly. And if I did manage to hit all the high Cs, I would lose control and hit a clam as I worked my way back to the middle register. I was surprised that Ramón kept on rehearsing the tune.

One day, after several hours at home woodshedding with the solo on "Barrigita Llena," I showed up at rehearsal and played it perfectly. I got a slight smile from the usually impassive Ramón. I was on cloud nine. It's all about the music, of course, and any woman who had nailed that same solo would have felt as good as I did. But at the end of the evening, two of the male percussionists walked over to shake my hand. It was not exactly my goal, but somewhere in the universe of Nuyorican machismo there may now be a tiny place for me.

Notes

CHAPTER 1 / How Buddy Bolden Blew His Brains Out

For this chapter as well as for the Preface, I have relied on the essential work of Donald M. Marquis as well as the oral histories in the Hogan Archive at Tulane University. Bruce Boyd Raeburn was extremely helpful throughout the time I spent at the Hogan.

1. *Carnaval* with Eastman Wind Ensemble (CBS Masterworks 1238066).

2. Roger Abrahams et al., *Blues for New Orleans: Mardi Gras and America's Creole Soul* (Philadelphia: University of Pennsylvania Press, 2006), 1.

3. Travis Jackson, review of *When the Levees Broke*, in *Jazz Perspectives* 1, no. 2 (2007): 221.

4. Daniel Hardie, *The Loudest Trumpet: Buddy Bolden and the Early History of Jazz* (iUniverse.com, 2001), 7.

5. Richard H. Knowles, *Fallen Heroes: A History of New Orleans Brass Bands* (New Orleans: Jazzology Press, 1996), 15.

6. W.E.B. Du Bois, *The Souls of Black Folk* [1903] (New York: Norton, 1999), 120.

7. Zora Neale Hurston, *Sanctified Church* (New York: Marlowe, 1998), 106.

8. Krin Gabbard, " 'Jazz': Etymology," in Barry Kernfeld, ed., *New Grove Dictionary of Jazz*, 2nd ed., 3 vols. (London: Macmillan, 2002), 2:389.

9. Max Roach quoted in Arthur Taylor, *Notes and Tones: Musician-to-Musician Interviews* (New York: Coward McCann, 1977), 110.

10. James Lincoln Collier, *The Making of Jazz* (New York: Dell, 1978), 173.

11. Alan Lomax, *Mister Jelly Roll: The Fortunes of Jelly Roll Morton, New Orleans Creole and "Inventor of Jazz"* (Berkeley: University of California Press, 2001), 57–60.

12. Donald M. Marquis, *In Search of Buddy Bolden: First Man of Jazz* (Baton Rouge: Louisiana State University Press, 1978), 70.

13. Pops Foster and Tom Stoddard, *Pops Foster: The Autobiography of a Jazz Musician* (Berkeley: University of California Press, 1973), 16.

14. Jelly Roll Morton, *The Complete Library of Congress Recordings* (Rounder CD 11661-1888-2).

15. Liner notes to LP recording, *Sidney Bechet, Grand Master* (Columbia 836).

16. Sidney Bechet, *Treat It Gentle: An Autobiography* (New York: Hill and Wang, 1960), 84.

17. Michael W. Harris, *The Rise of Gospel Blues: The Music of Thomas Andrew Dorsey* (New York: Oxford University Press, 1994).

18. Marquis, *In Search of Buddy Bolden*, 44.

19. Ibid., 105.

20. Bechet, *Treat It Gentle*, 83.

21. Jeff Nussbaum, personal correspondence, February 12, 2006.

22. Richard I. Schwartz, "The African American Contribution to the Cornet of the Nineteenth Century: Some Long-Lost Names," *Historic Brass Society Journal* 16 (2004): 61–88.

23. Ralph Ellison, "Blues People," in *The Collected Essays of Ralph Ellison* (New York: Modern Library, 1995), 284.

24. Eric Lott, *Love and Theft: Blackface Minstrelsy and the American Working Class* (New York: Oxford University Press, 1993).

CHAPTER 2 / From the Pyramids to New Orleans

Throughout this chapter I have relied on several excellent works: Edward Tarr, *The Trumpet* (London: Batsford, 1988); Anthony Baines, *Brass Instruments: Their History and Development* (New York: Dover, 1993); Don Smithers, *The Music and History of the Baroque Trumpet Before 1721* (Carbondale: Southern Illinois University Press, 1989); and Trevor Herbert, *The Trombone* (New Haven: Yale University Press, 2006), as well as the following articles by Niles Eldredge: "Evolution in the Marketplace," *Structural Change and Economic Dynamics* 8 (1977):

385–98; "Biological and Cultural Evolution: Are There Any True Parallels?," *Perspectives in Ethology* 13 (2000): 113–53; and "A Brief History of Piston-Valved Cornets," *Historic Brass Society Journal* 14 (2002): 337–91. I have also benefited from many stimulating conversations with the distinguished music historian and gender theorist Sherrie Tucker.

1. Leigh Dayton, "Rock Art Evokes Beastly Echos of the Past," *New Scientist* 1849 (November 28, 1992): 14.

2. A more detailed version is in the *Achilleid*, by the first-century Roman poet Statius.

3. Baines, *Brass Instruments*, 57.

4. Plutarch, *Morals* 150 and 362.

5. But see Smithers, *Music and History of the Baroque Trumpet*, Addendum 21.

6. Hervé Niquet and Le Concert Spirituel, "Water Music and Fireworks" (Glossa AOV58).

7. Some brass specialists insist that there are real differences between early cornets and the cornopeans, but there were so many differences among all the instruments being manufactured at this time that some cornets had less in common with each other than did a cornet with what was called a cornopean.

8. *International Trumpet Guild Journal* 16, no. 1 (September 1991): 17–26.

9. Al Rose, *New Orleans Jazz: A Family Album* (Baton Rouge: Louisiana State University Press, 1967).

10. Alexander von Humboldt, *Vom Orinoco zum Amazonas* (Wiesbaden, 1974), 293.

11. I thank Kathryn Kalinak for calling this scene to my attention.

12. Johann Ernst Altenburg, *Trumpeters' and Kettledrummers' Art* [1795], trans. Edward Tarr (Nashville: Brass Press, 1974).

13. Tarr, *The Trumpet*, 72.

14. Vinatieri's music was recorded in 2001 as "Custer's Last Band" with original instruments in the collection of the National Music Museum in Vermillion, South Dakota, just a few miles from Yankton.

15. Margaret Downie Banks, "A Brief History of the Conn Company," www.usd .edu/~mbanks/CONN4.html#Worcest, accessed August 18, 2007.

16. My sincere thanks to Nick DeCarlis, who consulted his archive of rare old price lists for this information.

17. Ingrid Monson, personal communication, October 12, 2006.

18. Sherrie Tucker, "Gender, Race, and Brass: Jazzwomen Trumpeting Modernity," paper presented at Jazz Roundtable Series, Rutgers University, Newark, N.J., October 13, 2005.

CHAPTER 3 / Louis Armstrong's Beam of Lyrical Sound

I am especially grateful for two superb books by Thomas Brothers: *Louis Armstrong's New Orleans* (New York: Norton, 2006) and *Louis Armstrong: In His Own Words*. I have also consulted biographies: Lawrence Bergreen, *Louis Armstrong: An Extravagant Life* (New York: Broadway Books, 1997), and James Lincoln Collier, *Louis Armstrong: An American Genius* (New York: Oxford University Press, 1983), as well as Armstrong's own *Satchmo: My Life in New Orleans* (New York: Prentice-Hall, 1954). In addition, I have benefited from Gary Giddins's fine narrative in his *Satchmo* (New York: Knopf, 1992) and from Jeffrey Magee's *The Uncrowned King of Swing: Fletcher Henderson and Big Band Jazz* (New York: Oxford University Press, 2005). I have also had productive exchanges with both Ricky Riccardi and Terry Teachout, whose forthcoming books on Armstrong promise to be thoroughly researched and highly original. I regret that Tad Jones will not read this chapter. It would be impossible to imagine anyone more devoted to Armstrong's life and work. He passed away a few months after we shared a meal in New Orleans.

1. Quoted in Gary Carner, *The Miles Davis Companion* (New York: Schirmer Books, 1996), 90.

2. Hoagy Carmichael, *The Stardust Road* (New York: Rinehart, 1946), 53.

3. Marie Cardinal, *The Words to Say It: An Autobiographical Novel*, trans. Pat Goodheart (Cambridge, Mass.: Van Vactor & Goodheart, 1983).

4. Toni Morrison, *Playing in the Dark: Whiteness and the Literary Imagination* (Cambridge: Harvard University Press, 1992), vi–vii.

5. Ralph Ellison, *Invisible Man* (New York: Vintage, 1972), 8.

6. Roddy Doyle, *Oh, Play That Thing* (New York: Viking, 2004), 135–36.

7. David Yaffe, *Fascinating Rhythm: Reading Jazz in American Writing* (Princeton: Princeton University Press, 2006), 7–8.

8. Gunther Schuller, *Early Jazz: Its Roots and Musical Development* (New York: Oxford University Press, 1968), 89.

9. Brothers, *Louis Armstrong's New Orleans*, 268.

10. Ralph Ellison, "Change the Joke and Slip the Yoke," in *Shadow and Act* (New York: Random House, 1964), 61–73.

11. Louis Armstrong, *In His Own Words: Selected Writings*, ed. Thomas Brothers (New York: Oxford University Press, 1999), 170.

12. Brothers, *Louis Armstrong's New Orleans*, 122.

13. Stanley Crouch, "Laughin' Louis," *Village Voice*, August 14, 1978, 45.

14. Brothers, *Louis Armstrong's New Orleans*, 269.

15. Brian Cameron Harker, "The Early Musical Development of Louis Armstrong, 1901–1928" (PhD diss., Columbia University, 1997).

16. Armstrong, *In His Own Words*, 27.

17. Danny Barker, *Life in Jazz* (New York: Oxford University Press, 1986), 59.

18. Giddins, *Satchmo*.

19. Jim Bishop, *New York Journal-American*, January 2, 1958, 17.

20. David Margolick, "The Day Louis Armstrong Made Noise," *New York Times*, September 23, 2007, Week in Review, 13.

21. Brent Hayes Edwards, "Louis Armstrong and the Syntax of Scat," *Critical Inquiry* 28, no. 3 (2002), 618–49.

22. Armstrong, *In His Own Words*, 114–15.

23. Nathaniel Mackey, *Bedouin Hornbook* (Los Angeles: Sun and Moon, 1993), 83.

24. The comparison has been made in more stolid fashion by Alfred Appel Jr. in *Jazz Modernism: From Ellington and Armstrong to Matisse and Joyce* (New York: Knopf, 2002).

25. Brothers, *Louis Armstrong's New Orleans*, 48.

CHAPTER 4 / Bending Brass

For Vincent Bach's story, I have relied on a thoroughly researched essay, "The Life and Work of Vincent Bach (né Vincenz Schrottenbach) 1890–1976: The Early Years to World War II," by André M. Smith, in *International Trumpet Guild Journal* (December 1994): 4–35.

CHAPTER 5 / Caution: The Trumpet May Be Hazardous to Your Health

An especially helpful reference book for this chapter has been Frederick J. Spencer, *Jazz and Death: Medical Profiles of Jazz Greats* (Jackson: University of Mississippi Press, 2002). Among the many scholars and players with whom I have spoken, I am extremely grateful to Paul Berliner, Randy Sandke, and Brian Lynch.

1. Mezz Mezzrow with Bernard Wolfe, *Really the Blues* [1946] (New York: Kensington, 2001), 260.

2. Lawrence Bergreen, *Louis Armstrong: An Extravagant Life* (New York: Broadway Books, 1997).

3. John Chilton, *Roy Eldridge: Little Jazz Giant* (New York: Continuum, 2002).

4. William Whitworth, "Lead Player," *New Yorker*, December 20, 1969, 43–61.

5. Lois Rosenfeld, personal communication.

6. Art and Laurie Pepper, *Straight Life: The Story of Art Pepper* [1979] (New York: Da Capo, 1994), 191–95.

7. Carl A. Vigeland, *In Concert: Onstage and Offstage with the Boston Symphony Orchestra* (New York: Morrow, 1989).

8. Vance Bourjaily, "In and Out of Storyville: Jazz and Fiction," *New York Times Book Review*, December 13, 1987, 1, 44–45.

9. Dorothy Baker, *Young Man With a Horn* (Boston: Houghton Mifflin, 1938), 138.

10. Jean Pierre Lion, *Bix: The Definitive Biography of a Jazz Legend*, trans. Gabriella Page-Fort (New York: Continuum, 2005), 23–24.

11. Robert Dupuis, *Bunny Berigan: Elusive Legend of Jazz* (Baton Rouge: Louisiana State University Press, 1993).

12. Charles Mingus, *Beneath the Underdog: His World as Composed by Mingus*, ed. Nel King (New York: Knopf, 1971).

13. Spencer, *Jazz and Death*, 19.

14. Nick Catalano, *Clifford Brown: The Life and Art of the Legendary Jazz Trumpeter* (New York: Oxford University Press, 2000).

15. Paul Berliner, personal communication, May 23, 2007.

16. Jeffrey S. McMillan, *Delightfulee: The Life and Music of Lee Morgan* (University of Michigan Press, 2008).

17. David French, "The Sidewinder's Coda," *Down Beat* 74, no. 1 (January 2007): 38–43.

18. Tom Perchard, *Lee Morgan: His Life, Music and Culture* (Oakville, Conn.: Equinox, 2006).

19. James Gavin, *Deep in a Dream: The Long Night of Chet Baker* (New York: Knopf, 2002).

20. John McDonough, "Flying High: Maynard Ferguson Played the Impossible

During His Illustrious Career," *Down Beat* 73, no. 11 (November 2006): 46–49.

CHAPTER 6 / Miles Runs the Voodoo Down

The biography of Miles Davis on which I have relied most consistently is John Szwed's excellent *So What: The Life of Miles Davis* (New York: Simon & Schuster, 2002). I have also benefitted from Jack Chambers, *Milestones*, 2 vols. (Toronto: University of Toronto Press, 1983–85), and Ian Carr, *Miles Davis: The Definitive Biography* (New York: Da Capo, 1999). *Miles: The Autobiography* was largely ghosted by Quincy Troupe and is of little use except as a guide to how the Miles myth has been constructed.

1. Amiri Baraka (as LeRoi Jones), *Blues People: Negro Music in White America* (New York: Morrow, 1963), 155.

2. Miles Davis and Quincy Troupe, *Miles: The Autobiography* (New York: Simon & Schuster, 1989), 7.

3. Paul Berliner, personal communication, May 21, 2007.

4. Ingrid Monson, "Miles, Politics, and Image," in *Miles Davis and American Culture*, ed. Gerald Early (St. Louis: Missouri Historical Society Press, 2001), 87–97.

5. Szwed, *So What*, 151.

6. Peter Manso, *Brando: The Biography* (New York: Hyperion, 1994), 619.

7. Richard Cook, *It's About That Time: Miles Davis On and Off the Record* (New York: Oxford University Press, 2007), 247.

8. Steve Waksman, *Instruments of Desire: The Electric Guitar and the Shaping of Musical Experience* (Cambridge: Harvard University Press, 1999), 188.

9. Paul Tingen, *Miles Beyond: The Electric Explorations of Miles Davis, 1967–1991* (New York: Broadway Books, 2001).

10. Richard Williams, *Miles Davis: The Man in the Green Shirt* (New York: Henry Holt, 1993), 171.

11. Albert Murray and John F. Callahan, eds., *Trading Twelves: The Selected Letters of Ralph Ellison and Albert Murray* (New York: Modern Library, 2000), 193.

12. Quincy Troupe, *Miles and Me* (Berkeley: University of California Press, 2000), 12.

13. Davis and Troupe, *Miles*, 366.

14. Pearl Cleage, "Mad at Miles," in *The Miles Davis Companion: Four Decades of Commentary*, ed. Gary Carner (New York: Schirmer Books, 1996), 214.

15. Robin D. G. Kelley, "Miles Davis: A Jazz Genius in the Guise of a Hustler," *New York Times*, May 13, 2001, Arts and Leisure, 7.

16. Szwed, *So What*, 403.

CONCLUSION / Beyond the Brute

Although I do not quote him directly here, Will Straw has had a powerful effect on my thinking, especially through his essay "Sizing Up Record Collections: Gender and Connoisseurship in Rock Music Culture," in *Sexing the Groove: Popular Music and Gender*, ed. Sheila Whiteley (New York: Routledge, 1997), 3–16.

1. The word that the Fool speaks in the film is *ciufile*, a nonsense word that Zampanò himself uses in his act with Gelsomina. Pretending to be a stupid hunter, Zampanò calls for his *ciufile*, a child's mispronunciation of *fucile*, the Italian word for rifle. In the act, Gelsomina corrects him and calls him *ignorante*. So, when the Fool laughingly calls Zampanò "Ciufile," he is implying that the strongman really is an ignoramus.

2. Lois Rosenfeld, personal communication, April 13, 2007.

Acknowledgments

First I thank my agent, Sydelle Kramer, who knows practically nothing about jazz but who gave me the great idea of a cultural history of the trumpet with special attention to the achievements of jazz musicians. If the result is less than monumental, it's not her fault. Denise Oswald at Faber and Faber has been a patient and cogent adviser as well as a first-rate editor. I'm also thankful for all the energy that Jessica Ferri has devoted to this book. Many thanks to Cynthia Merman and John McGhee for their scrupulous copyediting. Caryl Flinn, a superb music scholar in her own right, could have been devoting herself to more important pursuits when she found time to read an early draft of the entire manuscript. She then wrote a series of astute critiques that convinced me I had some major reorganizing to do. I hope she's pleased with the result.

As with my previous book, I owe much to David Yaffe, who reads everything I give him and then comes back with great suggestions for making the book smarter and wittier. Barbara File also read an entire draft and provided me with much-needed encouragement along with detailed criticisms. Edward Tarr, David Hajdu, Bo Winer, David Lionel Smith, John Szwed, Sabine Klaus, Robert Crease, Mary Francis, Mike Jarrett, Jeff Nussbaum,

Niles Eldredge, Eva Linfield, David Monette, Tom Brothers, Jeanne Bernard, and Brigitte King were all more than generous with their time and gave me help with different sections of the book. Sherrie Tucker continues to be an especially sensitive reader, always teaching me how to put gender analysis to good use.

At the archives, I enjoyed the seemingly limitless attentions of Bruce Boyd Raeburn at the Hogan Archive at Tulane University, Michael Cogswell at the Louis Armstrong House and Archives in Queens, and André Larson at the National Music Museum in South Dakota. At the factories, I was graciously guided by Tedd Waggoner at Bach and Conn-Selmer, Dave Monette and Dean Comley at Monette, Charles Hargett and Zig Kanstul at Kanstul, Stephane Gaudry and Pierre Riou at Courtois, Maurice Selmer at French Selmer, and Dave Surber and Larry Ramirez at American LeBlanc. Jeanne Bernard accommodatingly chauffeured me to the Courtois factory in the Loire Valley and then back to Paris to meet distinguished members of the Selmer family in their offices. Lewis Porter introduced me to the Historic Brass Society, where I met Jeffrey Nussbaum, who generously shared his archives with me and answered my naïve questions. Michael Kimmel took me aside and explained why the electric guitar had long ago surpassed the trumpet as the most overtly masculine musical instrument. Sabine Klaus gave me beautiful illustrations of how trumpet valves work, and Michael Bushnell put his substantial computer skills to work on my musical examples. Jacqueline Reich translated the Italian dialogue of *La Strada* so that I could get a handle on (pardon the expression) that film's phallic wordplay, and Niles Eldredge escorted me through his astounding collection of cornets and brass instruments. Will Friedwald invited me to play in his group long before I had any right to play with anyone except Jamey Aebersold. Woody Shaw III spoke to me at great length about his father's work and even let me play the flügelhorn with which Woody II once worked his magic.

For crucial bits of information, inspiration, and friendship, I thank Lynn Abbot, William Adam, Carolyn Appel, Joseph Auner, George Avakian, Ian Barber, Lisa Barg, Paul Berliner, Emily Bernard, Anne Beversdorf, Norma

Beversdorf, Justin Block, David Brackett, Cecil Bridgewater, Rebecca Gor-mezano Brown, Harriet Castraro, James Castraro, Eric Comstock, Stephanie Stein Crease, Stanley Crouch, Zeinabu irene Davis, Nick De-Carlis, Scott DeVeaux, Robert T. Eberwein, Brent Edwards, Steven B. El-worth, Barbara Fasano, Lucy Fischer, Mike Fitzgerald, Jane Gaines, Bernard Gendron, John Gennari, Fiona Goh, Ruth Goldberg, Pamela Grace, Harvey Greenberg, Farah Jasmine Griffin, Ian Harwood, Trevor Herbert, Herbert Heyde, Chris Holmlund, Sharon Huff, Andre Hurni, James Hurt, Travis Jackson, Tad Jones, Alexander Kafka, Avi Kandov, E. Ann Kaplan, Howard and Beverly Karno, Robin D. G. Kelley, Deborah Kempe, James Ketch, Bill Kirchner, Michael Landwehr, Peter Lehman, George E. Lewis, Ira Liv-ingston, Cindy Lucia, Ray Lucia, Brian Lynch, Joe Magnarelli, Jacqui Ma-lone, Joe Medjuck, Russell Merritt, Vera Micznik, Leslie Mitchner, Stewart Mitchner, Ingrid Monson, Dan Morgenstern, Mary Morris, Adrienne Mu-nich, Richard Munich, David Murray, Brenda Neece, Karen Oberlin, Larry O'Connor, Carol Oja, Robert G. O'Meally, David Ostwald, Jimmy Owens, Bill Ozier, Kenny Rampton, Doug Ramsey, Jacqueline Reich, Waldron Ricks, John Rommel, Jenny Rosenbaum, Lois Rosenfeld, Jim Rubin, Liliane Rubin-Braesch, David Sager, Randy Sandke, Dan Schlegelmilch, Loren Schoenberg, Christopher Sharrett, Bobby Shew, Maureen Sickler, Gene Sil-vers, Gabriel Solis, Lew Soloff, Mark Spencer, Bob Stewart, Jonty Stockdale, Dick Sudhalter, Graham Taylor, Louise O. Vasvari, Jans Wager, Jack Wal-rath, Ben Waltzer, Richard Wang, Chris Washburne, Howard Weiner, David Weiss, Susan White, Tony Whyton, Joe Wilder, Gretchen Willoughby, and the members of the Columbia University jazz orchestra.

At SUNY Stony Brook, I thank my chair, Robert Harvey, and my dean, Jim Staros. Mary Moran-Luba has for many, many years made my life much simpler by looking after everything for which I don't have the memory. I also thank Alinda Askew and Victoria Judd for being indispensable allies at the office.

In New York, it's always wonderful to spend time with Amanda Gabbard and Keith Everett Book. They take me for trips in their rocket ship.

William Luhr has been as fine a friend as anyone could imagine, even when we were hopelessly engulfed in cochairing a monthly series of seminars and coediting an anthology. By consistently calling up his capacious reserves of goodwill and finesse, he has made me a much more productive person. I will always be in his debt.

I regret that neither of my parents will read this book. Lucina Paquet Gabbard and Earnest Glendon Gabbard died during the years I was writing. They led rich, creative lives as teachers and then as professional actors. It's only now when they're both gone that I realize what extraordinary parents they were. My fondest wish is that a bit of what was good in them can live on in me. And finally, there is Paula. She read the manuscript with her usual critical perspicacity; she tolerated my early, horrifying attempts to make music on the trumpet; and for more than thirty-five years she has been everything I could hope for in a life companion.

Index